understanding human behavior
An Illustrated Guide to Successful Human Relationships

COLUMBIA HOUSE / New York

Editor	Nicolas Wright
Deputy Editor	Susan Joiner
Senior Designer	Stewart Cowley
Art Editor	Mary Cooper
Art Assistant	Jeff Gurney
Editorial Assistants	Mundy Ellis
	Sarie Forster
	John Moore
	Michael McIntyre
Picture Research	Diane Rich
	Hazel Robinson
	Paul Snelgrove
Editorial Director	Graham Donaldson
Production Manager	Warren E. Bright

contents

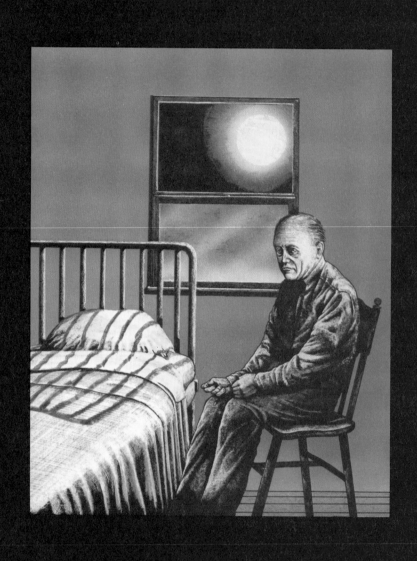

introduction

Marriage is a game of give and take. Those who play should know the rules and do their best to keep them. Of course, this is easier said than done. It may be a game of give and take, but it's also a game of chance, a gamble on the happiness of two different people. Recognizing the risks is half the battle, sensing the danger signals is vitally important, and dealing with marital problems in a mature, understanding way is essential to the continuation—and strengthening—of the relationship.

There are, of course, many ways in which the harmony of a marriage is threatened. Volume Seventeen of *Understanding Human Behavior* takes a look at one of the most common—and one of the most destructive—the seven year itch. The itch, or urge to seek solace in the arms of someone new, is something most people feel at some stage in their marriage. The figure seven is derived from statistical evidence that after this time a marriage tends to become less stable for all kinds of reasons.

A woman might feel her husband takes her for granted; a man might feel that the attractive, bright-eyed girl he married has turned into a nagging, lumpy housewife. Or possibly they're just bored with one another: their relationship is too steady, they feel too secure emotionally. But, whatever the reason for

(continued)

the itch in the first place, it needn't turn into a festering sore. All it takes is understanding. Volume Seventeen pinpoints the sensitive areas and suggests how they might be treated.

Volume Seventeen also explores the emotive world of group therapy, developed during World War II and now very much in the public eye. Of all groups, the encounter group is perhaps the best known. Here, instead of "talking" out a problem, you are encouraged to "act" it out of your system.

Does it work? The evidence suggests it does. But, as Volume Seventeen warns, if you are thinking of trying an encounter group, choose carefully. Most practitioners are genuine and well trained, but there are those who are interested only in parting you from your money.

Do you find the sight of someone slipping on a banana skin funny? If you do, do you know why? Volume Seventeen looks at humor in an apparently humorless world. It also discusses the physical and psychological changes wrought by adolescence and middle age; the impact of pop music; why little boys are exhorted to become "little men"; and why some people break into a rash after stroking a cat.

— The Editor

First fruit

All things must pass. But at the first flush of womanhood, need there be regrets?

Adolescence is potentially one of the most traumatic periods of life. Exactly how we cope with adolescence depends largely on two things: first of all the stability of the home and school environment, and secondly self-knowledge based on fact, not fantasy.

A good working definition of adolescence is the period between puberty (the time at which the sex organs begin to ripen) and maturity. Maturity in this case refers really to adulthood rather than physical maturity: an immature and adolescent girl can easily demonstrate *physical* maturity by having sexual intercourse and producing offspring. And so, of course, can an adolescent boy.

The period of adolescence in males is quite variable and has been put by some medical men as extending from the age of 12 to 25, whereas in women it is from 12 to 21. The psychiatrist Roger F. Tredgold, who subscribes to this view, is clearly referring to the emotional maturity process and indeed many young men will remain emotionally immature well into the twenties, victims of an extended adolescence. If such emotional factors are excluded, however, it would be reasonable to look upon adolescence as the period between 12 and 18 in women and 12 and 20 in men.

The clearest indications that adolescence is beginning are mainly physical changes. In girls these changes take place in approximately the following order. First, there is an increase in the transverse diameter of the pelvis. Until adolescence, although there are certain basic differences between the skeleton in boys and girls, they are not striking. Adolescence, however, primes the female pelvis at quite an early age for its function of childbearing and pregnancy. In fact it starts to widen before adolescence at about the age of seven.

The next physical change in girls is the development of the breasts. From childhood there is a difference in size and shape of the nipples between the sexes, but at some time between the age of nine and ten the breast develops what is called the areolar bud. The areola is the area of reddened skin that surrounds the projecting nipple in the female. This change in

Expression/Caroline Arber

shape is brought about in very early puberty by an increase in sex hormone.

Shortly after this the breasts begin to enlarge. To start with the breasts are mainly hemispherical. But as the girl matures one of three basic shapes gradually emerges which will remain

A highly romanticized view of life and a tendency to moodiness make adolescent girls hard to handle.

characteristic during adult life. These three have been described as bowl-shaped (or flat-breasted), conical, and

PAF International

At puberty boys and girls become aware of each other again after a period of studied indifference.

elongated (possibly even pendulous).

Strangely, there are very definite racial characteristics to the breasts. As far as the areola is concerned in most European women this is roughly disk-shaped once it becomes mature. In certain darker peoples the areola is much more cup-shaped and may even look almost hemispherical in African and Arab women. An exaggeration of this tendency is sometimes seen in Indian women. Similarly there is a wide variation in nipple formation, and knob-shaped, cone-shaped, cylindrical and extended fingerlike nipples all exist in mature women, and all are of course completely normal. The color of the nipple and areola starts to become more pronounced around the age of 12 to 14, although paler shades are present until the age of about 18 in most women.

Research has disclosed that 30 percent of mature women have red nipples, in 27 percent dusky brown predominates, in 20 percent the color is classified as reddish brown, rose pink in 15 percent and pale brown in

8 percent. It is important to realize this wide variation even in European women occurs because girls may be disturbed to find their nipples looking different from their peers and wonder if they are abnormal in some way.

Mound of Love

Perhaps it is worthwhile to remark that general body type has a very definite influence on breast size and shape. Generally speaking, women with fair hair and dark eyes have the most highly developed breasts, and girls with dark hair and light eyes are liable to fall into the small, flat-breasted type.

The next sign of puberty in girls is the appearance of body hair. This generally starts over the pubic area or, as it is classically described, the *mons veneris* (literally the mound of love). Hair under the armpits usually appears much later and is often not noticeable until after the menstrual periods have started. The physical characteristics of the *mons veneris* tend to vary greatly, and this is often another source of anxiety to girls during adolescence, who feel at times that they "look different" from other girls whom they see naked at school

or in changing rooms. Generally three factors contribute to its shape: first, the general bony framework of the pelvis, especially the angle between the two halves of the pubic bone, defines its general shape; second, the amount of fat that becomes deposited in this area at puberty creates the "bulge" of the *mons veneris*; and finally the density and color of the pubic hair is quite diversified. All these variables are largely determined by race.

Generally speaking, the pubic hair is denser in an area where it meets the outer lips of the vagina (the *labia majora*). Higher up it is more scanty. Almost always the upper limit of the hair in women is crescent-shaped, and the pubic hair in Western women tends not to extend very far upward toward the abdomen and navel. For the most part, women from Central European stock have a generous amount of fatty tissue deposited beneath the pubic hair which tends to raise the *mons veneris* above the surrounding areas, giving it a softly curving appearance. In Negroid races, however, the fatty tissue of the *mons veneris* is relatively undeveloped, and so this structure becomes much less prominent. Conversely, girls from Java, Samoa, Tahiti and parts of China tend to have an excessively developed *mons* compared with Europeans.

One common variation of the sexual hair in women that needs to be mentioned, if only to allay possible anxiety, is hair that extends from its normal boundaries upward toward the navel or downward onto the inner surface of the thighs. In fact, the pubic hair in brunettes is much more prone to extend upward and even to be found growing backwards between the legs toward the posterior part of the vagina and anus in very dark-haired women.

The color of the sexual hair in adolescence, as in later life, is often a matter of some discussion and is sometimes given quite erroneously as evidence that someone has changed the color of her hair. In actual fact statistics on this point, although rather few and far between, give the lie to this as an absolute rule. Neither is eye color necessarily related to the color of the hair, either on the head or on the genitals. Many dark-eyed women have light genital hair, as do girls who naturally have a very dark head of hair. Red-haired girls, however, are an exception to these natural variations. Their pubic hair is either red or light-colored, never dark or black.

Finally, the density and curliness of pubic hair often arouses curiosity and comparison. Generally young girls have very curly pubic hair, but once it has become fully grown, if they come from European stock, there is a tendency for this to become straighter as they get older. In other racial types there is a wide variation. A folklore belief that relates the density, color and curliness of pubic hair with either fertility or sexual appetite has now disappeared into the limbo of things best forgotten. In most girls, the full density and distribution of the pubic hair is not complete until a considerable time after the first menstrual period.

Stimulation Center

Alongside hair development in the *mons veneris* area during adolescence, there are other changes in the external sex organs. The external lips of the vagina *(labia majora)* become more prominent and darkly colored, especially in brunettes. If these outer lips are gently parted the inner lips, or *labia minora,* can be seen as pinkish strips of modified skin. In some girls these inner lips are much larger than in others, and there is then a tendency for them to protrude slightly between the larger lips. In many cases the *labia minora* become readily visible if the legs are widely parted or at times of sexual excitement.

At the meeting of the inner lips, in the front, a small vestigial structure called the clitoris is clearly visible in all females. In fact it is quite prominent in female babies, but then shrinks up in childhood. At puberty it tends to increase a little in size and becomes more sensitive to stimulation. Although it is minute compared with its male counterpart, the penis, it is capable of erection and enlarges during sexual stimulation or excitement.

The clitoris is well supplied with nerves and blood vessels, and during adolescence and throughout a woman's sexual life it is a major, but not the only, center of sexual stimulation. In the past doctors have overrated the part the clitoris plays in sexual pleasure. Many years ago, when women first started to wear panties, there was a tremendous outcry from some members of the medical profession because it was thought that even the merest touch of an undergarment in this area would be enough to transport a girl into a frenzy of "venal ardor"!

Between the top and the shaft of the clitoris there is a small fold or pocket which, during adolescence, tends to collect a whitish secretion called smegma. This, together with other secretions from the repro-

PAF International

ductive tract, contributes to the natural sexual odor of women, which, once again it must be pointed out, is a natural and not a shameful thing.

The first menstrual period usually begins between the ages of 10 and 16. Again, in different countries it occurs at different ages. In India the average age is 13.5 years, in Europe 13 years and in North America generally 12.5 years. But the age at which menstruation begins varies, often affected by general health. Generally speaking, the higher the social class the earlier girls menstruate; urban surroundings too seem to favor an earlier start to the periods. There is also a general trend towards earlier menstruation and physical maturity throughout the whole world. In Britain, the average age of starting to have periods has dropped from 17 to 13 during the last hundred years. What

The last word in clothes, make-up and male pop stars are all preoccupations of teenage girls.

is more, it is still decreasing by one month every two and a half years.

Menstruation naturally enough signifies a fair degree of maturity of the female reproductive apparatus. This whole system undergoes a rapid maturing process, starting about two years before the first period. This internal ripening process sometimes brings adolescent worry with it, because before the periods actually start there is often a rather thick vaginal discharge, and sometimes there are aches in the pit of the stomach probably caused by the developing womb "trying itself out" and contracting.

Alongside all this physical development in girls, there are quite profound

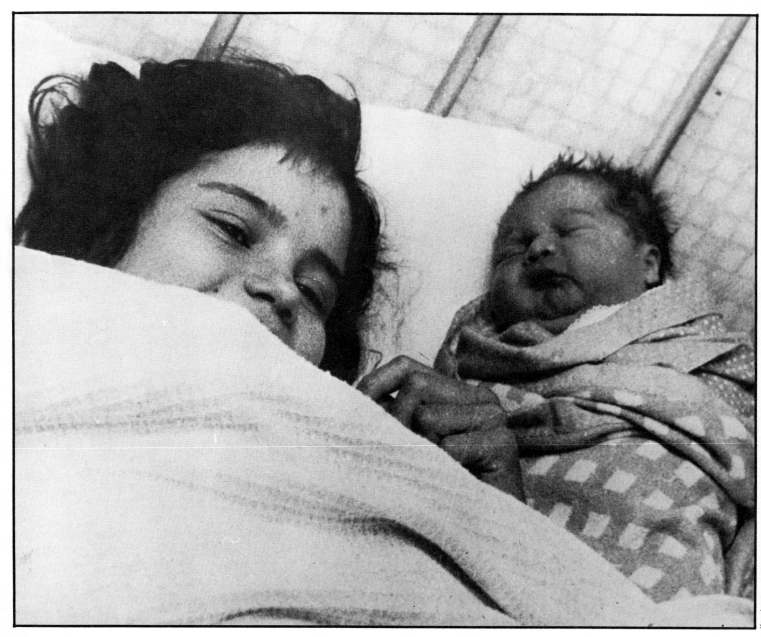

Keystone

psychological and emotional changes in most cases. These are quite variable, but generally speaking it is a time when the exuberant, tomboyish and giggly schoolgirl starts to become selfconscious over her newfound femininity. Different girls react to their changed appearance in very different ways. Some will dress to hide as far as possible their developing breasts, others appear almost to flaunt their new badge of womanhood: both attitudes are completely normal.

Nearly always, at this time, girls become interested in their appearance. Often they become introspective, moody and secretive. They have suddenly a new curiosity about life, and the imagination often runs riot. With her grown-up appearance, the adolescent girl *feels* she is grown-up and often finds it difficult to accept authority. She resents discipline and the need to obey orders; tempers and tantrums directed against parents are

all too often the order of the day.

At this time the adolescent girl usually changes her mother as confidant for a girl of her own age. Often this develops into a very deep relationship between the two girls which may, to others, appear to be something in the nature of a homosexual liaison. Even if this does occur it is nothing to worry about, but in most cases the relationship does not develop quite so intimately.

This close girl-to-girl bond is particularly obvious at a time when girls feel their first sexual stirrings, and there is a certain amount of evidence to suggest that, when there is no such female pairing in adolescence, a girl may precociously take a male partner, first as a confidant, and then as lover. Another fairly common feature of female adolescence is a sudden and inexplicable "crush" on an older woman, possibly because of an often forgotten characteristic of adoles-

In 1971, an Argentinian girl of ten gave birth to a healthy 6 lb. 8 oz. baby boy after a cesarian delivery.

cence in both sexes: a sudden increase in intelligence and a desire for intellectual stimulation.

One common preoccupation of adolescent girls is the hymen and their virginity. Although the two are linked in one way, in another they are totally dissociated. A girl with an intact hymen may not be a virgin. Or a girl with a ruptured hymen may be completely virginal, for the term virgin means quite literally a woman in a state of chastity. Structurally, the hymen is a delicate and incomplete membrane that guards the entrance to the vagina. It has one or more openings through which the menstrual flow escapes. The shape of the hymen varies considerably, with, in medical terms, four common types: the annular or ring-shaped; the crescent-

shaped; the septate or doubly perforated; and the cribriform, which has many small openings. Once the hymen has been ruptured—be it by an internal tampon, the fingers, or by intercourse—it looks roughly the same as all hymens.

Unless the opening of the hymen is very large, the initial sexual intercourse nearly always tears it and there is a slight loss of blood. A girl who has a tight hymen, or the rare cribriform hymen, may need help from her doctor before the vagina can be entered painlessly by a tampon, the finger, or an erect penis.

Because girls have rather more "highly differentiated" bodies than boys, they are more prone to abnormalities of development during adolescence. Sometimes they show a sudden increase in weight and may develop very pronounced "puppy fat." This does occur in boys but it is very much rarer. This overweight condition gives the subcutaneous fibrous tissue a tendency to split in places, especially around the breasts, buttocks, thighs and upper arms, and ugly reddish purple stripes tend to appear. These later fade to silver and are much less disfiguring. Undoubtedly puppy fat is due to a mixture of hormone imbalance and overeating during adolescence. Provided the appetite is sufficiently curbed and the diet is right, puppy fat disappears by the age of 20.

Adolescence is a difficult time for parents and older brothers and sisters as well as for the adolescent herself. Those who have had a "good" adolescence always say that it is because affection and trust have taken the place of orders and aloofness in elders. Adolescent girls always feel better if they are continually occupied and have a personal responsibility for something, particularly an animal. Another aid to an easy adolescence is for parents to encourage, as far as possible and in the kindest possible ways, the breaking of the old child-to-parent bonds and ties. Indeed many wise doctors and psychologists believe that unless the mother-daughter relationship is cut at some stage, the girl will never be able to adjust to subsequent roles as wife and mother.

1933

Richard Hook

Encounter yourself

"Know thyself"—the advice given to the ancient Greeks by the Oracle at Delphi. This precept, which still holds good today, is the ultimate purpose of group therapy.

"The first time I went to the group, I was very nervous. I was lucky—I only had to wait three weeks—but I spent most of the time imagining how the others would react. I thought they'd be hostile. When I introduced myself, I was shaking with terror. The man opposite glared at me and said nothing for the whole session—an hour and a half." (Liz)

"As soon as she came in, I knew she was just the sort of woman I hate. There were five of us already; we'd been getting on well for a month, we didn't need anyone else. Then this stupid female sweeps in, smiling graciously, taking over. Every time someone said something, she'd jump in. She didn't wait for Dr. Henderson to lead us, oh no; she thought she knew better." (Bill)

These two views of Liz's first night at a therapy group could not be wider apart. Before her arrival, Bill had taken an active part in the group, showing sympathy, asking questions and generally taking on the role of the wise man. Liz usurped him; she was beautiful, dynamic and apparently independent of the group conductor, Dr. Henderson. For the next three sessions, Bill refused to speak.

"Eventually, I asked him why he was being so aggressive. He said that was a joke and that I was highly aggressive towards him, but he refused to retaliate; he said he believed in non-violence. Then he asked why there couldn't be some feminine women in the group. I didn't have to answer this as Diane took him to task by demanding to know what he meant by feminine—someone who'd feed into his fantasies?" (Liz)

"I went home so depressed. Those bitches had a field day. Even Diane went over to her side. All that baloney about Women's Lib—we're the ones who need liberating." (Bill)

Return to Childhood

Many themes arose during the lifetime of the group, but the hostility between Liz and Bill never abated. One evening, the conversation had been about parental expectations of their children. Liz told the group that, as the oldest one in her family, she had to grow up before her time and act as an adult towards the younger ones. Bill said that he had been the youngest, constantly babied as he suffered ill health during childhood.

The first glimmerings of an understanding between them started.

"You are just like my mother. You order people around, you step on their feelings, you think you own the whole world." (Bill to Liz on the twentieth meeting.)

"I don't feel confident. I feel scared most of the time. Everyone expects so much of me that I'm terrified that I won't be able to give it." (Liz two meetings later.)

"You think I'm *formidable*?" (Liz)

"Formidable? You're absolutely terrifying!" (Bill)

"It amazed me at first, but the idea of being a formidable woman began to sound good. The more I thought about it, the more I liked it." (Liz)

Stone Wall

"In my world, women are strong, men are weak. My mother dominates my father completely. He never dares to disagree with her; nor do I—I just keep quiet and let her rave." (Bill)

"But don't you see you're doing the same thing here? You react by sulking, putting up a stone wall, instead of saying what you think. I'm *not* your mother." (Liz)

Liz came to recognize her strength, Bill to realize that he was highly aggressive. In less than a year, by working through their conflicts, they learned more than either might have done in individual therapy. And that was only one single part of the group transaction.

The one thing you can be sure of in group psychotherapy is that no two groups behave exactly alike. It does not depend just on the orientation of the group conductor, but on the individual personalities of the members. What you learn cannot be planned for. Six to eight people meet, with their therapist, usually for one to two hours every week for one to three years. The discussion is free-ranging. Before acceptance, each member is told that attendance at group meetings is vital; that telling the truth about what they feel—however difficult it may be—is the only way to make progress; that important decisions and life changes should be communicated. Some conductors also insist that members should not meet outside sessions. From then on, the members (including the conductor) create the climate, "rules" and transactions of the group.

Therapy groups share with other kinds of assembly some typical patterns of group dynamics. Any organization has a tendency towards self-preservation: the absence or desertion of any member causes alarm; deviant behavior will call forth attempts at conformity. Different groups define "deviance" in their own way; for example, rudeness in a professional group may be deemed unacceptable. In Dr. Henderson's therapy group, an unwritten rule grew up that while it was fine for members to say that they were depressed or miserable (the opposite of most social group rules!) they received disapproval from the others if they expressed hope or happiness.

When a member called Jack was promoted at work and communicated his pride, the others did not respond, but talked about something else. He felt sore about it and pointed out what was happening. The others would not at first acknowledge the truth of his assertion but continued to dwell on their feelings of depression. Even when Dr. Henderson intervened, calling attention to Jack's claim, they were hostile. Without realizing it, they were playing "patients" and resented the notion of becoming happy. They all had something to gain from their unhappiness.

Diane, married with a small child, found it convenient to blame her husband and domestic situation for what she regarded as her failure to achieve. Bill made a cult out of failure; he preferred the glorious achievements of his fantasies to any minor success in real life—and had a vested interest in putting down signs of real progress in anyone else. Tom had discovered that if he was "ill" or incompetent, his family would pay more attention to him than to his clever younger sister.

Given the Cold Shoulder

That particular group norm could have been harmful if it had been allowed to persist. It took Jack and Dr. Henderson to force the others to see what they were doing. In the subsequent weeks, there were many fruitful discussions of attitudes to success and failure, and thereafter it was possible for members to bring in their good as well as their bad feelings to the sessions.

In addition to creating norms and preserving the existence of the group, most groups can reward or penalize their members by inclusion or exclusion. Sometimes it is the therapist who finds himself cold-shouldered. On one occasion, Dr. Henderson took a vacation—always a difficult time for therapy group members, who feel that while they are revealing themselves to the therapist, he is free to desert them. Everyone turned up late to the next session. They avoided his eye and talked among themselves. When he said, "You are all very angry because I went away," Liz replied, "What makes you think you're so important?" After that meeting, they all went off together for a drink (it was the sort of group that did not forbid members to meet outside), pointedly excluding the therapist from the occasion.

Shared Emotion

When Liz told the group she was thinking of leaving, she was rejected. Mary went so far as to say, "Since you're going anyhow, why stick around for the next two months?" As separations had always disturbed Liz, it was very much in her interest to remain long enough to work out the implications of leaving the group, but she was never again trusted by the members. From being a central figure, she was pushed to one side, and often what she said was ignored.

"It upset me very much. I wanted them to go on liking me, but to let me go. It was just the same when I left my parents' home and when I left my first husband. I knew I had to go, but I couldn't bear their pain and anger. By living through the group's reaction, I found out that I *have* to accept the consequences of my actions on other people, but that I'm not entirely responsible for them. I didn't worry about the others when I left—I reckoned that it was their worry. I still have plenty of problems of my own without taking on the rest of the world's." (Liz)

Another quality of groups is their capacity to generate shared emotion. In a therapy group, this emotion is used to change personalities and attitudes. Intellectual effort alone will not bring about the radical adjustment sought in a therapy group. Jack was highly intelligent and had some knowledge of psychology. He turned up to his assessment meeting before being assigned to the group with a full and accurate case history of himself. But until his feelings were involved, his theoretical knowledge did him no good.

He was in the group for nearly a year before he allowed himself any spontaneous emotion. All along, he had maintained that he was indifferent to the death of his father, some four years before. He said that he envied his mother because she felt grief; he envied group members, Mary, because she displayed anger, and Liz, because she kept falling in love, albeit with the wrong people. When he spoke like this, he could have been offering a drink or a cigarette for all the emotion in his face or voice.

The others tried to force him out of his overcontrolled way of relating to them, but they were unsuccessful. In time, they ignored him. Experimental studies of small groups show that communication with a deviant member (and Jack, by hiding his feelings, was going against the group norms) increases at first, but if he remains deviant, he will eventually be excluded.

Jack was silent for several weeks, then he burst out in a torrent of anger and hatred. He told the others of his fantasies of harm befalling them—

when Dr. Henderson took one of his vacations, Jack wished him dead. The force of his feelings shocked the others, but they came back the next week as usual, proving to Jack that his infantile fear of causing actual harm by his thoughts was unfounded. A little later, he was able to reveal that, as well as loving his father, he had been jealous of him and felt in some way guilty about his death. Once this was recognized, he could allow his grief to come through. Everyone cried that night.

The sharing of grief is a therapeutic experience for the group, but not all the generated emotions are necessarily beneficial. Depression, mistrust and suspicion can sweep through the

whole room. Tom noticed the microphone in the ceiling for the first time in the tenth week, though it had been there all along, and he was instantly convinced that all the sessions were bugged. In fact, the permission of members is always asked if recordings (usually for teaching purposes) are to be made, and they have the option to refuse. But Dr. Henderson's explanation was not believed. As a skilled leader, he was able to turn the incident to good account, by encouraging everyone to talk out their fears, but some flavor of doubt remained among the members for the next three weeks.

Therapy groups are different from ordinary social or work groups in that members are given the chance to bring out feelings and thoughts that we usually have to suppress. Even with our closest friends, we tend to live up to their expectations and to edit out anything unflattering to ourselves. The same forces are at work in therapy. Liz felt obliged to live up to her image as the competent one, until she felt safe enough to admit that she sometimes wanted to be looked after. Dependency had not been encouraged in her when she was a child, and she had not allowed herself to recognize her need. Bill constantly blamed his mother for keeping him by her side; at last, he admitted that it was really the other way around —he was afraid to leave her.

Terrible Tirade

Truthfulness operates not only in the recognition of long-held attitudes and beliefs, but in the expression of immediate emotions. These are often of an aggressive or sexual kind. Diane found it easy to express anger, but difficult to convey warm feelings. It took her a year to say that she had any feelings towards the therapist. Even then, what she said was, "I need to fight you—but I need you to win." Bill felt an almost constant rage, yet he schooled himself to appear mild. The day he broke out in a tirade against women was a breakthrough for him. He expected that some terrible retribution was in store, and nothing happened. Time after time, different members of the group trembled at revealing "forbidden" thoughts, then wondered afterwards what all the fuss had been about.

David Levin

Behind the gregarious and confident mask may lurk a nervous wreck with an inferiority complex. Constructive criticism from others can help him to come to terms with himself.

Therapy groups frequently conspire to avoid painful or difficult areas of experience. In the early sessions, there is a strong temptation to keep the talk at a social level. When the group is in a hospital, the inpatients tend to complain about the food, the schedule for the day, anything except what they *really* feel. Getting in touch with their feelings is one of the first tasks for most people undergoing psychotherapy. It sounds too simple. Surely, you might think, grown-up people know what they feel? But often, in fact, they do not.

Vulnerable Victim

Children are spontaneous about their feelings, but we train them out of it pretty quickly: tantrums meet with disapproval; hostility is frowned on, sexual interests are actively discouraged. Many of us, not particularly neurotic, cannot express our needs in a direct way, especially if they seem bound to be frustrated. Most people need more love than they get, for example, but it is not realistic, in adult life, to demand the sort of total, unconditional love that an infant gets (if he is lucky). Still it is important to know if that is what you need, if only to cope better with the reality.

As a group gets more sophisticated, it develops new ways of avoiding pain. All neurotic defenses once served a purpose: letting them drop is a painful business. One way to maintain some protective barrier is to talk about things already solved. Another is to victimize one member of the group. Jack left Dr. Henderson's group when his company moved to another part of the country. After consultation with the others, the therapist brought in a new member, Hugh. Changes in the composition of any group often provide new learning opportunities and fresh insights; the familiar pattern of a new baby clamoring for parental care and attention is reestablished.

This particular new baby was very difficult. He was older than the others (most people in therapy are under 35) and his main problem was an inability to make decisions. Everything in life, from picking a tie out of the closet to choosing a career, was intolerably difficult for him. He was just as muddled about making sound emotional assessments, so he tried to behave as if the group were an ordinary social gathering. Yet he always asked for rules and guidance, and then grew very frustrated when none were forthcoming.

Eventually, he became the scapegoat for the group. The others attacked him to the point where he stayed away from the sessions. Even in his absence, they spent more time complaining about him than looking at *why* he caused such violent reactions. Liz was the first to admit that what she hated in Hugh was what she hated in herself—a wish to hold on to all her options. Bit by bit, they acknowledged jealousy and identification. He was only doing what they all wanted to do: turning to Dr. Henderson for a magic solution to their problems.

Dr. W. R. Bion, one of the pioneers of group therapy, deliberately used to withhold himself from the group. Most members looked to him for a lead and showed anger and fear when they were *not* told what to do. But the whole purpose of any psychotherapy is to enable clients to help themselves. Hugh's naive demands echoed the child in the other members, a weakness they would not readily admit to but were quick to condemn in him (turning the harsh spotlight, incidentally, away from themselves).

Group therapy developed during World War II. Originally, many groups were oriented towards individual analysis, emphasizing the relationships of individual members to the conductor rather than the complex interactions of the whole group. The sort of material introduced is the typical matter of psychoanalysis—free association, transference, resistance and the interpretation of dreams.

Mirror of Life

The study of group dynamics in the 1940s brought about a different sort of therapy. A perceptive group may deal with dreams and childhood experiences, but only in so far as they are relevant to the current group behavior. The group is a mirror of realistic, pertinent outside life; instead of only one object (the analyst) to react to and project upon, each member has six to nine others to relate to. For those who have never had a safe relationship with anyone else, the "sharing" of the leader may be too difficult. These patients may start in individual therapy and then move on to group therapy.

Apart from the practical advantage —economy of time and money—a group can offer unique experiences to its members. It is a more democratic setup than the patient-therapist relationship. Members have the chance to give something as well as to receive help. For people whose confidence has been lowered, or who have suffered from depression, this is a reassurance, and it increases their

social effectiveness. It is also more difficult to fool several people than one. Each person has his own perceptions of what is going on, and the most helpful insights do not always come from the conductor.

In a group, the status of "patient" is more tolerable than in the one-to-one situation. Individuals do not always feel at a disadvantage. This causes problems for those who *want* to be "ill," but even they can improve in a self-help atmosphere. Self-awareness, reflected by several people, increases with understanding the others. Compassion and tolerance can grow. It takes time, of course: if you are thinking of joining a group, do not expect instant results; it may be six months before you feel even slightly changed.

Sense of Direction

Does it work? The research results are confusing. It is difficult to assess improvement of patients, and even more difficult to compare the results with other forms of treatment. Many people, however, feel that they benefited from their groups. When Dr. Henderson's group finally ended after nearly three years, all except Hugh claimed that they felt and functioned better. Liz was freed from the crippling fears that made her work nearly impossible; she moved into a more responsible job and found that her marriage improved. Bill was still living at home but had grown much less dependent on his mother (he even stayed out some nights!). Diane got pregnant again, and admitted that she preferred to stay home and look after her children. Mary finally left her passive husband and found her new life much more satisfying than the old one. It is difficult to know if these changes would have occurred anyway, but the members were firm in their belief that the group, by enabling them to understand themselves, had helped them to make important life decisions and to give their existences more direction.

When all is said and done, unless you are marooned forever on some desert island, personal happiness is dependent on the success of your relationships with other people and what goes on beneath the veneer we call civilized behavior. Encounter groups attempt to give people a chance to explore this "underworld" in controlled circumstances so that mistakes are not too traumatic. Life with others is easy only when you have learned to be truly at ease with yourself.

Bebopalupop!!!

In the fifties, war babies were teenagers with money in their pockets and a taste for wild music . . .

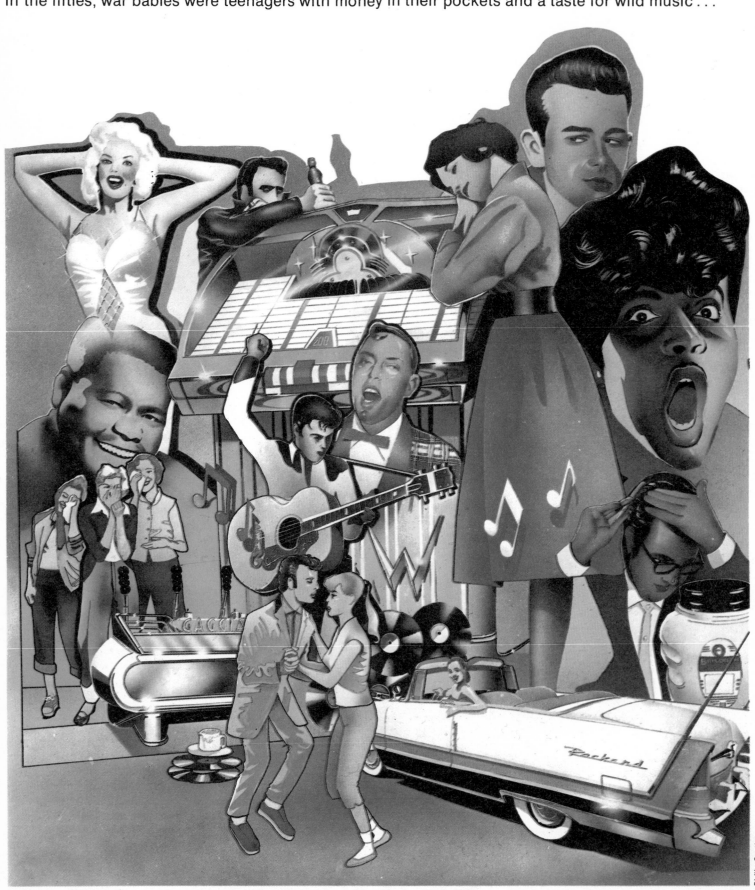

Philip Castle

The prevailing mood of the Western world in the fifties was lightheaded, slightly dotty. Postwar restrictions were gradually loosening their grip and the sorrows and bereavements that the war had brought were gradually dissolving in the general spirit of optimism. Once again there was fun, comfort, affluence and a return to family life.

And there were children, millions and millions of them: the war babies, and above all the postwar babies of the bulge. The children who reached puberty in the fifties had been born into an atmosphere of universal anxiety, of austerity and blind patriotism. In Europe many had grown up to expect that their homes would be wiped out suddenly and their neighbors killed by bombing, or that they would be separated from their families when the cities were evacuated. In the United States many of them grew up in homes where father was simply a photograph that would never come to life.

War was their norm, and when it was all over they had no fond memories of the good life to fall back on. While their parents returned with relief to

the life-style of the prewar days—the same old standards, a good education and a good job; the same old amusements, the big bands and the crooners —the kids kicked their heels and looked on. The chain had been broken: no longer did the youngsters try to emulate their seniors and long to be grown up, to wear the same clothes, cherish the same ideals. The war cut them off from their heritage.

They were waiting, albeit unconsciously, for something to turn up—something new, something of their own, something to identify with. And along came pop.

Before pop arrived, society had been divided by vertical lines separating people of all ages into black or white, rich or poor, upper class or lower class, educated or uneducated. It is too much to claim for pop that it did away with these barriers: it did not. But what it did do was to draw a thicker, blacker dividing line *horizontally* across society which for some years created a greater schism than all the rest—the gulf between youth and maturity, teenagers and grown-ups, pop and antipop.

"The Youth Problem" was the talking point of the age, discussed by eager sociologists, anxious parents and disapproving politicians alike. Pop was not the youth problem, not the cause of it, but one of its many

Top left: The man who started it all— Bill Haley and his famous kiss curl. Left: Elvis the Pelvis before he cleaned up and joined the army. Below: Wild scenes at an Elvis concert. The policeman, typical of the conformist older generation, is plainly horrified by such behavior.

Dezo Hoffman

Keesee Phototrends

symptoms. It was a symbol which the outraged could point to, and more than that it was a rallying cry for the teenagers, a peg on which to hang their floating allegiances. It gave them their own identity.

It was so exciting. Over the years pop has become tamed; it has been explained, commercialized, intellectualized, justified, and classified, in some circles, as art. But in the beginning it came on like an explosion — of noise, action, violence, sensation. The fallout from that explosion is still, twenty years later, drifting gently to earth — infiltrating the faraway realms of art and literature — and is called "pop culture." But the original explosion had nothing at all to do with culture.

Rhythm and Blues

The bomb went off in 1954 in the United States with Bill Haley and the Comets and a song called "Rock Around the Clock." Haley was an unlikely character to lead a revolution. He was flabby, he was cute, he was white, and he was no teenager. He was a country and western singer to begin with, playing the small-time radio station circuit for six years until, in 1951, he switched to a style of music that had, until then, been the preserve of black singers playing to a predominantly black teenage market: rhythm and blues.

Rhythm and blues was strong stuff. It did away with romance, with moon and June, and replaced it with the hard facts of life, with sex and raw passion. It did away with lilting strings and came up with savage saxes and twangy electric guitars, with beat and bombarding noise. It came to the white kids not from the safe, comfortable world of their parents but from the dangerous, violent world of the urban Negroes, and once they had got a taste of it they would not let it go.

Bill Haley was not alone in sensing the new white market for rhythm and blues. In 1951 Alan Freed, a radio DJ from Cleveland, Ohio, had begun to prick up his ears at the sounds the kids were dancing to, and even buying, at the local record shop. Until then, black music and the black record chart had been very much a segregated affair, but suddenly the kids were forsaking the gloss and polish of the white music for the gutsy beat of the black. Freed pushed a new program on his station. It was called

Chuck Berry, one of the giants of rock and roll, blended blues with pop and still keeps on rocking.

"Moondog's Rock and Roll Party," and rock and roll was born.

Publicity is an industry. It thrives on news, and even when the news is shocking — is "deplored," is condemned — it still gets through. In the fifties the opportunities for spreading news had never been so good: not just newspapers, not just radio, but now television as well. What might have remained a localized trend twenty years earlier became a nationwide talking point overnight. What happened in Cleveland, Ohio, because of the publicity it got, might just as well have happened up the road for kids all over the United States. And what happened was that Alan Freed had organized a "Moondog Ball" with live black groups playing rhythm and blues: when over three times as many kids turned up as the Cleveland Arena could hold, and when black and white kids were seen to rub shoulders in the crush, the "Moondog Ball" was canceled in a storm of outraged authority and racist fervor. For a while it looked as though Alan Freed might be arrested.

As the adult world tut-tutted over their newspapers at this event, the spin-off — for the teenage world — was a determination to do the opposite, to join in with all those thousands in Cleveland, to find out what rock and roll was all about.

Teenage Rebel

The "Moondog Ball" affair happened in 1953, and it was in 1954 that Bill Haley scored the first big hit for rock and roll. In itself "Rock Around the Clock" was not very different from the big-beat, small-content disks he had been cutting (and more or less failing with) since 1951. The difference, and what made it such an overwhelming hit with the kids, was that the press — primed by the goings-on at the Cleveland Arena, made an issue out of it. Rock and roll became something that parents, worried by the boredom and unconventional behavior of their children, homed in on as the root of all the dissent, it became a platform for churchmen and politicians and it dug itself deep into the teenage world.

What really made Bill Haley and his song into the campaign cry for young America (and a year later for young Britain) was a movie, *The Blackboard Jungle.* The film world was among the first to reflect the restlessness and boredom of postwar teenagers. James Dean encapsulated the spirit in *East of Eden* and *Rebel Without a Cause,* and Brando was the rootless tearaway of *The Wild One.* In *The Blackboard Jungle* a new element was added to the "youth" theme. It used rock and roll on the soundtrack, and to set the scene—of a school where rebellious teenagers, black and white, come eventually to be loved and understood by a sympathetic teacher—there was Bill Haley and his Comets playing "Rock Around the Clock."

That blew the scene wide open. Kids flocked to see the film and journalists wrote articles on what the teenage fuss was all about. When it was shown in Britain in 1956 there was dancing in the theater and so much jubilation on the streets that it was termed a riot by the press. In the States cinema proprietors were so affronted by audiences getting to their feet and dancing that they stopped the projectors. But that could not stop the exuberance—cinema seats were torn up and the kids went wild. The press went wilder, ignoring all the peaceful showings of the movie, broadcasting only the violence. The dividing line between age groups became firmer, all the more because teenagers were ignoring the old class and race structure. In the Deep South, where racial segregation was most hallowed, copies of "Rock Around the Clock" were publicly burned. Rock and roll became the cause for the rebels, not very well articulated perhaps, not very worthy, but deeply significant to its adherents. It meant being young and wanting to find a brand new way of doing things.

The Pop Revolution, as it has been called, was under way. What it needed was a leader. Bill Haley had done the groundwork, but he was too soft, too fat, too old and too professional to make a hero. He reminded the kids too much of the old-style entertainer. He lasted longer in Britain than in the United States, but by 1957 he was finished. And by 1957 there was a new and definitive leader of rock, Elvis Presley. Haley had introduced to the ears of the world the new sound. Presley brought before their very eyes the image of the new generation. He *looked* right: he was tough, he was sexy, and he was one of them.

Elvis was truly king of the teenagers, and it was he who made the Unilateral Declaration of Independence for their new nation. In 1956 he recorded "Heartbreak Hotel," and

One hundred police were called out to dispel rioters in Copenhagen after a showing of the film *Rock Around the Clock*. Around the world, rock 'n' rollers clashed with authority.

within six months it had sold eight million copies and he was blessed with a correspondence of ten thousand fan letters a week. He became the property of all his followers: he said it all, not just with his raw, agonized and infinitely sexy voice, nor just with the way he moved, his explicit wriggling riveting your eyes to that famous pelvis. He appealed not just to pubescent girls and not just with sex. He was the image of how any teenager could be: wild, unbounded, different—but nonetheless rich and famous. Elvis was all right, he was on your side.

Of course there had been superstar singers in the past, like Frank Sinatra and Pat Boone. But their songs had been polished with professionalism, the emotions they expressed cloaked in romance. No white singer had been so explicitly sexy, reflected such thrilling male prowess that the boys could identify with. Nor had any white singer offered such a breathtaking contempt for his women that turned girls' knees to water and made them squeal all the louder.

Elvis was tough and he was flash and he had style, a style that became the prototype for kids from then on. And once the initial impact had been made there was no stopping pop. Many of the older generation tried—and failed. And many others grew rich on the pickings.

Age of Affluence

No wonder youth was a problem in that decade: the world was so full of young people with time to kill. No wonder rock and roll became an issue in the press: it was sensational, it made such good copy. No wonder that rock and roll and teenagers together spelled such an irresistible market for business men: corporately and individually, the kids had so much money to spend. And for the first time, the under-21s outnumbered the rest of the world's population.

Compared to the deprivations of the war years, the postwar fifties were years of affluence for society as a whole. It was an age where material symbols of wealth—the TV, the automobile, the house, the freezer—began to count for a great deal, and these adult preoccupations were more than reflected in the interests of their kids. Clothes, radios, record players, hairdos, and motorbikes formed the essential, and usually portable, paraphernalia of the well-set-up teenager. Most important of all were the "wheels," particularly in the United States. Begged, borrowed or conned

out of your harassed parents, you had to have a car—preferably a convertible.

The car was vital, and it was significant too. It made teenagers more independent and put them firmly into the consumer bracket, with entertainments and cafés designed solely for the young, while the car radio blared out teenage rock and roll from teenage-orientated radio stations. The teenage boom might not yet have much influence over the leaders of the nation, but it cast a spell over the commercial world. The record industry was soon to outstrip the Hollywood film industry in terms of size and profits, and everything concerned with rock was hot property.

Goose with the Golden Egg

Elvis had had two money-minded men to help him on his way up. One was Colonel Tom Parker, a wheeler-dealer from way back, with a quick eye for Elvis's image and publicity. The other was Sam Phillips, an ex-DJ who ran a small record company, Sun Records. (In 1957 Elvis told *Hit Parade* magazine how he joined up with Phillips: "'You wanna make some blues?' he suggested to me over the phone, knowing I'd always been a sucker for that kind of jive.") The Colonel was a skillful manager, and Sam Phillips was a producer with a feeling for the teenage market. Between them they had turned the poor boy from Tupelo into millions and millions of dollars, and everywhere smart businessmen inside and outside the music industry began to look for the goose that was going to lay their own particular golden egg.

Rock and roll became an industry, especially in the northern states of America, where record promoters had begun to read the mood of the youngsters with deadly accuracy. First they took a beat—*the* beat, rock and roll music. Then they took a list of ingredients for the song: teenage love, parental opposition, the hassle of still being at high school, good grades, bad grades, jukeboxes, ponytails and sneakers. And they found a group to put the song across. So they had hits—and hit groups like the Coasters, Dion and the Belmonts, Danny and the Juniors, and Frankie Lymon and the Teenagers, who would last them a good month or two until another novelty came along. Out of the South and the West emerged more genuine pop heroes—Buddy Holly, Eddie Cochran, even the black singer Chuck Berry, who, though they were all more or less molded by their backers, tended to mean more as

individuals and bring their own originality to rock and roll.

Meanwhile, Britain was just waking up to the pop explosion and beginning to think of creating homegrown stars. The kids knew about it: they had responded to American export rock and roll and they were just waiting for it to happen in Britain. Youth in Britain had a rather ominous air, less cosseted, more deprived and shocked by the war years, far meaner. All this was summed up in the Teds, or Teddy Boys, who actually did roam the streets in packs and distinguished themselves by their flamboyant style of dress (a parody of the high-class Savile Row tailors' latest fashion—three-quarter-length jackets, velvet collars in the Edwardian style, hence the name). Not by any means was every British kid a Ted, but all of them, in some degree, reflected the preoccupations and the neuroses that went into the Ted mentality. All of them had a frustrated energy to use up and nothing suitable to spend it on: the Teds rid themselves of it by identifying "enemies" and fighting battles. All kids were looking for an identity, something to define their role: the Teds formed gangs, swore blood brotherhood. All of them were deeply concerned with themselves, what to copy, who to be: the Teds were out-and-out narcissists, with their immaculate, heavily greased DA hairstyles, much attended to with the benefit of every reflecting shop window they passed.

Grass Roots

What the British music industry offered these waiting millions, and what they (at first) lapped up like water in the desert, was the delightful Tommy Steele.

Tommy was a simple boy from Bermondsey, southeast London, so the publicity spiel ran, found singing one day at the Two "I"'s coffee bar in Soho. Suddenly he became the hottest singer in Britain, 18 years old and a true cockney rocker. In fact, he had only ever had one record, "Singing the Blues," at number one in the charts, and it bore little resemblance to rock and roll. In fact, he never really spoke to British youth at all and quickly disappeared into theater and the show-biz mecca, the London Palladium. But for a while, and by dint of clever promotion by his manager John Kennedy, he rocked them both at the grass roots and in the press, so glad were they all at the emergence of a truly British rock and roll star. He was falsification from beginning to end, not in himself, for he was and is a charming man of diverse talents, but in the way he was put across. Nevertheless he marked the start of the British pop industry, an industry that was going to lay down the law, with the Beatles in the sixties, to the rest of the world of pop.

After Steele, other British contenders came thick and fast—each with his own slight variation on the theme. Where Tommy was a lovable idiot, Cliff Richard was a winsome lad, the bland and pettable "Living Doll" of rock. Where Billy Fury—as his name was designed to suggest—was the inarticulate but basic raw essence of rock (along with Marty *Wilde*, Rory *Storm*), Adam *Faith* was sensitive, thoughtful, articulate, a pop philosopher.

Laying the Groundwork

Adam Faith gave the clearest clue to the way pop would develop. He was short, blond, delicate and extremely good-looking, and his songs—"What Do You Want? (If You Don't Want Money)" and "Poor Me"—were far from being great rock blockbusters. They were odd, slightly vulnerable, but cleverer than most. He was pounced upon by the media as a new, completely original phenomenon, a thinking pop star, who might have the answer to the problem that vexed the minds of the nation—the Youth Question. So he appeared (sandwiched between luminaries from the Establishment) on John Freeman's TV chat show "Face to Face" and spoke quietly and surprisingly articulately of books, of classical music . . . of sex before marriage.

Faith became—probably unconsciously—the first interpreter to the adult world of the so-far incomprehensible language of noise, beat and rhythm that had been the private preserve of teenagers. He took the first step across the line dividing the teenage from the adult world. Parents regarded him with little more than a mild curiosity, but the hungry media were fascinated. Perhaps they sensed that he was doing the groundwork for pop which would eventually lead to the grateful acknowledgement of the Beatles as "Members of the Order of the British Empire."

Mean and moody, James Dean (top) lashed out at his long-suffering mother in *Rebel Without a Cause*. He and Marlon Brando (right) symbolized the disaffection and non-conformity of youth in the fifties.

Warner Bros.

John Garrett

Sexploration

Parents are often upset by infantile sexuality, but it's just a natural part of growing up.

At what age does a child first become aware of its own sexuality? The question has not yet been finally answered because among the medical profession, parents and educationalists there is still no consensus. Some doctors would put the age as early as one year while others believe that sexual awareness does not really begin until much later. Most medical men, however, concur with the theory that by the time a child is five it has known some sexual feelings—and parents' observations bear this out.

The differences of opinion arise largely out of the difficulty in defining sexuality. Does it mean, for example, merely noticing the difference between the sexes—that little boys have penises where girls have none—or does it imply a sexual experience—that is to say, excitement or stimulation of the genital regions? Many parents have seen their children "playing with themselves" as early as 18 months; what they cannot ascertain is whether the infant's sensations are sexual or just part of the normal exploration of the body. Certainly infant boys are capable of erection, but again it is hard to say whether this is sexually induced or merely the result of a change in temperature, involuntary friction, or possibly even a simple, preparatory reflex action.

The greatest obstacle to ascertaining a small child's sexual experiences is his limited vocabulary. Without the

Above: "Why do they keep telling me silly stories about birds and bees?"

powers of complicated speech or the ability to conceptualize, the small child is unable to communicate many of its experiences, including sexual ones. As one mother put it, "My little boy of two always giggles when he touches his genitals and says 'nice', but then he says that about ice cream and rain as well!" What does seem clear though is that, whether specifically sexual or not, the small child gets some pleasure from stimulation of the genital region, and it is vital for parents to recognize this.

Social constraints are such that adults would be severely censured if they touched their genitals in public. But a child is unaware of these constraints. Nevertheless many parents are very intolerant of such "naughtiness," even if the child is within the home, in bed, bathing, or merely playing. Their censorship may be restricted to words—telling the child not to do that or frowning disapproval—or it may take the form of physical disapproval, such as a slap or pulling the child's hand away. In transmitting his own inhibitions, the parent who reprimands a child may be doing untold harm to his sexual development.

Naughtiness in the Nursery

There is no longer any doubt that almost all fears and inhibitions—as well as feelings of security—start in the nursery. Parents who make a child feel that he is being naughty or disgusting by touching what to him is just another part of his body put the child's future sex life at severe risk. This is a point that cannot be overemphasized. The adult who dislikes animals almost certainly learned to do so from his parents, or possibly because he had a bad experience with one as a child; similarly the adult who fears or is repelled by sex, even if at a subconscious level, is likely to have had parents who also felt this way.

Psychologists have said that it is a normal part of development for the child of eight or nine to believe that sex is a little naughty, something to be tittered at. Most children have known the furtive pleasure of "inspecting" each other behind the school sheds, or making Jane-from-around-the-corner take her pants down, but this is a passing phase for all but the eventual pervert, such as the voyeur. But if the child has been led to believe that sex really *is* dirty, something that no respectable adult approves of, then explorations behind the sheds become far more sinister.

Adults tend to think that sexuality in childhood or the years immediately before puberty, if it exists at all, is of a fairly insubstantial nature, and yet if memories are to be relied upon, many people have had enormously exciting sexual contact in their early years. "One of the most thrilling memories of my life has to do with childhood sex," one woman mused. "I can remember it graphically. I was eight at the time, and living in the country. My cousin—a girl nine months older than myself—and I decided to leave home and camp out in the country. Two friends who lived nearby, both boys, volunteered to come with us to set up the tent and

make a fire. We went only about half a mile away to some woods we knew. It was all a great adventure, heightened of course by the knowledge that home was only a short distance away so we were in no real danger—and by the fact that the boys were with us. One of them, Robert, I liked very much. I was teased at school because everyone knew I liked him, and though he was very standoffish and gruff, I suspected he liked me too. Anyway, we got the tent up, somehow, though we couldn't get a fire going. We sat around feeling very grown-up, talking, joking and drinking pop.

"Then my cousin said she had something she wanted to show Peter, winked at me, and led him off into the woods. I can still see Robert's face, very red and pouting. 'I don't want to go into the stupid old woods. I'll stay here with this silly thing (meaning me) instead.' He stuck his hands in his pockets and strutted around whistling, then like the Sheik of Araby suggested nonchalantly we go into the tent. Even talking about it brings back the feeling—incredible, breath-holding excitement, a tummy that felt as if it had just gone over a hump-backed bridge, and a *very* hot face.

"When we got inside he kissed me and pushed me to the ground; then he lay on top of me—we were both fully clothed—and held my arms down and kissed me again. 'Now you're my girlfriend,' he said, got up and took my hand and said, 'Come on, it's too hot in here.' As soon as the others came back he let go of my hand and behaved as though nothing had happened, but Peter kept grinning at me and asking Robert if he'd 'done it', until Robert told him to shut up.

Vivid Memories

"There couldn't have been a more innocent charade than that, and yet it was incredibly sexual. The amazing thing is that Robert still remembers it, yet it all happened 22 years ago. He's married now too, with children, but still lives in the same area, though I've moved away. But we met last Christmas in the street and both laughed about that day in the tent. 'I was really crazy about you, you know,' he said, 'even though I didn't know exactly what to do with it!' Robert's memory confirms that, far from being the fantasy it could have been, Jenny's experience was a vivid reality.

Another memory sheds further light on the influence an early sexual experience can have. John's first conscious sexual excitement occurred when he was only six years old. "I

come from a large family, and my older brothers and sisters used to have to cart me around with them quite often. On one occasion my ten-year-old sister was left in charge of me for the afternoon. She and a girlfriend and my younger brother and I went off to play in the fields behind my house. The girls were very giggly, I remember that, and my sister's friend kept teasing me about being a big boy for a six-year-old. I *was* tall for my age, but like all children I was embarrassed to be talked about.

Dirty Minds

"At some point we all sat down and the older girls started giggling among themselves and then Clara, my sister's friend, told me she was going to show me something very special, but only if I kept very still and quiet. She then took all her clothes off and danced very slowly in front of and around me, waving her dress in the air and looking at me all the time. She could only have been about ten, too, but she had very tiny breasts and very long hair. I thought she was the most beautiful girl I had ever seen. After awhile she put her clothes on, and she and my sister told me I was not to tell *anyone* what had happened, which of course I didn't . . . or not for years. But I kept the memory of that afternoon forever. I once asked my younger brother if he remembered the incident, but he asked me what on earth I was talking about and suggested that I was just imagining it all.

"So when I was about 17 I approached my sister. She denied the incident immediately and told me I must have a dirty mind, but she turned scarlet as she was talking and left the room quickly—all the proof I needed that it had really taken place."

One psychological theory has suggested that the elements of exhibitionism and voyeurism are in some degree an integral part of human sexuality, and certainly these elements seem evident in a lot of childish sexual experiences. The idea of "showing" oneself can be translated not only as a desire to shock or thrill, but also as a way of asking approval or recognition of one's own attractiveness. Watching a display of sexuality can also be a way of learning, though if the child cannot cope with his reactions, or if he is punished for looking, there may be serious repercussions. One girl remembers the strong physical fear she had to grapple with at her first adult contact with a man; and she could trace this back to an event which happened when she was only four.

"My brother and his wife lived with my parents and me. My brother is 21 years older than I, and when I was four he had been married for a year, though most of that time he was away at sea. He was home on leave, and one morning I walked into his bedroom—I had been in the habit of going into my sister-in-law's room and talking to her or occasionally being read a story. But this morning I interrupted them when they were about to make love—though that's not what I thought at the time. My brother's penis was erect and when I came in they looked up. My brother was very cross, but my sister-in-law's reaction was violent. She shouted at me to get out and then burst into tears.

"Of course now I can understand that she was frightened and embarrassed, upset to have their love-making interrupted; but at the time I couldn't see what I had done wrong. I also thought my sister-in-law was in pain, because she cried. I went on seeing that incident in my mind's eye for years, and I suppose I worked out that the cause of her distress had something to do with my brother's penis. Many years later, when I was about to be made love to, I had a totally involuntary reaction of terror. I pushed the man—who until that moment I had felt very attracted to—and rushed off. At the moment of penetration I suddenly saw my brother and sister-in-law all those years ago. 'He's going to hurt me,' I thought, 'like my brother hurt her.'"

This girl's reaction illustrates the damage that can be done to a child's mind by an unexpected, uninterpreted, and therefore frightening view of sex. As many doctors and psychologists have discovered, the sex act can seem like an act of aggression to a small child, and for this reason it is inadvisable to let him see his parents making love. Even a passionate kiss can be frightening to an infant who is unable to distinguish between what is fierce but pleasurable and what is fierce and painful.

Naked and Unashamed

Parents do have an enormous responsibility to bear in what they teach their children about sex: what they let them see, what they show their approval of, and what they condemn. Starting with the premise that the one thing they must avoid is instilling feelings of guilt or disgust, there still remain a number of other choices they have to make. For instance is it sensible to let a child see his parents nude? Most experts believe that it is, for in hiding the body, or suggesting that there is embarrassment or shame in nakedness, they will automatically transmit these feelings to the child. This does not mean that the parents have to put on a brazen display of nudity. One girl, whose parents were in fact nudists, said, "I was wholeheartedly bored at the sight of the naked, middle-aged body by the time I reached puberty. I didn't find it repellent sexually, but I used to wonder why on earth women with big floppy bosoms didn't put a bra on. If nothing else they would have been a whole lot more comfortable. And when I first saw a beautiful male body in the nude it came as something of a shock, since most of the ones I had seen were anything but!"

Most children go through a stage when they insist on privacy when dressing, undressing or bathing. This

PAF International

Little girls and boys soon discover that their bodies are different and naturally want to know why.

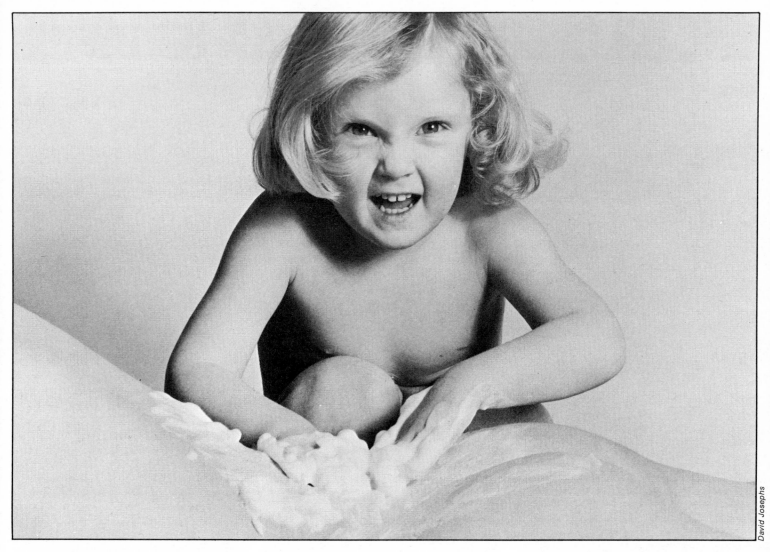

David Josephs

may be due to natural modesty; it may be because they are suddenly aware of their own sexuality and wish to explore it privately. The parent who opposes this "modest" stage in particular can do even more damage than the one who has always been reserved about nudity. Privacy—on every level, including sex—is vital to development.

The problem many parents feel most concerned about is masturbation. Like it or not, doctors and psychologists who are in any way enlightened know this to be a normal part of a child's development. Put at the most simple level, people—including children—have to learn what is pleasing to them before they can learn how to please someone else.

Step by Step

Possibly one of the best maxims to use as a guideline in teaching children about sex is "Do what comes naturally." Children are very astute and can often sense discomfort or embarrassment, even if they do not have the vocabulary to explain it. Screwing up courage to tell a child about "the birds and the bees" has been an abortive occupation, as many a parent

has discovered. What *is* important though is to see that the information is *available* to the child, even if it is not given personally.

One doctor has very clear ideas on the parents' attitude to sex and children. "No running away from the problem, that's rule number one. After all, if little Jimmy asks you about his homework, or why a tree is like it is, you try to answer him, don't you? In the same way you must always try to answer questions about sex—as honestly as you can, but in your own way. Doctors and educators often tell you to trust your intuition as a parent before any 'outside' advice, and this also applies to sex education.

"Second point: Answer only as much as you are asked. There is no advantage in explaining the mechanics of daddy's erection if all you've been asked is where a baby comes from. Take it step by step, and if you feel you cannot do a good job, stall. By this I don't mean evade or lie—but try to give an explanation you feel happy with, and if necessary refer the child to the other parent. Children are very quick to notice unease in a parent, and though they may not be

A child should not grow up to think that the naked body is shameful.

able to explain it they will make associations between the subject and the distress and store it away.

"Rule number three: Never chastise children for 'playing with' their genitals—even if it is causing you a little embarrassment. You can suggest some other activity or, better still, ignore it. But to express disgust could eventually prove positively harmful to their sexual development. By the time they are nearing, or at, puberty —but preferably just before—children should know the basic facts about sex—their own and the opposite sex as well, even if they have no siblings. They should know how babies are born and grow, what the penis and an erection are, and the reasons for the menstrual cycle. Although not all doctors would agree, I think they should also know about contraception: what some of the methods are and their purpose. Half the babies in the world are born through ignorance of the facts of life. The least we can do as parents is to see that our children are not among the ignorant."

ENCYCLOPEDIA OF HUMAN BEHAVIOR

FORMANT
The particular quality of a vowel which allows it to be discriminated from other vowels.

FORMICATION
Prickly skin; the sensation of ants (*Formicae* in Latin) or small creatures crawling over the body.

FORNICATION
Sexual intercourse between people not married to each other.

FOSTER CHILD DELUSION
The belief that some children have that their mother and father are not really their true parents. This is often a temporary delusion and is related to the child's feelings of insecurity within the family.

FOVEA
An area of densely packed cells in the center of the retina in the eye which sends the most detailed visual information back to the brain. Foveal cells are almost all sensitive to color and are known as *cones*.

FREE ASSOCIATION
One of the main techniques used in the system of psychotherapy developed by Sigmund Freud, known as psychoanalysis. In his pioneering work, Freud came to believe that neurotic conditions are caused by conflicts within the personality which have been repressed into the unconscious mind. Here the individual, or his conscious self, may no longer ''know about them,'' but because they are still conflicts they lead to disturbances in his personality and mental life which he simply cannot control. The neurotic condition could be relieved only by bringing the material out of the unconscious, identifying it and taking steps to resolve the conflict. To get at this unconscious material Freud at first used hypnosis but later abandoned this in favor of dream interpretation. He also developed the technique of free association in which the patient, relaxed on a couch and spoke aloud any thoughts, no matter how shocking or absurd, that came into his mind. In a smooth psychoanalysis, inhibitions between the patient and the doctor would soon break down, and through the free association some of the repressed unconscious material would begin to come to light. Free association is still one of the major tools of today's psychoanalysts.

FREE-FLOATING ANXIETY
A vague sense of anxiety which does not appear to be attached to any particular person, object or event, but which plagues many people suffering from mild neurotic or depressive conditions.

FREQUENCY
A measure of the number of occasions that a particular event repeats itself in a fixed period of time.

FREUDIAN SLIP
An unconscious error in speech or writing which Freud believed gave an insight into what the speaker was really intending to say, rather than what he would like his listener to have heard.

FREUD, SIGMUND (1856-1939)
The outstanding Austrian psychologist who made many important contributions to understanding the human mind. He realized that motives and desires are often the product of unconscious forces within the mind and therefore not open to conscious voluntary control; that many of the peculiarities of human behavior and mental disorders are caused by conflict of powerful mental forces within the unconscious and therefore unidentifiable by the individual; and that the material of dreams gave important insights into the workings of the unconscious mind. He also developed psychoanalysis, a powerful if controversial tool for the identification and treatment of psychological disorders. Freud's ideas met with bitter opposition when he first launched them in the latter part of the nineteenth century, and only his fierce persistence, tremendous industry and refusal to be intimidated by the opposition of his colleagues allowed the ideas to develop to their present state, where they are a main prop of modern psychological theory.

FRIGIDITY
A woman's inability to get pleasure from sexual intercourse.

PAF International

FRONTAL LOBE
The large mass of the brain behind the forehead of the skull. It has an important role in rational thought and, to some extent, in control of the emotions.

FRONTAL LOBOTOMY
Cutting the nerve fibers of the frontal lobes of the brain. This is a drastic and irreversible surgical technique which gives some relief to seriously depressed or anxious patients. It is also known as *leucotomy*.

FROTTEUR
Someone who gets sexual pleasure principally from rubbing up against clothing of someone of the opposite sex.

FRUSTRATION
Any condition which follows the blocking of a basic drive, such as hunger, thirst, sexual desire or other psychologically orientated need.

FUGUE
A longish period of amnesia, almost always caused by psychological stress or conflict, in which a person may wander from his home and even become momentarily unaware of his identity.

FUNCTIONAL DISORDER
Any breakdown in a physical or psychological mechanism for which no organic cause can be discovered. Neuroses are the best example; no change in brain or body pathology lies behind them, and they appear to be related to the individual's inability to adjust to the world.

FUNCTIONAL PSYCHOSES
Major psychological disorders which are not supposed to have any organic origins. Schizophrenia and the manic-depressive psychoses were once believed to fall into this category, but evidence now shows that changes in the body's biochemistry are the most likely causes of these disorders.

FUSION
A uniting of two different things; in particular the brain's ability to blend the two slightly differing images fed to it by the eyes.

G FACTOR
The name given by the psychologist Charles Spearman to basic intellectual ability—the kind of thing which it is believed intelligence tests measure. There is considerable controversy over whether the G factor really is one single ability or a combination of many different ones.

GALTON, FRANCIS (1822-1911)
A British psychologist much influenced by Darwin. He was a pioneer of mental tests and the use of statistical methods in psychology.

Mary Evans

GALTON WHISTLE
An extremely high-pitched whistle which only the most sensitive human ear can detect. It is normally audible only to children, young adults and dogs.

GALVANIC SKIN RESPONSE (GSR)
A minor change in the electrical state of the skin which occurs during emotional reactions. This change can be detected if electrodes on the skin are hooked up to a sensitive recording device, and in this way a rough measure of an individual's emotional state can be made. The GSR, which is also sometimes known as the EDR *(electrodermal response)*, is an important part of the "lie detector."

GALVANOTROPISM
A tendency for a living organism to move towards an electric current.

GAMBLER'S FALLACY
The belief that, in supposedly random games like roulette or dice, sequences of numbers occurring together are somehow related to each other. The fallacy lies in assuming that, if heads comes up ten times in a row in flipping coins, this long sequence implies that heads is more likely (or *less* likely) to occur on the next throw than tails. In fact, in a genuine game of chance, the probability of heads or tails turning up on any throw is absolutely equal and has nothing at all to do with how many times either has come up in the past.

GAME THEORY
The study of games, and human strategies for playing them, in order to make predictions about social behavior, and mental processes in general.

GAMOPHOBIA
The abnormal fear of marriage.

Zip Art

GANGLION
A group of nerve cells.

GANSER SYNDROME
A tendency to give absurdly incorrect or silly answers to even exceedingly simple questions. This technique is most commonly seen in people trying to fake mental illness.

GANZFELD
An experimental situation, generally a small curved room or dome, in which the individual can see no corners, edges or variations in light or shade. Peculiar hallucinations and perceptual disorders tend to occur under such conditions.

GASTRIC NEUROSIS
A "nervous stomach," caused by anxiety, stress or conflict.

GATING
Interference by one sense with another. When we look closely at something, for example, we fail to hear the ticking of a clock.

GAUSSIAN CURVE
In statistics the so-called *normal distribution curve.* Typically found when factors such as height, weight or IQ scores are plotted. In the case of IQ, the peak of the curve represents the number of average individuals—those with an IQ of 100. The peak declines sharply but equally on either side so that there are roughly the same number of people with IQs of 110 as with IQs of 90, and a lesser, but equivalent, number with IQs of 120 and 80.

GENE
A tiny structure that together with the chromosomes, of which it is a part, forms the basic mechanism of inheritance in humans and animals.

GENERAL ADAPTATION SYNDROME (GAS)
Widespread change in the body's hormonal system brought about by stress.

GENERAL PARALYSIS OF THE INSANE (GPI)
Severe, progressive psychosis due to long-term effects of syphilis on the nervous system (also known as *general paresis).*

GENERAL PSYCHOLOGY
The main theme of psychology itself—the study of the laws of human behavior.

GENERAL SEMANTICS
The study of the way people use and understand symbols and language.

GENERALIZATION
Forming a principle which applies to one individual or circumstance and then extending it to apply to many.

GENERATION
The average reproductive life span of human beings, normally taken as between 30 and 35 years.

GENETICS
The study of the mechanisms by which humans and animals hand on characteristics through the reproductive system.

GENICULATE BODIES
Clusters of nerve cells which act as "junction boxes" in the brain, particularly for neurons from the visual senses.

GENITALS
The sexual or reproductive organs, especially the external organs.

GENITAL ZONES
Highly sensitive areas of the body in the neighborhood of the reproductive organs.

GENIUS
Someone with exceedingly high intelligence or creativity. Anyone with an IQ over 160 is generally classed as "genius level."

GENOTYPE
A characteristic which is shared by a biological group, like the tendency for Scandinavian people to be blue-eyed.

GEOMETRICAL ILLUSION
One of a whole range of peculiarities of visual perception in which geometrical shapes appear distorted despite the fact that the observer "knows" them not to be so. It is the universal nature of these illusions that makes them so fascinating to psychologists, who believe them to be clues about the brain's visual recognition mechanisms.

GEOPSYCHOLOGY
The study of the influence of environmental factors, such as climate, and terrain, on personality and behavior.

GEOTROPISM
A mechanism by which animals position themselves in a manner appropriate to the pull of gravity.

GEPHYROPHOBIA
A special form of *agoraphobia* (fear of open spaces) in which the individual is frightened to cross a bridge.

GERIATRICS
The study of psychological and physiological problems associated with old age.

GERIOPSYCHOSIS
A severe mental disorder caused by deterioration in the brain and nervous system as the result of old age. It is sometimes known as *senile dementia.*

GERMINAL PERIOD
The first phase of life in the embryo, in particular the two weeks following conception.

GERONTOLOGY
The study of old age.

GERONTOPHOBIA
An abnormal fear of old people or of becoming old oneself.

David Levin

Masculine mystique

"Be a man!" little boys are urged from the earliest age. A man is brave, strong, and virile—altogether superior to the "weaker sex." Men never cry, and if they are gentle they risk being called a sissy. Gee, it's tough being a man when you're shackled to an outgrown model.

For a long time man had never had it so good. Although he would not admit it, women as housewives were the backbone of society. Their job was clearly defined and straightforward: managing the household and bringing up children. After all, for women, there were far fewer opportunities for advancement than today. Though their horizons were limited, they knew what they were doing, and why they were doing it.

But this docile subservience in a sexually segregated society could not go on for ever. Women eventually struck out against the supremacy and arrogance of a male-orientated society which kept their intelligent and capable sisters boxed up in an unnatural state of idleness and boredom. Their determination brought its re-

ward. Eventually, they managed (theoretically) to achieve for all women equal rights to men. At the beginning of the century in the United States and Europe, concurrent movements were taking place and emancipation was established (at least in law if not in custom) for many millions of women.

But how do you free the mind? How do you liberate people from centuries of attitudes and prejudices about the sexes? Take our attitude to love and marriage. The poet Byron asserted that "man's love is of man's life a thing apart; 'tis woman's whole existence." This sounds to a woman's ear very much like the typical male viewpoint—a convenient rationalization for some of society's stereotypes about differences between men and women with regard to love, sex,

and the division of labor within the family. It means that women are prepared to work full-time in the service of love. Self-denial is the norm.

Supremacy Syndrome

In the early 1900s, marriage was a very unequal partnership. Father was head of the household, with mother and children way down in the "pecking order." Where this type of paternalistic male attitude still persists, it is generally held by men who are afraid they will somehow be less manly if they show kindness or consideration to a woman. Desmond Morris, zoologist and author of *The Naked Ape,* has stated that in Victorian days the male-supremacy syndrome involved lack of respect for so-called "inferiors." "Women, dogs, horses

1951

Mary Evans

were treated in a way men would never dream of treating other men. But today men are more manly, biologically, in that they are more loving to women. A man has to know how to assert his dominance without brutality." Even this statement is ambivalent, but the increasingly widespread rejection of the "masculine mystique"—the fear of tenderness and gentleness—is highly significant. The modern husband can embrace the "feminine principle" and be loving and domesticated, without being an effeminate sissy.

Crass Classification

Such changes have been remarkably rapid. Professor Ronald Fletcher, a sociologist and author of *The Family and Marriage in Britain,* has observed, "In the late twenties and early thirties there was a marked difference between the things men did and the things women did. Today men and women do things together. The new egalitarianism in marriage—this mutual consideration between two equals—has brought a new inde-

pendence and freedom to both sexes. This is a tremendous improvement. Men, I think, actively want this. A man now doesn't want to have a woman who is a sexual object only and just does his washing. He actively wants a relationship with an equal person who can talk with him about his interests." There remain the few who regard a wife as some sort of possession to do with what they will —like the man who locked his wife in the cellar until she promised to stop wearing miniskirts!

The trouble is that human beings find it convenient to classify each other into groups, and once we have sorted people—despite their rich individual differences—into simplified mental "categories" we think of them as *all* alike. And then we put values on our labels. "Men are only interested in one thing," say the women. "All women think about is getting married," say the men. "They're all the same," say the women. "They always think of themselves first—they're selfish, inconsiderate, undemonstrative and un-

Over port and cigars, gentlemen discuss matters of importance.

romantic." "Women," say men, "are possessive, overemotional, illogical and vain." You would think men and women were different species. Disillusionment, frustration and unhappiness that sometimes end in marital breakup can be the result of misunderstanding between a man and a woman.

The stereotype that suggests that we really *are* different in fundamental attributes and needs goes fairly deep. In a sense, the strength of these attitudes is not surprising. Male and female roles and expectations are conditioned and indoctrinated from early in life through the vital processes by which the young learn sex-role standards—the behavior and attitudes culturally appropriate to their sex. They also acquire "gender identity," the feeling of maleness or femaleness. Gender identity and sex-role standards are "printed" indelibly on the youngster during childhood; after only a few years a child is strongly committed

Marshall Cavendish

to shaping his behavior to what the family and society dictate as "appropriate" to his biological sex. Once this sex role is learned, it is not easily altered. The die is cast, pretty well, by the age of seven, if not earlier. Genetic or hormonal influences play only a secondary part in the process; upbringing and indoctrination into a sex role have the overriding influence.

Virility Obsession

Several theories have emphasized the role of identification. A child is said to be identified with a model (perhaps the father) if he is more likely to match that model's behavior than anyone else's. This matching behavior is more extensive than mere imitation. The child behaves as if *he* were the model, even in situations where he has seen the model in action. He also does this in a relatively comprehensive manner, adopting the model's values, beliefs, attitudes and life-style, as well as matching particular forms of behavior.

The view of many social learning theorists (like Dr. Jerome Kagan and

Dr. Albert Bandura) is that the child's experience with parents (particularly parents of the same sex) critically determines how he subsequently learns his social role. Parents (especially fathers) place great emphasis on the manly virtues. Boys have a more inflexible sex role to play than girls; they have the added difficulty of being required to shift initial identification with the mother over to the father, in order to acquire the appropriate masculine attributes.

A boy is under pressure from parents and teachers to do certain things, behave in certain ways, and is required to actively prove his maleness. At the same time he is curbed if he is overaggressive. So he is caught in a vicious circle—nothing he does is right. On the one hand he is being egged on; on the other he is being held back. He is caught up in the mystique of virility. This word virility has several connotations apart from the sexual ones we usually think of. It imparts the notion of strength, power, energy, vigor, potency and force and, in particular, dominance.

He's busy solving the world economic crisis—she's only keeping house.

To be sexually virile and manly is regarded as so important in our society that not to be so is a disaster. This obsession with sex and virility affects the way we bring up children —in particular, the disproportionate emphasis we place on virility in boys. Girls are allowed the leeway to pattern themselves after boys, in some respects; but boys are not allowed to behave like girls. Girls may wear skirts *and* trousers, but can you imagine a boy in a dress? Girls may have masculine-sounding names like Toni, Steve, Jo, Jackie, and so on, and can play with boys' toys and indulge in boyish activities.

Because of the inflexibility of the masculine role, boys are more aware of sex-appropriate behavior than girls. A boy's gender role is a matter of great concern to parents (especially to fathers, who place great emphasis on the manly virtues, and to mothers who through force of circumstance have to bring up their boys without a father). Parents worry that, if he shows some "effeminate" gentleness or "girlish" interests, the boy may not identify himself as a male. They may also worry that their child is homosexual. These inflexible attitudes mean that psychological pressures are at work to maintain differences, from early in life.

Though various pressures and expectations make them difficult to rear, male children are still highly valued by parents, and particularly mothers. Mothers sometimes spoil their sons and make them feel that females are their satellites—thus increasing the boys' self-importance. It is ironic that the same women who complain at length about the selfishness and self-centeredness of their husbands at the same time—quite unconsciously—indulge their male children and thus prepare their own dubious fate for another generation of wives. The really doting mother is storing up trouble for her daughter-in-law. Why should a wife in this situation want to match the mother and be a sort of willing slave? After all, it is her husband, *not* her son, and they are not treated the same! The trouble is that some men do expect their wives to duplicate the maternal role. But, today, many women reject the combined roles of childbearing handmaiden and little "earth mother" to the entire family.

Threatened Identity

A survey of married women showed that most of the wives were aware of undergoing changes in themselves as a result of being married and having children. Several felt that, as a result of being completely tied to the home while their children were young, they had been forced to re-adjust more drastically than their husbands. Sometimes resentment crept into the discussion. A wife's identity and individuality as a woman and not just as a housekeeper and mother is more seriously threatened by domestic pressures than a working man's identity is ever likely to be. One woman felt that her marriage would definitely not survive the birth of another child, because that would mean she was doing nothing but satisfying others for yet another five years. "I think of myself as always giving—either to my husband or my child."

In some homes you simply are not aware of any questions like "The baby's crying and yelling again—who's going to see to him this time?" Husband and wife operate so smoothly as a team that they convince you

they are one unit. Elsewhere husband and wife always seem to be asking, "Am I having to do more than my share? I'm not getting a fair deal!"

If a radical change is to take place in man's place in the family, it must begin with the child. At a very basic level, learning how to become a good father begins in childhood, with the experience of having observed a good husband, and of having had a good father. But if the personal experience of these relationships has not been happy, then a useful start is to try examining the reasons for success and failure. Some fathers are unthinkingly trapped in patterns of behavior which can be traced back to childhood experience. For instance, boys are not normally encouraged to look after younger children. They tend to think of it as a restriction rather than something to be enjoyed. But if a boy's parents can remedy this situation by allowing him to demonstrate his skill, knowledge and experience to younger children, then they may do much to promote a basic foundation for fatherhood.

Too Much Togetherness

The new approach of giving the father a real place in all the activities of family life is not without its problems. A fact we have to face is that the divorce rate has almost doubled in ten years. Experts have suggested a possible reason for the increase: it may well be, in part, symptomatic of new partnership problems, of men and women having to learn to live and work together in new ways. Sociologist Professor Donald MacRae believes it was in the fifties that men discovered home was quite a good place to be. "There was simply more to stay in the home for—television, better food, greater warmth. All this went hand in hand with greater prosperity. There was more money about. A man could afford to decorate, to become a home handyman. The family car became a normality of life. Holidays became shared experiences. Suddenly men found themselves not just providing for but sharing in the home." And yet this togetherness puts a great strain on the individuals in a partnership.

Togetherness can be excessive. If husband and wife are to develop in their own right as individuals, they cannot do *everything* together or they may feel trapped. When men try to articulate their reasons, the gist of it seems to be that they crave a temporary escape from the feminine principle—the world of tenderness

and gentleness which men sometimes find cloying or even suffocating—into the more robust, rough, even uncouth masculine ethos. Rightly or wrongly, men (or at least many of them) feel threatened. They feel alienated by the work they do and the lives they live in a huge, impersonal technological society. For many men it seems that their work and their roles in life are emasculating. It is a relief for them to withdraw for a short while into the company of other men and into the masculine fantasy and wish-fulfillment world that males provide for each other. There have, of late, been many books and articles written about the "masculinity crisis" and the "flight from women"—emphasizing man's search for his lost identity.

Masculinity Crisis

As Myron Brenton puts it—in a book *The American Male: A Penetrating Look at the Masculinity Crisis*—"A man trapped is a man whose freedom —in effect, his virility—is being taken from him. This attitude shows up when a man has to deny his dependence on a woman to insist, 'It is she who needs me, not I who need her.' "

Karen Horney, author of *Feminine Psychology,* states that the mother, with her dual critical-nurturant role, is obviously a very potent figure in the evolution of attitudes towards love. As the first love object in most people's lives, her influence is thought to be very persistent—affecting even adult behavior. In males, there are various residual effects of this primary love. They recoil from the forbidding female. They have a childlike, happy sense of release when in each other's company in clubs, sports, and war—free from women and particularly wives, the unconscious symbols of chastising mothers. For men often regress in each other's company, behaving more like adolescents than grown men.

Margaret Mead points out the inescapable truth (in her book *Male and Female*) that if women are denied the right to use their minds, their sons suffer as well as their daughters. She goes on to argue that an over-emphasis on the importance of virility and male dominance (the whole cult of *machismo*) will in the end make the lives of men as incomplete and machinelike as an overemphasis on the females' reproductive functions makes the lives of women: "It is possible to say that, to the extent that either sex is disadvantaged, the whole culture is poorer, and the sex that, superficially, inherits the earth, inherits only a very partial legacy."

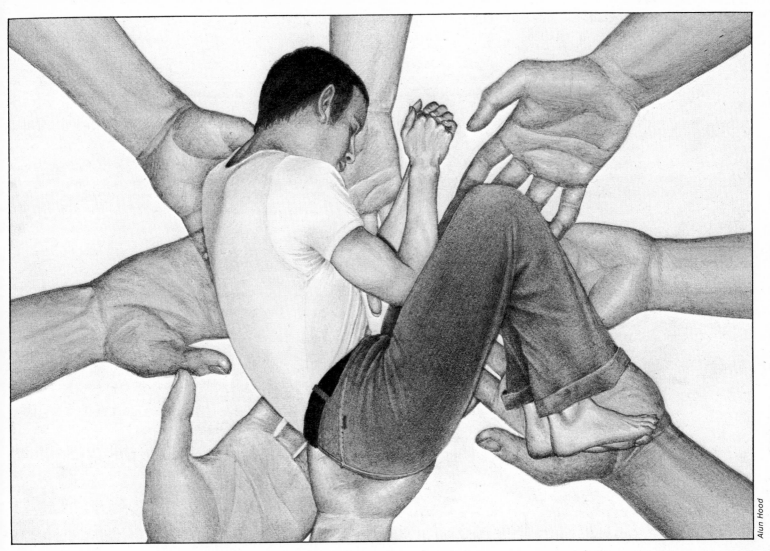

Alun Hood

No man is an island

We all need a helping hand now and again to bolster our flagging egos. Encounter groups
are made up of people with problems who take it in turns to focus on one individual
and buoy him up. And so they get by with a little help from their friends.

Imagine over five hundred psychiatrists, counselors and psychologists, all barefoot with their eyes tightly screwed up, picking their way gingerly across the banqueting room of a large hotel. Imagine them selecting a partner, still keeping their eyes closed, and tentatively touching the hands and face of the other. Those who managed to cross the purple-carpeted floor without being chosen by anyone are matched up by the therapists standing around the edge.

Such a scene—and this took place in Britain—would have been unthinkable ten years ago. Yet a conservative profession was ready to explore a new form of group therapy that had swept the United States. What is different about encounter groups? One of the most immediately striking differences

between encounter groups and more traditional therapy groups is that nonverbal communication is encouraged.

In the traditional group, six to eight people sit with their therapist and talk about their feelings. In an encounter group, you are encouraged to "act out" what you feel. Instead of saying, "I feel angry," you can punch a pillow, yelling as loud as you like. If you want to show sympathy, you can take the hand of someone or cross the room and put your arms around him. The effect on someone used to the restraint of ordinary groups is exhilarating—or terrifying.

Sensory awareness is among the stated aims of some encounter groups. Most of us are unaware of our own body signals, and those of other people. Our socialization trains us,

if not to suppress, at least to refrain from expressing feelings too spontaneously. Consequently, we lose touch with what we really feel and develop the capacity for denying truthful directness. Social distance is a feature of our society; touching, except in special relationships, is forbidden. Yet contact, real physical contact, seems to be an important human requirement.

Group Grope

In an encounter group, the usual taboos may be lifted. Of course, this could merely be a cover for crude sexual groping, and in some groups, and with some individuals, this is so. But in most groups with properly trained leaders, contact and freedom of physical expression are a genuine way to counteract alienation. Some of the techniques used involve trust, physically expressed, among members. In a group of eight, members may be asked to choose the person they most wish to relax. The selected person stands in the middle, with all the others around him. He closes his eyes and lets himself fall back, into the waiting arms of another member. He will be passed gently from hand to hand: he learns that the others will not—literally—let him down.

Touching Experience

"I thought it was crazy at first, and I was annoyed that I had been chosen. It suggested that I seemed tense. It was very difficult to let go in the beginning. My back was rigid. Then a strange feeling came over me; I felt that all my worries were being taken away and I let go. When it stopped, I felt regret and great gratitude." (British psychiatrist, age 45)

A more complicated version of the same experience is for the chosen person to lie down, while the others kneel beside him, stroking his body. Gradually, they lift him up, making a hammock of their arms, swinging him slowly, raising him three or four feet, then gently replacing him. Sometimes, they sing and hum, each his own tune, making a strangely beautiful sound.

"I'd never heard anything like it. Five hundred people or so, all singing something different. You'd think it would be a hideous din—yet it wasn't. It was like mermaids, or the music of the spheres. Not quite earthly." (Clinical psychologist, female, age 29)

Even with people who normally shun direct physical contact, once the first distaste is conquered, the opportunity to touch is welcomed. Because we often lie with words, even without realizing it, any member of an encounter group can stand behind another and say for him what he *really* seems to express with his body. The interpreter may be wrong, and the selected member can protest, but once you are sensitized to nonverbal cues, you can tell with great accuracy what is going on under the surface. You have to accept, of course, that others may do this to you as well.

The second main way encounter groups differ from other therapy groups lies in the function of the leader. In psychoanalytic groups, the leader tries to be a blank screen on which the various members can project their significant figures. The less the leader shows himself, the better his technique is supposed to be. Other kinds of group leaders monitor the discussion, try to keep the group climate a healing one, and offer interpretations. In most encounter groups, the leader is called a "facilitator" and his job is to ease communications. He does not hide behind a professional mask but brings in his feelings too.

Psychiatrist Carl Rogers points out that disturbed persons, or those who need the group more than it needs them, do not make good facilitators. The presentation of the leader as another human being can relieve or frighten the group: very dependent clients like to be given a lead; they *want* to feel that the therapist is an expert who will tell them what is wrong and what to do about it. The very lack of structure in encounter groups can produce anxieties, but a good group will usually help the individual work them out.

Usually, encounter groups last for a short time. They may involve a whole day, a weekend or an entire week. However, it is more usual for psychotherapy groups to be conducted in weekly sessions for periods of one to three years. Some encounter groups are marathon sessions, lasting for 24 hours or more. The experience is intensified, so that insights and new patterns of behavior which would take much longer in conventional groups can happen much faster.

Difficult to Deal With

The changes most often reported by participants are new depths of communication, increased self-awareness, and more loving tolerance towards others. Whole families may join a group; but even when only one member does so, the benefits are shared. One father said that he was able to talk to his son, to see him as another person, for the first time. A young mother who had been irritated by the constant quarreling of her two daughters was able to respond to them so much better that one child asked her, "What did they do there? Teach you to be nice to kids?"

Occasionally, if only one marriage partner goes to an encounter group, the other finds the new openness of communication too difficult to deal with. It used to be very rare for a husband and wife to be in the same group, but it is becoming more usual. If one partner feels that this would be inhibiting, it would be better for them to go to separate groups, then bring their experiences together.

The changes do not always last, and unfortunately we do not have enough research evidence to know what conditions and personality types make for the most lasting changes. In a group of managers, one man admitted that he had gone back to work after the group, full of a new, open and cooperative spirit, but that, three months later, it was all too easy to slip back into the old patterns. For some, the experience has the intensity of religious conversion, but that does not last forever either.

Factors which probably play a part in the degree of long-term change are the amount of dissatisfaction with old attitudes; the quality of the experiences in the group; and the amount of effort it takes to put new ways of relating into practice. Emotional arousal and group support make personality change easier. Where it has been a matter of losing fears or developing confidence, encounter sessions make their most dramatic impact.

Feelings of Jealousy

One woman of 40 came along to a weekend encounter in a state of quiet desperation. She was a schoolteacher, good at her job, but always bypassed for promotion. The principal was a dominant woman who struck fear into her heart, in much the same way as her tyrannical mother had done all her life. Barbara looked as defeated as she felt. She dressed dowdily and shrank away from contact.

By the end of the first day, she was struggling against feelings of jealousy towards a young, pretty, married woman who seemed to get most of the male attention. These feelings came out in some bitter remarks: "You don't know what a problem is. You've been spoiled all your life, anyone can see that. You act like a child; you think the world is just for you to play with."

The younger woman burst into tears. The group discovered that less than a year before her baby had been killed in a road accident and she had suffered badly from depression since that time, blaming herself for leaving the baby carriage in a place which should have been safe. A truck had mounted the curb and backed into a wall, crushing the baby.

Barbara felt completely hateful and ashamed; she could say nothing. She turned away, intending to leave. But instead of rejecting her, the group brought her back. They all sat up very late, holding each other for comfort, talking from time to time about guilt, loss and jealousy, but in a personal, not an abstract way. Barbara told them about her young sister, who was always the favorite. She was the pretty one, while Barbara was the clever one.

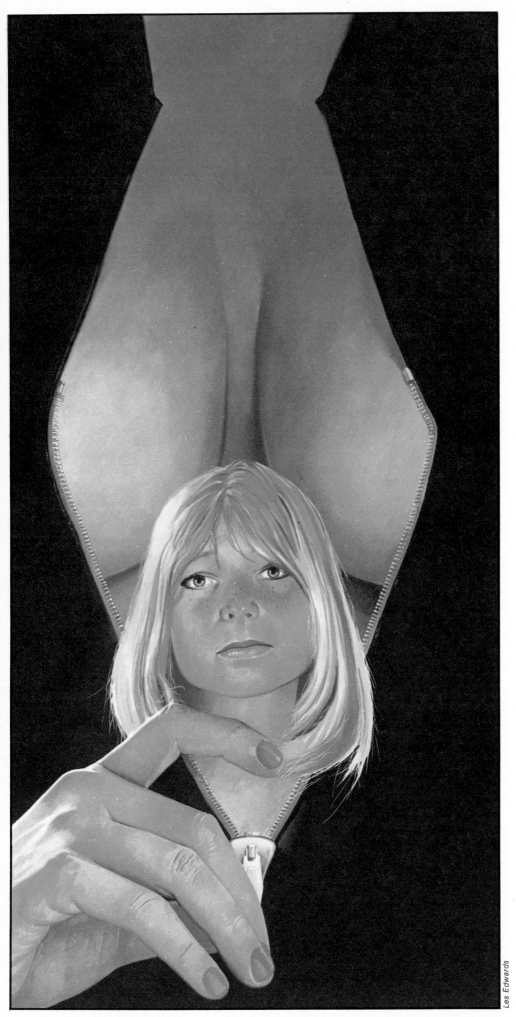

Les Edwards

She had never really felt like a woman, but some kind of neuter. It was not an unusual story, but telling it in an atmosphere of trust helped Barbara to see that she *could* be loved; that under her shyness and self-deprecation was a rage about being left out that had intensified with the years.

On the following day, one of the men said thoughtfully, "You could easily be beautiful, Barbara. All you need to do is like yourself a bit. You look lovely right now, open and glowing." It was true—all human beings look beautiful when their face is open, and even the best features can look ugly when the face is closed.

Need for Comfort

Barbara went back to school in a new mood. She handed in her resignation and found a better job where she was appreciated. She renewed real contact with her sister, and bit by bit she started doing things that she really enjoyed.

The old fears come back from time to time. "I hear my old whining, self-hating voice put down my new efforts, but I think about the group and keep going until the destructive bit shuts up. My life may not look very different from the outside, apart from the job, but it *feels* different inside. I enjoy it; experience gets straight through."

Why do people go to encounter groups? Barbara was typical of one kind, who feel dissatisfied with themselves and the lives they have built, but are not sure what is wrong. Unless they are very rich, such people would not usually consult a psychiatrist, nor are they "neurotic" in the clinical sense. They manage; they hold down jobs; but they have a sense of wasted potential. Rather than a "cure," they are seeking personal growth: ordinary life may seem too superficial. Certainly the mushroom growth of encounter groups suggests that many people feel the need for meaningful contacts.

If you are thinking of trying an encounter group, choose carefully. Most practitioners are genuine and well-trained, but there are some whose only interest is in parting you from your money or, worse still, living vicariously through other people's emotions. Sometimes, in the course of a group, an individual's problems are exposed but not worked through. Then the unfortunate person may feel worse instead of better. If Barbara had

Group therapy may strip her of her false image to reveal the little girl inside. Daring to show yourself is vital to emotional development.

1957

been left in full knowledge of her anger and jealousy, without being helped to accept them, she could have broken down completely.

The range of techniques in encounter groups varies greatly. Some groups incorporate nudity, meditation or psychodrama. Others concentrate on massive attacks on participants' defenses. But most groups go through similar stages of development, whatever their particular orientation. At first, there is a "milling around" period, with no one quite sure what to expect. People eye one another warily and look to the leader for guidance. There may be some warming-up games, like walking blindfold across the room and pairing up.

Truth Game

If the original group is large, it is soon divided into much smaller subgroups, and this is where the real learning begins. Unless all the members are sophisticated in group techniques, there is a social stage of politeness. The facilitator may say something like, "Here we are. We can make anything we like of this group"—which seems like no help at all to the anxiously waiting members. Eventually someone will break the ice, suggesting introductions, and it all begins. Something will always break through the original resistance.

In one group, it was the refusal of a woman to give her name or any personal details, as she wanted to be known only for what she was in the group. This annoyed the people who had already introduced themselves. They felt belittled, and exposed.

Very often, the first real, immediate feelings to arise are negative ones. When we meet people in everyday life, we usually have a "liking" or "not-liking" response, but etiquette forbids us to make the "not-liking" clear. In an encounter group, you are encouraged to be truthful. This can be very hard at first if the not-liking is directed towards a pathetic member.

When this happened in one group, everyone automatically behaved well to Stan, who was eager to please, unsure of himself, and with his every move begged for sympathy. After a couple of hours, when people were interacting more freely, they were still being "nice" to Stan, until one young man said, "I feel awful about saying this, but I'm getting mad with Stan. He is so blasted pathetic." One or two were censorious about his statement, but the rest admitted that they, too, felt resentful of Stan's demands and his helplessness.

Cruel? In another setting, maybe—but in the group Stan had to face up to the way he manipulated people. Eventually he gained some insight into why he so often felt let down. He made real progress, getting around to voicing *his* annoyance, with some of the others, something he could not do before. He went home less pathetic, feeling like a real adult person at last.

When hostility is expressed in a group, it can be harsh. This is where a skilled facilitator is needed, to ensure that it does not go too far—or not far enough. Usually people in encounter groups move from expressing hostility to realizing why they feel so strongly about others. It could be that the other reminds them of someone in their outside lives, or that what they hate in the other person is actually a trait that they dislike in themselves. From this realization grow bonds of understanding and sympathy and the group develops a healing capacity.

Carl Rogers points out that self-acceptance is the beginning of change. Yet self-acceptance is dependent on acceptance by other people. In this truth lies the power of the group (it is so for any group, but the intensified conditions of encounter situations generate more emotion). The members often share painful memories and experiences with each other, knowing they will not be rejected. Out of the pain of self-revelation grows a sense of trust and of release and the feeling of isolation fades. Increasingly, the real selves come through, with the support of the whole group. People who started off disliking each other frequently end up with a mutual compassion.

Three-Day High

Each person receives feedback about how he operates socially: some of us can be amazingly unaware of the impression we create. It is an exhausting and sometimes overwhelming process, if taken at all seriously. If treated like a kind of parlor game, it is a waste of time. For those who remain skeptic and uninvolved throughout an encounter, it seems a missed opportunity.

At the end of the session, the usual sensation is one of joy. Having worked through things together creates a strong feeling of unity and hope for future change. "I was high for three days after. Even when I came down to earth, it wasn't a letdown feeling. I was changed, nothing could take away what had happened to me." (Housewife, age 36)

"I was full of the milk of human kindness for a couple of days. Then I realized that it had all been a con; people aren't basically loving at all. Why should they be? Away from the group, the world was just the same. I felt annoyed with myself for being taken in, even for a short time. But it was kind of interesting while it was going on. It wasn't real, though." (Executive, age 28)

Off with the Facade

If you have lurid visions of orgiastic weeks in California, you may be surprised to know that encounter groups are widely used in industry, churches, education and even government. In industry, they have proved useful in creating an open climate for problem solving. Executives who have experienced sensitivity training are often able to build up better communications between departments and help their employees work together more effectively.

Church personnel find that pastoral care and counseling are improved by the insights they gain into themselves and others. "It made me much more human in my approach, and I learned that my authoritative manner often works against what I try to do. I guess I learned a lot about my own problems, too. I have not changed overnight, but I think I can get through more easily to people now. At least, I'm working on it!" (Roman Catholic priest, age 38)

Teachers find their relationships with students and colleagues improve, making cooperative work easier. "I couldn't stand having another teacher in the room. Team teaching seemed a good idea in theory, but in practice I wanted to close my door on me and my kids, with no one else there. It was lack of confidence, and a bit of maternal jealousy, about *my* class. Now, after the group, I can appreciate the help of my colleagues, and I'm much more ready to take a risk and stick my neck out. No one's cut it off yet!" (Woman teacher, age 45)

What you get out of encounter groups depends partly on what you need. Whether the gains are personal or professional (though most professionals who attended work-oriented groups said that they gained as people, too), you have to be prepared to be honest, to take responsibility for your own feelings, and to risk showing yourself as you really are. Hanging on to your facades, even if it feels more comfortable, will box you up and prevent growth.

Paddy Eckersley

Learning to love

Our parents' relationship acts as a mold in which the forms our own love takes are cast.
Failure is thus not always ours alone but is handed down through the generations.

Sexually, our parents leave an indelible mark on us—partly because of the inherited physical stamp we bear, partly because of the emotional lessons we learn from them.

Physical differences can play a significant part in sexuality. A woman so beautiful that conversation stops whenever she enters a room may develop a view of the relationship between physical attraction and love that is quite different from a homelier girl's. A tall man is regarded differently from a short man, and this affects his assessments of himself and others. He may develop a sense of authority and grow used to taking the initiative in sexual matters; or, on the negative side, some women may reject him as a potential sexual partner just because he intimidates them.

Because people tend to look like their parents, they may find themselves becoming involved in the same type of sexual situation. Two people with fair skin, for example, shunning the holiday sunlight, may strike up a relationship in a darkened bar or discothèque—just as their parents did.

"When I met Bernie," said Joy, "I was 19. And with two years' experience as a cabaret dancer behind me I thought I was a real old-timer. My legs were my fortune—you can see they're still good. They say you never lose good legs whatever happens to the rest of your looks—'right up to the armpits' was the phrase the men in the audience used.

"Bernie was one of those men. He brought in a party of out-of-town salesmen one night—and came back

by himself the next. We weren't meant to date the customers, but it's not too difficult to let someone you like know where you can meet—accidentally. Within about three weeks we were engaged, Bernie arranged with the club manager to release me from my contract, and we were married in under a month. I wired my mother— 'Bringing husband home'—and took Bernie to meet my parents.

Like Mother, Like Daughter

"When we walked in the house, my mother was in tears—but it wasn't anger; she really wanted to make sure we'd be happy together. Then she started to tell me about the way she and my father met—it was almost more romantic than me and Bernie, and I'd never known. She'd been modeling stockings—it's those legs again—and my father was a buyer with one of the major outlets. Within two weeks of meeting he'd taken out a license and they were married as soon as they could. My grandparents wouldn't see them, apparently, and that was why my mother was crying. She was determined I wouldn't be rejected in the way she had been. But I was far more excited by just how similar our experiences had been—and without my knowing about it."

Legacy of Love

Much the greater part of parental influence, however, is psychological. And this influence can operate equally through foster or stepparents or other adults who become closely involved with a child's upbringing. Children become imbued with a sense of values, a feeling of how to act, which they derive in great part from the way their parents behave. Later they may rebel against these values and will certainly adjust their acceptance of them in the light of their own adult experiences. But this legacy does form the framework within which they will come to terms with their own developing sexuality and may affect much of their adult sexual behavior.

The prime influence on the child's developing sexual personality comes from his observations of his parents' relationship. However the parents treat each other, that, to the child, seems the only way possible for a man and a woman to interact. And if, in later life, the child decides a different form of relationship is preferable, it can mean learning a new set of responses. A person who comes from a "cold," apparently asexual, background, for example, may find that even within a sexual relationship this psychological "coldness" persists.

The significance of the parents' behavior stems from the close relationship the child develops with mother and father individually early in life. The most important man in a child's life is the father, the most important woman the mother; and the way they act as individuals and as a couple governs the child's picture of how a man or a woman ought to act.

"My parents were in love and you could tell it," Jennifer said. "When I was young I didn't know that was what it was—I only learned how to label things later—but I already knew that some children had parents who seemed to be carrying on some internal war, and others would be all over their kids but almost ignored each other. Ours were very involved with each other—it meant we children became very independent early because they preferred to see us as small adults and an extension of their relationship rather than something that interfered with it.

"It's a pattern I've carried on into my own married life. Before I met Erik I'd had a number of affairs—very pleasant but not overwhelming emotional experiences. My parents had shown me that there were levels of love, and I was happy to share the pleasure of sex with someone I found attractive without thinking that this meant I must be in love.

"With Erik I knew it was more than sex and pleasure—although they're very important—right from the start. In some ways our relationship duplicates my parents', but I think we've extended it and gained some advantages. They were so close that other people hardly counted—they had friends, but somehow when they were with them there was this feeling that everyone else was superfluous.

Rewarding Relationship

"Erik and I are freer. We probably spend more time together, actually relating to each other, than most couples; but we have interests of our own. I spend a lot of time working on an education project I'm planning and Erik designs new computer hardware, and we have a number of close friends, people we'll spend hours with discussing—well, discussing what it is that makes a relationship rewarding, as often as not."

The way parents show their love for each other and for the child can have a very great effect on the purely sexual aspects of the child's later life. A mature adult displays what Erich Fromm, the American psychoanalyst, labels the ability to love—and that includes the ability to feel loved.

A child brought up by undemonstrative parents who satisfy every material whim but never make any spontaneous gesture of affection can become an adult who remains aloof from emotional involvement. Sex, if sexual relationships are indulged in at all, becomes an impersonal slaking of a physical urge. However effective the bodily stimulation offered, the emotions do not come into play and he or she never experiences the full

Marshall Cavendish

A youngster's outlook is heavily influenced by the attitude his parents take to one another. If they are natural and don't suffer from hang-ups, the child will grow to have a healthy view of sex and marriage.

PAF International

release of total orgasm. Wilhelm Reich, author of *The Function of the Orgasm,* believed such a person would become irredeemably neurotic.

Emotional Exploitation

In other cases parents might feign affection and be overdemonstrative. The child can detect the hypocritical motives behind hugs and kisses that always seem to have some ulterior aim—will you do this? are you going to side with Mummy or Daddy? For the adult, sex becomes just another mode of emotional exploitation. The partner is brought to a state of sexual expectation that makes him or her easy to manipulate, and then favors are extracted—agreeing to visit an unpleasant relative, the gift of a new mink coat, or just a sense of domination can all flow from this form of sexual bargaining.

When the parents themselves have a mature relationship and express their love for their child without restraint but without false effusiveness they prepare the way for the adult appreciation of love. The child acquires the ability to respond to affection and to expect that others will value him or her as a person. Without this internal feeling of personal value there is always a danger that an adult will attempt to compensate by "forcing" a succession of other people to fall in love with him or her, substituting sexual desire for an intimation of intrinsic worth—and running the risk of being labeled Don Juan or nymphomaniac as the conquests pile up. With parents who demonstrate how to feel and how to act, the growing child establishes a model of emotional behavior that governs his or her own developing sexual personality.

This boy is outgoing and happy because his home life is firm and secure. His parents see to that.

Parental attitudes towards sexuality itself are, however, the most important influences on their children's sexual behavior. Reactions to parental attitudes vary widely: from Aleister Crowley, the English necromancer, who throughout his life conducted his sexual affairs as though he was embracing exactly what his puritanical parents would have forbidden; to the shrinking child-wife whose attitude towards men remains exactly what her mother told her it should be; to the liberated adult whose life is free from sexual dogma imposed by parental decree but reflects the valuable advice and example they have given. And adults—not their parents—must actually take responsibility for their own sexual behavior, although it may reflect the combined resultant of the influences of parents and others.

Parents who do not disguise the fact that they make love and are able to accept the sight of the naked body with joy—although without going to the excesses of forcing nudity, or especially the sight of love-making, on their children—are likely to instill an open and welcoming attitude about sex. The adolescent may adopt a supercilious attitude towards his or her parents' continued sexuality: "Think of it. They're 50 years old and you can still hear their bedsprings creaking every night after they've gone to bed. They ought to act their age, not like a couple of horny teenagers." But this is a passing phase and as an adult the parents' example is remembered—and suggests how rewarding a relationship can be.

Sex Secrets

One of the difficulties inherent in any sexual relationship is just this— each stage is completely new to those involved. From the first experience of love-making through the growing intimacy of a long-term relationship to the settling down into life together each step is into the unknown. The knowledge that another couple—the parents—made the same journey and found, and continued to find, pleasure in their sexual relationship is reassuring. The children of such parents are likely to accept sex easily as an important and sustained part of an emotional relationship but will not turn it into a magical totem that is meant to solve every problem.

When parents themselves are secretive about sex—and possibly show embarrassment when others show an interest—their children, too, can acquire the same furtiveness that may continue into adult life. There can be some stimulation in the idea that sex is a bit shady, a secret activity a couple share without letting the world know: but to base a relationship completely on an act viewed as distasteful will impose an intolerable strain.

An adult may overcome harmful attitudes instilled by the parents by contact with others who have developed healthier attitudes to sex. But discovering a mode of sexuality different from the parental relationship is a matter of luck, of realizing that there are many different kinds of experience and of learning how to react to the influences of others.

In some cases, the example set by the parents may reappear in their children in quite specific ways. In a self-fulfilling analysis the child-adult says, "My parents were like this; therefore I am condemned to act as I do." The rationalization may provide a convenient excuse for behavior that is actually painful to others or help a person conceal a belief that his main relationship in life is no longer viable.

Annette was intelligent and, as a young girl, strikingly beautiful: a career, heady romances, and a life that seemed all excitement were hers. She married an admirable man and quickly had three children—and then the other side of her brilliant nature began to show. As her children grew and her husband devoted himself more and more to work, she indulged in a series of affairs. Her children became used to meeting handsome but unknown men who would whisk their mother away to obviously exciting assignations. Eventually she moved out of her husband's house—the children were now teenagers, almost adults—and continued her rackety life untouched by responsibility.

"Going to a party with my mother was an amazing experience," said Donald. "About half the men in the place would dash forward when she arrived, and then they'd hang around obviously wondering what kind of relationship she had with the others. When I met Magda I thought, 'This is the woman for me'—I'd had a couple of affairs so I thought I knew what I was talking about.

In the Blood

"Then Magda got pregnant, and one night, when she was about six months gone and sex had become a bit difficult, I stayed out drinking with some guys from work. One invited me back to his house and somehow or other I managed to have sex with his wife out in the kitchen while he had fallen asleep in the living room—I still don't think he ever knew what happened. I saw his wife again—and then met a friend of hers. With Magda getting more unwieldy day by day, before I knew what was happening I seemed to be setting up quite a harem.

"The bubble had to burst. But when it did I didn't care. 'It's in the blood,' I told Magda. 'You knew what my mother was like when you married me. If that's the way it is, that's it.' Magda left me—with the new baby. But I'd sort of resigned myself to it happening. You have to live your fate —and with my mother that's my fate."

Parents have two apparently specific influences over the way their children develop sexually. Sex instruction—father sitting down to talk to son, mother explaining to daughter —is often seen as a straightforward exposition of how things ought to be. But sex education is far more complicated than a single session of the birds and the bees, and the parent who undertakes to guide an adolescent towards sexual maturity with a half-hour talk is already demonstrating an approach to sex that will cause the child difficulties later.

Sex education is a continuing process, and it helps if the child receives advice from both parents about the emotional concomitants of being a boy or a girl. Some straightforward information is necessary—how you carry out sexual intercourse, the methods of contraception—but the context within which this is put conveys far more about sexuality than the pure biological instruction.

Anxiety Area

Later the parents may attempt to guide or even control the adolescent's explorations into sex. At one extreme they may help the adolescent discuss the emotional problems he or she is experiencing for the first time, ensure that information about contraception is available, and trust the young adult to act responsibly. At the other extreme, they may impose a curfew, screen boyfriends or girlfriends, and even inspect their child's clothing after a date to ensure nothing untoward occurred. Other parents may ignore what is happening—but by refraining from discussing sex, they allow their child to flounder into and out of just as much sexual confusion as he or she can manage.

But, as with sex education, these "controls" are symptoms of the entire relationship between parent and child —and of attitudes to sex. Banning friends of the opposite sex will do little to deter the adolescent who has already decided to rebel against parental values, but it may warp the life of someone who has no desire to thwart parents at all. Making contraceptives available will do little to help the adolescent who has learned from the way his or her parents behave that sex is an area of anxiety, not joy.

As adults we are like our parents— in our sexual attitudes and behavior as much as any other area. They have influenced us and we are often willing to accept that influence. But as adults we can question our parents' ideas about sex as much as we might query their opinions about politics or fashion. And if we disagree there is every reason why we should change our feelings about sex.

Robin Clifford

Chrysalis kids

Boys and girls grow up—time takes care of that. But whether it is a painful process or
not depends upon many factors. For puberty can be a period of happy exploration—or misery and
inhibition. What is it that makes the difference?

Girls mature into women in different ways. Puberty may be delayed, so that a girl does not develop her sexual characteristics and start her periods by the time she is 16. For about one girl in a hundred, puberty does not occur by this age (a perfectly arbitrary figure), but rarely is it delayed past the early twenties without obvious physical reason. Always, however, a physician should be consulted.

Precocious, or early, puberty is sometimes more of a worry. A precise definition of early development is again necessarily a little arbitrary, but broadly speaking it is considered to be the onset of menstruation, accompanied by other evidence of maturity, such as the development of the breasts or the appearance of pubic or other sexual hair, before a girl is ten. In such cases general physical development is also accentuated. Bones that normally keep on growing until the late teens suddenly complete their growth spurt, so that the girl commonly remains unusually small. General intelligence and mental function may be retarded, or advanced, by this very early puberty.

In all cases of precocious puberty a thorough medical examination with special reference to the pituitary, the adrenal gland and the ovaries should be carried out. Often it is advisable to refer the girl to an endocrinologist. Nevertheless, in about 90 percent of all the cases of precocious puberty, no organic cause is obvious, and the condition is "constitutional."

Mother at Five

Precocious puberty may very occasionally cause a medical sensation: a little Peruvian girl called Linda Medina started her periods at a very early age and had a baby when she was only five years eight months old.

Regular menstrual periods are among the latest features of puberty to be established in adolescence. The very first period may be short or long, and a little or a large quantity of blood may be lost. Thereafter the menstrual cycle is often very irregular. Sometimes periods occur frequently (which usually does not worry anybody) or infrequently—which may produce a certain amount of anxiety. A more or less regular pattern often takes anything up to three years to establish itself, and 20 percent of teenage girls experience gaps of anything from two to twelve months between periods.

Wide Variation

Even when girls are in their late teens, "regular" menstruation is something of a misnomer. Each girl tends to find a pattern of menstruation that is highly individual and yet quite normal despite wide variations. Any cycle of between three to five weeks is common, although the large majority of women have periods at around the familiar 28-day interval. However, whenever records are kept over a long period of time, in normal and healthy girls, occasionally cycles are found to occur in which the periods may be anything from 2 days "early" to 28 days "late." Clearly a woman's internal biological clock, although quite

marvelous in many ways, sometimes loses or gains "time."

In the same way that periods are irregular in their spacing, particularly in adolescence, there are also wide variations in the amount of blood that is lost in quite healthy, normal girls. Periods are expected to last three to five days but gynecologists accept anything from two to seven days as normal. The total amount of blood loss is on the average 25 to 30 milliliters, but again a survey of normal women shows a variation of from 5 to 100 milliliters.

Menstrual pain, or more general physical disturbances associated with menstruation, can be an upsetting facet of adolescence. It is customary for the medical profession to consider that the degree of such upset during menstruation is dependent to a large extent on the individual's determination to lead a normal life during her periods. There is something to be said for this traditional attitude which is, generally speaking, agreed upon among both women and men doctors, provided that it does not lead to an unfortunately unsympathetic handling of a girl who experiences a lot of difficulty, for frequently the discomfort has its roots in genuine physical

or emotional disturbance.

Only about 3 percent of young adolescents sail through the development of womanhood without menstruation taking any effect on their young lives, and only 20 percent of mature women are completely free from discomfort or minor upsets as a result of menstruation. In Britain and the United States, 50 percent of women below the age of 30 experience pain in the stomach, pelvis, or back during or before their periods.

Other common manifestations of menstruation include tender and sore breasts, irritability, temper tantrums, lethargy, poor concentration, or sometimes excitability, especially of a sexual nature. In 50 percent of girls, the bowel function changes, constipation being the rule before the period is due and then more frequent motions passed during the time of the period. There is sometimes a tendency towards frequent urination before the periods are due, and often girls complain of vague feelings of nausea, and a few are actually sick. Statistics show that there is an increase of accident proneness, mental disturbance, and even suicide associated with the menstrual period.

Awful Acne

A less extreme but more common accompaniment to adolescence is the appearance of acne spots on the face, an annoyance to teenage girls and boys alike. Nobody knows for sure what causes the acne of adolescence. It begins at puberty and generally speaking if it is going to be a problem it is at its worst at around 19. It tends to run in families and is associated usually with a greasy skin. In all probability acne is a result of a disturbance of sex hormones production.

It must be remembered that in both sexes male and female sex hormones are produced, and during the time of sexual ripening levels of these within the bodies of both girls and boys are constantly changing. But alongside sex hormone factors go emotional ones. Dermatologists give many examples of the emotions affecting the skin. A French doctor way back in 1785 wrote that marriage cures acne, and there is no doubt that the change from a stressful insecurity of adolescence to a happy marriage helps the body to settle its skin down.

Luckily today the teenager prone to acne need not suffer in silence as a variety of treatments, both old and

The Picture Library

Early adolescence is a time of growing interest in the opposite sex.

PAF International

new, are available for the alleviation of this distressing complication of adolescence. Perhaps two erroneous folklore beliefs may be dismissed with reference to acne: it is neither a sign of constipation nor that the victim is practicing masturbation.

Masturbation is another characteristic common to adolescence in both sexes. It is most unusual for a boy to pass through adolescence without masturbating, and in all probability the same is true of girls. Such adolescents who do not masturbate either have an abnormally low sexual drive, have led such a sheltered life that no one has ever mentioned or discussed

the subject, or have not been sufficiently enterprising to discover how to do it themselves. Masturbation is, of course, an entirely harmless alternative to sexual intercourse.

One theory that still holds sway, both with some adults and adolescents, is that masturbation leads to loss of energy and drive. This stems from the view that semen is a "vital fluid," the loss of which somehow depletes the body's vital forces. Nothing, of course, could be further from the mark. Repeated masturbation in the male simply leads to a smaller ejaculate and, if pressed to extremes, to a temporary lack of sexual interest,

Youth clubs give young boys and girls a chance to meet informally.

so the whole process is self-limiting.

Except for masturbation, the adolescent changes that occur in boys are, compared with girls, rather less spectacular, although they are no less dramatic to the person in question. By the time a boy is 11, he has already reached 80 percent of his adult height and his shoulders tend to broaden considerably. The penis gets longer and somewhat thicker; the voice, although not technically broken, is rather deeper. Boys in early adolescence are usually very serious about games (but not girls) and enjoy "gang" behavior. During the next two years growth is very rapid, four or five inches being added to the height.

Pubic hair starts to grow at about the age of 13 and the testes enlarge considerably. Occasionally a transient swelling of the breasts occurs. At this stage nocturnal emissions or "wet dreams" occur and sometimes masturbation starts too. Mutual masturbation between boys at this age sometimes takes place and should not be thought to be evidence of homosexuality. At around this time the larynx enlarges, the "adam's apple" becomes more prominent and the voice breaks. Usually this period between 13 and 14 is one of readjust-ments. Existing relationships tend to break up and the boy finds new friends, often concentrating on a "best friend" who acts as a confidant. Generally speaking, a boy of this age becomes more protective towards his mother, rejecting temporarily his father whom he sees as a rival.

Between age 15 and 16 the texture of the skin changes and acne may become a problem. Growth is still rapid but rather less so, about four inches being added to the height. For the first time usually, a boy becomes clothes conscious, and teenage fashions and modes are suddenly important. The heterosexual phase has now fully developed and girls are of great interest. For the next few years the developing male goes through at least three stages in his relationships with females. Exactly how long he stays in each is quite variable, and not all males "complete the course," some remaining arrested at one stage perhaps forever.

The first stage is very definitely polygamous, a stage during which sexual curiosity together with a desire to "get" girls drives the boy to mix with several girls of his own age. How far such relationships go depends on many things, not the least being the sexual mores of the available females. In these days of much greater sexual freedom it is likely that a greater degree of sexual exploration takes place than it did, for instance, 25 years ago. Sometimes as a result teenage pregnancies complicate the picture, and it is important to realize that marriage is almost always disastrous.

Puppy Love

The second stage in the development of the boy's sexuality is a romantic stage, in which one girl attracts him predominantly. This is the age in which adolescent "love," with all its heartbreaks and upsets, worries young people. But it should not be forgotten that even at this stage, say at 17 or 18, young males are not emotionally ready to establish a lasting love relationship.

Young adolescent men and women often pose the question as to whether it is a good idea these days to "sleep around" and, in this way, find the ideal mate. The only real answer is to point out that this type of behavior is really an extension of the most immature sexual curiosity stage of adolescence and is not a sign of sophistication.

By the time a boy reaches the age of 18 he is very nearly full grown. He will now have to shave fairly regularly, in most cases, though he is not out of adolescence by any means. He is sexually mature, however, and sexual needs are often very pressing unless a devotion to sport or a hobby like motorcycles or cars has persisted.

By now the common male behavior patterns of adolescence will have gone through several phases. First, the young adolescent boy is often shy and "tongue-tied," especially in the presence of strangers, and later on with girls. He tends to believe everybody is watching him, and blushing is

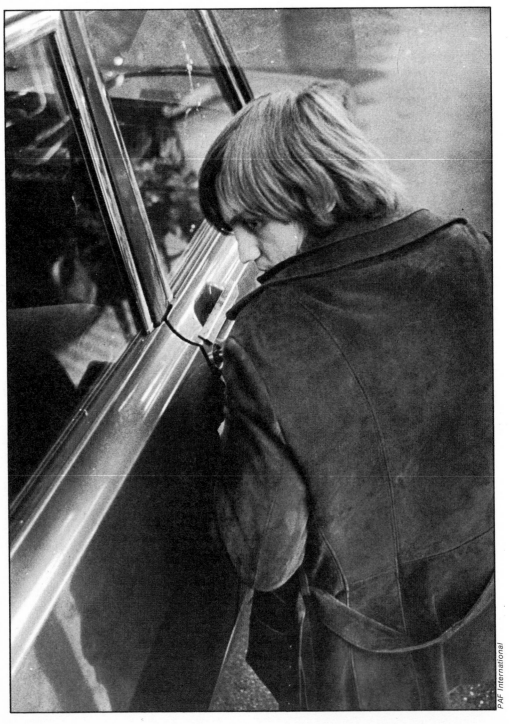

PAF International

Adolescent rebellion against authority sometimes includes petty crime – or even stealing cars.

very common, as it is in girls; he is preoccupied with the impression he is making on others. Next, there often comes a period of general churlishness, sulkiness and obstinacy, which is really a preamble to the final stage where the adolescent male tests himself against authority.

Exactly how the individual plays this part depends on many things. Parents are good and safe opponents and often provide exactly the test of will that is needed. Teachers come into it too in certain social systems, and less so, fortunately, do the police. Authority in general is often threatened in antisocial ways that are often inexplicable to the uninitiated. The adolescent who finds no challenge at

home or at school will often seek it more directly against society in the form of minor, or even major, vandalism, rowdiness at sports events, and "gang warfare" in one shape or another. To a large extent adolescent, drug taking is initiated because of its illegal background and antisocial nature, and the same is true to a lesser extent of adolescent bad language and swearing.

Finally, a few points of more medical interest figure in the adolescence of both sexes. Nutrition is extremely important during the whole of this time mainly because in both sexes there is extremely rapid physical growth.

The two main nutritional diseases of adolescence today are obesity through

poor nutrition and a basically emotional problem associated with food called anorexia nervosa. In this case, primarily for emotional reasons, an adolescent turns away from food. This is almost entirely a disease of young girls and can be fatal.

Cry for Help

A common, tragic complication of adolescence is unwanted pregnancy or venereal disease, usually gonorrhea. Both are usually brought about, even today, by a mixture of bravado and ignorance. Sex education of a sensible type is still not available to the majority of the adolescent population in most civilized societies.

Mental disorders secondary to adolescent stress complicate many young lives. Often the basic fault in such cases lies not so much with the adolescents themselves but with others. If parents are either grossly overprotective or completely undemonstrative, the effect on the adolescent psyche can be quite profound, leaving the victim unable to handle developing emotional reactions, and causing the telling symptoms of anxiety, overdependence, guilt, or aggression. Often adults still find it difficult or even impossible to crack the code of adolescent misbehavior and nervous upset.

Psychosomatic disorders are unfortunately very common in adolescence. The stresses generated by psychological tensions then tend to "funnel into" a target organ. The psyche seems to be saying, "I cannot make my complaint in any language I know, or that people will listen to, therefore I will disturb the way my body works. That should fix it." And so symptoms related to the heart, like breathlessness or pain in the chest, and to the alimentary system, like overeating, undereating, dyspepsia, wind, constipation and so on disrupt young people's lives. Likewise the central nervous system may be upset and such symptoms as giddiness, tremor, faintness, migraine, or a feeling of being "run-down" predominate. Skin complaints like dermatitis, itching skin conditions, and even phobias about "picking up" infectious skin diseases are similarly psychosomatic in origin during adolescence, turning a time that should be pleasant and rewarding, even exciting, into something very much less of a joy and more of a drag.

Two of the possible pitfalls of puberty: anorexia nervosa (left) and obesity (right).

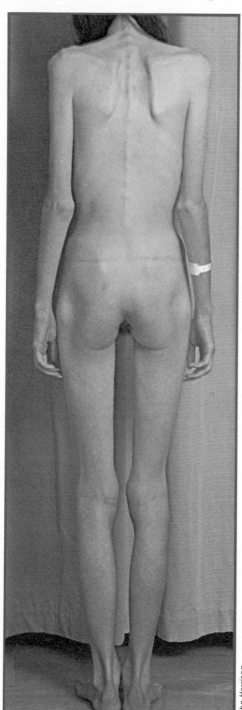

John Harrison

John Harrison

Twist and shout

With roots raw and raucous, pop grew up to flower power, and busy bees came to get the money.

In the United States, where rock and roll was born, the freshness and originality of pop music had begun to wear off by 1960, while Britain—a couple of years behind—was still bowled over with the new discovery.

The leaders of the rock revolution had all somehow disappeared: Elvis Presley in the army, Chuck Berry in jail, Buddy Holly and Eddy Cochran both dead. The American pop scene was wide open for Tin Pan Alley to get back in business, and what it was producing was little more than an updated version of the professional but predictable music it had been churning out before rock.

The pop bandwagon was crammed with businessmen, each devising a new sound, a new face, a new image, a new dance, each manipulating the media to sweep the States with yet

another new trend. Most of the trends during that period were seven-day wonders: however good the publicity machine, however heavy the investment, few of the attempts at reconstructing rock paid off. What they lacked was a real and recognizable center, a focus for the kids' enthusiasm. Something to identify with, someone to idolize, someone to tell the real truth about being a teenager. And that is where the Beatles came in.

Beatlemania Begins

In December, 1963, the London *Sunday Times* critic William Mann declared the Beatles "the greatest composers since Beethoven." Earlier the same year the *New Statesman* had, with equal fervor, derided them— "Those who flock around the Beatles, who scream themselves into hysteria,

whose vacant faces flicker over the TV screen, are the least fortunate of their generation, the dull, the idle, the failures. . . ." Both these emphatic, though diametrically opposed, reactions came within a year of the Beatles' first number one hit record, "Please Please Me."

The phenomenal speed with which the group took a hold on national and then worldwide opinion can be compared only with the explosive velocity of the early rock and roll cult in the United States. But their penetration into the hitherto sacrosanct pages of serious journalism was something new. In the ten years since Elvis Presley had first hit adult society over the head with his raucous music, the intellectuals, the parents, the journalists and the sociologists had been primed—and now when the

Camera Press/Keystone

Beatles let out their first rallying cries to the kids, it was not only the kids who heard it.

In retrospect, all the earnest attempts of the (by pop standards) elderly fans to interpret, to "understand" the Beatles seem faintly ridiculous. Early Beatles numbers— "From Me to You," "Twist and Shout," "She Loves You"—had no pretensions to subtlety, either in lyrics or in music. The only way to understand them was to dance: the only people who *could* understand were the kids, who instinctively knew that the Beatles were talking directly to them, about them and for them. They were the new representatives of youth, self-made, working-class and completely without hypocrisy. They had created their image for themselves and they stuck to it.

The fact that these elected delegates of youth were able, for years, to command the attention of the adult world without losing prestige in the eyes of their fans is an indication of their integrity. No publicity machine would gobble them up, as it had done Elvis, to regurgitate them smooth, polished, and professional. They knew

that their trump card was doggedly to "do their own thing."

Just as the Beatles were becoming an accepted topic for serious musicians to talk about, and at the same time winning for the younger generation's enthusiasms the dubious accolade of pop culture, "society" and the transatlantic jet set began to take up pop as well. While intellectuals pursued pop with sometimes inappropriate seriousness, the fashionable set followed it with a rather patronizing enthusiasm: few smart London dinner parties in the early sixties failed to include, as a curious conversation piece, a short excerpt from the latest Beatles album; in New York Greta Garbo and Noel Coward, Tennessee Williams and the Duke of Bedford could all be found twisting away at New York's Peppermint Lounge.

Swinging Sixties

It was as if the battle, that had been raging since the adult and the teenage world had declared war on each other over the issue of rock and roll early in the fifties, had suddenly quietened. The adults had been outnumbered and overwhelmed—and

Above: The Beatles became gods of the pop cult in the early sixties: nothing they did could fail. They experimented with life-styles and moved easily from pop concerts to composing to filmmaking. The Queen invested them with MBEs, America gave them a tickertape welcome. But in the end the group couldn't take the strain of adulation and, like their music, lost their impetus, their genius and their direction.

seemed to be following the adage "If you can't lick 'em, join 'em!"

There are many ardent adherents to the old-style, raw and compelling sound of rock that would pinpoint this as the moment pop lost its guts. Certainly it is the moment when young protesters against the adult way of life—now suddenly finding they were being listened to—began to put their ideas into words. If the rock explosion had been the first inarticulate cry for recognition, for an identity, then the new pop era—which granted that recognition—presented the opportunity to look for that identity.

So in the sixties—glorious to all those who happened at that time to be

1970

Left: The Beatles played to capacity crowds wherever they went. From the moment they appeared on stage, thousands of fans screamed in frenzied adoration — often drowning out the music of their idols. Above: Flower power v. fire power.

the "right" side of 20—there was a veritable burgeoning of style, of experimentation, of talent, of new philosophies. This was a generation of prosperity, with the time and the economic means to develop new concepts in art, dress, and life-style, as well as music; designers and journalists and photographers as well as musicians all had a chance to say their say—and an audience to say it to.

This was a generation that did more than any other since the Industrial Revolution to do away with class barriers, when it became—in Britain at least—positively trendy to be working class; the improved education and comparative prosperity that their parents had granted them provided the tools and helped remove the inhibitions. Every youngster could feel that he was in with a chance to make his mark on the world.

The pop scene in the sixties became more and more fragmented as the kids explored their separate avenues to the future. Many of them turned out to be nothing but blind alleys, whereas others continue to influence the Western world.

The first manifestation of the new outlook was "Swinging London," now a byword which covers a multitude of bright and adventurous innovations of the time, as well as a multitude of sins. Corny in retrospect, the image of Swinging London raises a giggle of derision or a groan of embarrassment: nevertheless it provided an arena for all sorts of creative people before it became unrecognizable under the high gloss of commercialism.

There was Mary Quant, who revolutionized the idea of *chic*, from a shamefacedly cheaper variation of the sophisticated—and adult—Paris fashions into an assertive, and defiantly cheaper, sexy proclamation of youth: short skirts, definite colors, no-nonsense city clothes, which left room to move and made corsets an anachronism. Bazaar, Mary Quant's boutique in the King's Road, Chelsea, defied girls to look like a cut-down version of their mothers and led the way to Biba, a tiny shop with inimitable style that eventually took over one of London's largest and most luxurious department stores. The art deco mausoleum where acquiescent teenage girls used to have their mothers choose their new tweed two-piece is now crowded with teenagers choosing clothes for themselves; from a bastion of the establishment, the grandiose old building has been transformed into an emporium of youth.

A similar, though less kindly, fate has overcome Carnaby Street. John Stephen, the clothes designer exclusively for men, was the first to find it, and, as boys began to appreciate the low prices and distinctive style of his kind of gear, he was joined by others until the tiny Soho street became a mecca for every lad in London. Clothes were of paramount importance for awhile, identifying the wearer immediately as one of the "in crowd" or a "square." The race was on to see who could stay on the crest of a trend. The main thing was to be young, happy and basically frivolous—frivolity that, of course, has laid Carnaby Street wide open for commercial exploitation and turned it into a tacky travesty of itself.

The reason London swung was that it swung for everyone of the younger generation: mass production was no longer a dirty word, it had style. The

David Gahr/Time

Bob Dylan, the leader of pop protest, wrote words and music which reflected troubled times.

cheaper the clothes, the more were produced. The more produced, the greater the opportunity for new designers to muscle in; the more designs, the greater the interest. Fashion photographers like David Bailey and Terence Donovan put zest into the styles; beautiful long-legged, shining-haired girls like Jean Shrimpton epitomized the image.

There *was* an elite of Swinging London, but the elite was not defined by the old rules of class and privilege alone. "Society" sloughed off its dignity awhile and fell over itself to woo the self-made princes of pop.

Although "high society" might embrace the stars of pop with open arms, society in the shape of law and order had eventually to curb the license that Swinging London had fostered. The central issue was drugs. "Soft" drugs such as hashish had been a common feature of the habits of jazz musicians for decades. In the sixties the effect of drugs was recognized in the work of both the Beatles and the Rolling Stones. The Beatles became more introspective, more contemplative, and the Stones more and more outrageous. But drug taking was no longer limited to the relatively small clique of musicians; it spread among young people everywhere. Whether the effect was good or bad, whether the widespread use of marijuana broadened horizons or dulled the senses, blunted the cruel edge of ambition or dwarfed the possibilities of a generation, it certainly had the effect of reopening the rift between the young and the old.

In the United States particularly, pop society identified the freedom to use drugs as its cause. LSD, which for a brief period had seemed able to break down the dreary barriers between the real and the imaginary for thousands of West Coast hippies and make everything possible, became a cult. Those who had tried it came together in sunny California and formed a kind of sect, a family who shared a common secret experience. They established communes and put their seal on a nonaggression pact—not only among themselves but with the rest of the world as well. When their intentions met with opposition they would reply with flowers. The most evocative reminder of "flower power" is a photograph published in the *Washington Star* which shows a line of militia looking in bewilderment at

Syndication International/Picturepoint/Rex Features/Keystone

the butts of their rifles. In each had been planted a flower—by the hippies they had been sent to control.

"Flower power" now seems little more than a ludicrous, naive and misguided fantasy, for it was quickly taken up, exploded by the press, and as quickly cast aside. But although the fashion itself lasted no longer than the 1967 "silly season," it reflected a more substantial and more deeply rooted shift in pop culture from the material to the spiritual. Swinging London had been a bubbling response to the discovery that the young could compete with their elders in matters of material and commercial concern—and win. Flower power rejected the very rules of that competition, offering not a variation on a theme but a new theme.

The theme was, as everyone knows, "love and peace" and was possibly the result of the deenergizing effect of drugs, though far more likely it was the reflection of the anxieties that college kids were feeling during the

politically fraught years of the sixties: the arms race, the Bay of Pigs, the assassination of President Kennedy . . . and the powerlessness of the new generation to get through to their leaders. All they could do was protest, and leading them was the first "pop philosopher," Bob Dylan.

Dylan took pop a long way from rock and roll, although in later years he returned to "the backbeat you can't lose," picking up the electric guitar for the first time on stage almost twenty years after Elvis had used it to fanfare pop into the world. His origins were in folk music, and his strength lay in writing lyrics that became catchphrases for his generation. Perhaps, as many people suggest, Bob Dylan was in reality as cynical as the next millionaire; perhaps what he traded in was indeed only simplistic, marketable propaganda. But he gave to pop a coherent voice, to his many successors he gave a precedent: meaning took first place

Carnaby Street—Swinging London, 1966—and some of the people that changed style and life in the sixties. Clockwise from top left: Twiggy, boyish girl model; two gear birds who followed fashion's every whim; Pete Townshend, lead guitarist of The Who; and designer Mary Quant, who started it all with her miniskirt.

over sound. And to his fans—whether sincerely or not—he gave food for thought rather than mere sensation.

Pop culture has now so many offshoots and is now so ingrained in our society (as the teenagers of the fifties come to make the decisions that affect the world of the seventies) that it is fast becoming difficult to identify as a separate entity. It is now a part of the lives of kids and parents alike. The cause of the pop explosion may be easy to describe, but the effects—the fallout—will continue filtering imperceptibly into our lives for all time.

Heather Clarke

Family man

Happy ever after but for worry about the wife, the kids, the mortgage, the job. . . .

Man has often tried to present himself as a reluctant candidate for marriage and family life. He likes to see himself as hooked or trapped by the wiles of a cunning woman.

Where women's parties for a bride-to-be are usually joyous, congratulatory and expectant affairs, the stag sessions for the prospective groom usually have the atmosphere of a wake. They tend to be maudlin, nostalgic occasions, mourning the old free bachelor days, soon to be gone forever! These are the assumed attitudes, the expected role playing.

What are the realities? In the sober light of a recent survey carried out by Gallup pollsters these attitudes look a bit phony. Some 82 percent of boys aged 15 to 19 believed that mar-

riage was *important* and that 23 is the ideal age to get married. Another fact which suggests that many men are poseurs in their statements about their loss of bachelorhood is that there is a drop of two years in the average age at which men marry—and this has occurred in much less than a decade. Two out of every three divorced men remarry. So much for Dr. Samuel Johnson's cynical conclusion that second marriages represent "the triumph of hope over experience."

Of course, the "institutionalized" role of husband and father within the family, to which men are committing themselves with such apparent reluctance and abandon, has changed in the last two or three decades. Increasing educational opportunities

for women and better career prospects have given them a higher status in the home; the nuclear family with both husband and wife in professional jobs is no longer the exception. Coupled with this is the growing authority of the mother and the lessening of the father's authority within the home, particularly in decisions on education and discipline of the children. Nineteenth century wives had small option but to bow to the commands of the father of the family. Few could afford divorce. Today, the balance of power has shifted significantly. Many husbands and wives start off with every chance of cooperating with each other fully and enjoyably in a more evenly balanced, egalitarian partnership.

But there are sources of tension that can undermine their coalition. The husband takes into his marriage what he remembers about his mother and father and *their* family life. These impressions shape his attitudes towards his own home. He may want to be different and "progressive" and yet he remembers fondly his mother's competent management of their home. She had an old-fashioned, traditionalist view of the roles of husband and wife. The man was the head of the house and if he was not up to it, he was made to feel that he was.

Mother and Mistress

Most husbands probably like the idea of a traditionalist wife, nurturant and loving, deferring to their male superiority while shielding them from the dreariness and perplexity of household problems. Psychologists tend to agree that what these men really want is to find their mothers again in their wives. As children, it was mother who fed them, protected them, organized them and made them comfortable. At one level they want this, but at another level (the sexual one) they may recoil from it if the process goes too far.

Poor woman, she has to be *all* things to her man: the mother figure on a pedestal of virtue; domesticity itself in the kitchen; a bit of a "tart" in bed. This dichotomy cannot always be sustained by those men who require it (it is too much like incest); some women cannot make the transitions required by the dual roles of mother and mistress. A husband—even one who does not indulge in this sort of compartmentalizing—may see that the pretty, sexy girl he married has become a rather ordinary and faded housewife. Familiarity can breed contempt. (He fails to notice that the bloom of carefree youth has deserted him too.) The qualities of mind and personality that first attracted him to his wife are out of sight, hidden behind a facade of routine. And unless a wife realizes that her husband is looking at her with these new eyes, and makes an effort to look at herself with an equal objectivity, she may find that her husband withdraws a little from her, seeking elsewhere new interest and amusement (and this does not necessarily mean sexually). This can only too often happen; yet an overreaction against becoming a "vegetable" can lead to difficulties.

The wife who attempts to interest her husband by becoming genuinely knowledgeable herself, developing a powerful achievement drive, may up-set her husband considerably if she competes too successfully. It is sadly true that many men dislike their wives to be too intelligent and think that an intellectual woman is unfeminine. But a woman with interests beyond the home and family is likely to be stimulating company—and to give no chance to the depredations of boredom.

In any event, it may be the man who proves to be something of a let down. The person she thought during her courting days to be highly intelligent, driving, and ambitious may in fact be a rather straightforward, ordinary man who does not know nearly as much as he likes to pretend, and whose drive is more a matter of talking than doing very much.

Pressures on a marriage can come from a wife who is too houseproud. The home is still her main territory: if pride in her home runs rampant, she may become critical of anything which fails to meet her standards. She plumps up the cushions immediately after her husband gets up and makes him take his shoes off in the living room. The house looks (and feels) like a museum. Women compete mainly in their appearance, their children and their home, but as children grow up and become independent, they often become a less satisfactory source of pride. This is the time when there is a danger of a wife becoming excessively houseproud and making her husband feel like an interloper in his own home. If she becomes too obsessional about the tidiness of the place, he may retreat more and more from its rigors.

Talking It Over

Marriage—when successful—can be the most joyous and secure of relationships; the partners share each other's lives, communicate their most intimate thoughts and deepest feelings to one another. A survey of married people showed that what was crucial in modern marriage was the satisfaction of psychological needs rather than the traditional economic ones. Good communication was seen as a vital function of modern marriage. Everyone questioned stressed the importance of talking to each other, except for one wife who would not have married the same man again and felt she was "just plodding on to a silver wedding anniversary with nothing left to talk about." All mentioned talking (and, equally important, listening) as a way of getting over difficulties. They differed only in when and how they used communication.

One happily married couple went for long periods when they did little talking apart from domestic pleasantries, but were quick to analyze any problems that emerged. Any difficulties would usually come to the surface when unsuccessful love-making signalled the dissatisfactions of either partner. A quarrel often followed, which precipitated a lengthy "all-night" discussion during which their problems were usually resolved. In the case of another couple, the wife had found that her husband was too moody to reason with in the "heat of the moment." She had learned that it paid to wait until he had calmed down, even if it took several days, and then broach the subject tactfully. Even the most dissatisfied wife felt that the one good thing about her marriage was that she and her husband could always talk to each other. She did not like her husband, but both were completely open to each other.

Active Involvement

A newspaper survey reported that a majority of British couples believed that the enjoyment of talking with one's marriage partner was more important than having satisfactory sexual relationships. Newspaper surveys are not always reliable indicators of fact, but the importance of having good communication between a man and woman who have to live together is sufficiently self-evident to make the findings of a survey by a respected team of American social scientists rather alarming. On average, an American husband and wife will talk to each other for 16 minutes, in total, per week! (excluding any three-cornered conversations involving the children).

Having children constantly underfoot can sometimes be a hindrance to communication in a marriage, but often they provide such a strong focus for mutual feelings that conversation can become all but superfluous, especially when both partners are actively involved in their care. The contemporary young middle-class husband, as he fulfills his paternal role, may assist his working wife with the feeding or bathing of the baby. Such notions of fathering are alien to earlier times and other species. Throughout the animal kingdom, males play little or no part in the care and nurture of their offspring. Anthropologists, studying human societies, believe that men learned to develop a relationship with their children as a result of setting up long-term living arrangements with one or more women. So the family unit was

1975

established, whereas most male and female animals come together for mating purposes and then part. In fact, humanity took a long time to discover what fatherhood was. There are 40 weeks of pregnancy—a long period of complicated, mostly invisible, activity—dividing the moment of conception from the birth of a baby. Our earliest ancestors did not know that the two events *were* connected. Indeed, it is only comparatively recently in our history that scientists managed to discover that both father and mother contribute equally to the genetic heritage of their offspring.

Traditional Role

Patterns of fatherhood naturally differ throughout the world, and there is a variety of meanings to the term father. The Imperial Roman paterfamilias held even the power of life and death over his wife and children; his womenfolk as late as the fourth century did not have personal names, only the family name prefaced by "the elder," "the younger," to indicate their place in the family hierarchy.

In India, it is still traditional for the man to bring his wife into his parents' home, where she becomes a servant. He lives with her only at night and has little to do with his children, although his authority affects their environment. The classical Indian joint-family system, in which the immediate families of a set of brothers formed a joint cooperative unit, left little real authority to each brother as a father.

The Irish farmer had little contact with his children before the age of eight. At that age, the boy came under his father's supervision and remained subservient according to the father's wish. Later on, the father arranged his marriage and his future—and the daughter's also—to further the interest of the family.

The men of the Trobriand Islands nurture the households of their sisters, not their wives. Male Mentawie Islanders continue to work in their fathers' households until their own children are mature. Meanwhile, these children are looked after by their mother's father and fed by their mother's brothers. The father of the early twentieth century in London's East End was informally subject to the authority of his wife's mother.

Originally men were dependent upon agriculture for subsistence, growing what they needed to eat for themselves, and supplementing this by animal husbandry or hunting. Thus, men lived in tiny family or tribal units which were ideal for such a way of life. A peasant farmer's child can help his father in the fields; in fact he will probably be expected to do so, since his labor is valuable to the family.

A Polynesian child is given his own canoe as soon as he is able to swim, which is about the time that he has learned to walk. He is soon expected to help with fishing along with enjoying himself in play. A boy of six among the Masai of East Africa is expected to be able to look after several cows by himself in a region where both cattle and humans may be prey to attacks by lions or leopards. But in an industrial society like ours it would be difficult to think of any real contribution that a young child can make to his family's material well-being.

Western society is becoming increasingly compartmentalized as specialized social groups become larger and people's social contacts increase. For instance, a man's role in the work situation may have nothing to do with his role as a father and husband or as a member of the local sports club or political party.

The most frequent barrier between father and child is the father's work schedule. Many fathers, because of long-term goals, sacrifice time with their families only to find that they have lost their children, at least psychologically, in the process. They may end up with financial security but a very empty family life.

In some cases, modifications in the daily work routine may be possible to ensure his fuller participation in family life, but all too often work is used as an excuse for avoiding family responsibilities. Many fathers who are competent and active at work feel totally inexperienced and ineffectual at home with their children. Of course, each family has to assess its priorities, but it is important that both the husband and wife agree about decisions which affect the amount of time the breadwinner is away.

Out in the Cold

Henry Biller, associate professor of psychology at the University of Rhode Island, has examined the father's contribution to family life and concludes that any new father should be encouraged to spend as much time as possible with his wife and child. The earlier he can feel involved with the child, the more likely will a strong relationship develop between them. He believes that having a child should be a careful decision for both father and mother, and before the child is conceived the prospective parents ought to feel a joint commitment.

This mutual interest should carry on through pregnancy, though it is easy for the father to begin feeling useless at this stage. Too often all the attention is focused on the expectant mother, and the "expectant" father is left out in the cold. It helps for husbands to be involved in prenatal visits to the doctor and then, if the hospital allows it, to be with their wives during labor and in the delivery room, where they can be of enormous support. A father can be very important to his child's development even in the first year of life, but such attitudes to fatherhood are extremely radical.

Masculine Influence

Fathers have been neglected in the clinical literature until fairly recently. It is perhaps significant that we have only the feminine word "mothering" to denote the tender and nurturant care of children. The importance of the father in the home and his influence in producing positive mental health—or maladjustment—in his offspring have been largely minimized by researchers, reflecting the matricentric status of child rearing in Western society. There is increasing evidence, of late, that fathers play a much more active role in rearing their children (in all its aspects) than researchers thought or fathers were prepared to admit.

While it is true that it is "mama" who has more contact with the child when he is very young and her influence is often predominant, we now know that father-child relationships are vital and sometimes the predominant influence. Both parents influence their children's development, and which parent is more important varies with the child's age, sex, temperament and environmental circumstances. Furthermore, it is not always meaningful to regard the influence of each parent as separate and independent. The mental health of one parent may influence the other and may also influence the marriage relationship. The family consists of individuals and pairs of individuals, but it is also a social group of its own and needs to be considered as such.

The father provides a model for the boy learning the masculine role. In addition to his supportive role for his wife, he is a protective and nurturant figure to the child. He is less protective and caring in the tender, softer maternal style, but he is the model for the nurturant attitude men take towards women. He also teaches the boy masculine pursuits and hobbies, perhaps introducing him to masculine social groupings, such as sports teams, scouts, hobbies, or clubs. The father's importance in the home is greatest in our small Western "nuclear" families where there can often be lack of contact with other adults.

The opportunities the child has to spend with *both* his mother and father together are of crucial importance. A child forms much of his attitude towards relationships between men and women by watching how his mother and father behave towards each other. The effective father values his wife's role and respects her opinions, rather than showing off his masculinity (perhaps in an unconscious attempt to impress the child) by constantly asserting his superiority in argument or discussion.

The parents' respect for one another and their ability to talk openly and honestly will also help a child's development. The more consistent they can be, the more secure will the child feel. He will be reassured if he senses that his parents are largely in agreement about their approach to his upbringing, though, of course, parents are not always going to carry on in perfect harmony.

It cannot be emphasized enough that the most effective way to teach a child appropriate behavior is by exposing him to effective models worth emulating, and the behavior of the mother and father is most significant. If they are continually arguing with each other, it is difficult to expect their child to respect the feelings of others. The learning of a sex role is helped by the child's desire to identify with a model of the same sex.

But this is but one means by which appropriate sex-role behavior is learned. Most boys and girls have many opportunities to learn a masculine or feminine pattern of behaving, even when the same-sex parent is absent. The mother may have brothers, or other male relatives of her own generation, who can serve as masculine models. Neighbors, teachers, other children, can all help to provide masculine relationships.

Mothers are particularly worried about the problems of being mother *and* "father" to the child; for example, in the case of a boy, they may be concerned about their ability to provide discipline and a model for the normal development of his masculinity. To reassure mothers, it should be emphasized here that, while the loss of a father increases the risk of a child becoming delinquent at adolescence, fatherless juvenile delinquents are a *very* small proportion of the total fatherless group. Family background is only *one* of the main factors involved in delinquency. There is, in particular, evidence that a very inadequate father may have more unfavorable effects upon the child than the absence of a paternal figure.

Male Model

Children in fatherless homes often make believe that they have a father—usually softer, kinder and more friendly than the original. But another supposed effect—the homosexual tendencies of fatherless boys—has been very much exaggerated. If the mother is having a struggle, the male child may *have* to assume an adult male role very early in life, to replace the missing father.

Perhaps more important than the absence of a male model for the boy reared by his mother will be the attitudes she expresses about the boy's father in particular, and men in general. Derogatory remarks about males, if they are repeated over and over by a mother who is the authority in the family, may produce strong feelings of self-doubt in the boy, particularly about his budding manhood. Or, if the child is a girl, she may grow to distrust all men. If a reasonably relaxed relationship between divorced parents is possible, visits and outings with the father can overcome the mother's fears about the amount of masculine contact the child is getting and can contribute to a more healthy family atmosphere.

A warm relationship between father and daughter will help to produce a balanced adult woman.

PAF International

ENCYCLOPEDIA OF HUMAN BEHAVIOR

GESELL, ARNOLD (1880-1961)
An American psychologist who did pioneer work in child development. He was one of the first people to realize the value of studying identical and nonidentical twins in order to separate the effects of heredity and environment.

GESTALT PSYCHOLOGY
An important school of psychology founded in the early twentieth century which provided an alternative point of view to the Pavlovian and behaviorist approach fashionable at the time. The Gestalt psychologists stressed that the brain plays a dynamic, active role in perception, learning and other aspects of behavior and is not just a complex, passive, stimulus-response mechanism as Pavlov and others implied. Their main experimental approach was the study of visual perception, and it was through this that they coined the famous phrase "The whole is more than the sum of its parts." For example, a number of dots drawn together in the form of a circle are only a collection of points in terms of stimulation on the retina, but nevertheless the brain perceives them "as a whole" and describes or recognizes them as a circle. The important point here is that the "roundness," or "circularity," of the dotted figure is supplied by the brain and is obviously something much more than just a collection of dots. This fact may not seem particularly earthshaking now, but it produced a revolution in psychology when it was first put forward. In support of their argument for the brain's active part in perception, the Gestalt psychologists also developed and classified a series of "laws" of perceptual organization *(continuity, contiguity, goodness of figure,* and so on). The three founders of the Gestalt school were Max Wertheimer, Kurt Koffka and Wolfgang Köhler. Köhler was also well known for his remarkable studies of thought processes of chimpanzees and for his discovery of the *aha reaction.*

GESTATION PERIOD
The time a living organism spends in the uterus from the moment of conception to birth.

GHOST
A disembodied being supposed to be the remnant of a dead person or some manifestation of his spiritual existence. Belief in ghosts is still exceedingly widespread, though there is no scientific evidence for their reality. Most people who honestly claim to have seen ghosts have probably been suffering from one of a large class of hallucinations to which the brain is subject.

GIFTED CHILD
A child with a very high degree of intelligence or creativity, though not necessarily at genius level. Anyone with an IQ between 130 and 150 would normally be placed in this class.

GIGANTISM
Huge stature and physical growth normally caused by an extremely overactive pituitary gland.

GLAND
Any organ in the body which discharges substances either into the blood stream, into an organ, or outside the body itself. The most important of these are the endocrine glands, which pump hormones into the blood at times of stress.

GLANS
The end of the penis or clitoris.

GLAUCOMA
An eye disease characterized by an increase of pressure from the fluids inside the eye, leading to blindness.

GLIOMA
A kind of brain tumor.

GLOBUS HYSTERICUS
A neurotic complaint in which the individual feels that he has a big lump or blockage in his throat affecting his swallowing or breathing.

GLOSSOLALIA
Babbling speech, often sounding vaguely like a foreign language and typical of certain religious trances or hysterical states. It is sometimes called "speaking in tongues."

GLOVE ANESTHESIA
Loss of sensitivity in the hand over an area roughly covered by a glove. This is a neurotic or hysterical condition easily diagnosed as such because the sensory nerves which would be affected if the anesthesia were real would not be concentrated on the hand as a whole. Patients, of course, do not know this but assume that if one side of a hand is insensitive, then the other must also be.

GONADOTROPIC HORMONE
The hormone produced by the *pituitary* which controls the growth of sperm and eggs in the *gonads.*

GONADS
The sex glands—the *testes* in the male and *ovaries* in the female.

GOODNESS OF FIGURE
One of the so-called Gestalt "laws of perceptual organization." If a visual stimulus is exposed briefly, the brain will simplify the perception as best it can. A slightly oval figure will be seen as round, a vaguely wiggly line as straight. The Gestalt argument was that the brain likes figures to be "good" or neat and simplifies them whenever it can.

GRAND MAL
Major epileptic attack—as opposed to *petit mal,* a minor attack—accompanied by loss of consciousness and spasms.

GRAPHIC LANGUAGE
An early form of communication using symbols such as employed in "picture writing."

GRAPHOLOGY
The study of the relationship between personality and handwriting styles. Present evidence suggests that it is doubtful whether anything very deep can be said about personality from examining handwriting, but that identification of an individual through his handwriting *can* be achieved.

GRAPHORRHEA
A meaningless stream of handwriting, often typical of certain psychoses.

GRASPING REFLEX
The automatic clutching movement made by the hand when the palm is touched. This reflex is present in most babies at birth.

GRAY MATTER
The name given to the masses of nerve cells in various parts of the brain, and principally in the outer layer known as the *cerebral cortex.*

GRAYOUT
Partial loss of consciousness—as opposed to total loss: blackout—in which the visual field goes gray. This is generally due to reduced blood supply to the brain.

GREGARIOUSNESS
A tendency of people or animals to wish to gather together into crowds.

GRISELDA COMPLEX
A psychoanalytic term used to refer to an abnormal desire by a father to prevent his daughter from leaving home or getting married.

GROOMING
A ritual act in which one animal plucks parasites, dead hairs or feathers from another. Occasionally, grooming precedes mating behavior.

Spectrum

GROUP MIND
The phenomenon supposed to arise when a large number of animals of the same species gather together and apparently act with a common purpose. The idea of a group mind was once popular because it seemed impossible to see how colonies of ants or huge flocks of birds could behave in the same way without apparently communicating with each other. Another theory proposes that group activity of this kind is coordinated by special signals which are not readily detected or understood by humans or other animals.

GROUP RIGIDITY
The tendency of a group to maintain common policy and collectively resist pressure from outside to change it.

GROUP THERAPY
An approach to psychotherapy which involves a group of patients, who under the guidance of a trained therapist attempt to identify and understand each other's problems. This is often very effective treatment for patients, such as alcoholics, who have previously suffered from shame over their illness which they had considered to be unique.

GUSTATION
The sense of taste—one of the weakest human senses and more dependent upon the sense of smell than most people realize.

GYNANDROMORPHISM
The abnormal occurrence of both male and female characteristics in one individual.

GYRUS
A fold or wrinkle in the cerebral cortex or surface of the brain.

HABIT
A response or pattern of behavior which has been learned or acquired in an organism's lifetime.

HABITUATION
The process by which an inappropriate response becomes gradually eliminated when it no longer serves a function. To give a simple example, if a person moves to a busy road his sleep is at first disturbed by traffic noise but in due course his brain ceases to pay attention to the sounds.

HABROMANIA
An abnormal state of elation.

HALLUCINATION
A vivid perceptual experience, generally featuring sight or hearing, which is so real that the observer does not appreciate at the time that it is not objective, a part of the real world. Hallucinations are experienced by only one individual at a time and are induced from within, perhaps by drugs or mental illness or in the transition period between sleeping and waking. They need to be distinguished from *illusions*, which are commonly experienced disturbances in perception and are caused by some ambiguous feature of the environment that is misinterpreted by the brain.

Camera Press

HALLUCINOGEN
A drug such as LSD or mescaline which can induce hallucinations.

HALLUCINOSIS
An illness, often caused by alcoholism or brain damage, in which the patient suffers from persistent hallucinations.

HALO EFFECT
A sociological term which refers to the tendency, when interviewing or assessing a person, to allow favorable impressions made early in the interview to have a beneficial influence on later judgments.

HAMARTOPHOBIA
An abnormal fear that one has committed or will commit a grievous sin.

HAMMER
One of the tiny bones that make up the hearing mechanism of the middle ear.

HAMPTON COURT MAZE
A complicated maze of hedges at Hampton Court Palace in England dating from Tudor times. It is significant to psychology because the first mazes built to study animals' learning strategies were exact miniature models of it.

Woodmansterne

HANDICAPPED
Refers to a child or person suffering from some physical or psychological condition sufficiently severe to make it difficult for him to compete with others of his age.

HAPLOID
Those body cells which have only half the normal number of chromosomes—principally sperm and ovum cells.

HAPTIC
Relating to touch or skin senses.

HAPTOMETER
A device for measuring sensitivity to touch.

HARD COLORS
The reds and yellows.

HARMONY
Groups of figures or sounds which seem either to "work together" or provide a pleasing effect.

HASHISH
The narcotic drug *cannabis indica*.

HAWTHORNE EFFECT
A sociological term which refers to the way people behave differently when they know they are being studied in an experimental situation.

HEAD BANGING
A curious habit in which babies or very young children bang their heads repeatedly and rhythmically against a hard object, often in their sleep. This is often more annoying to the parents than dangerous to the child.

HEARING
Detection of sounds by the ear and their perception by the brain, technically known as *audition*.

HEART NEUROSIS
A common neurotic condition in which the individual suffers from "heart pains" which have no physical origin or basis.

HEBB, DONALD OLDING (1904-   )
Outstanding Canadian psychologist who is best known for his theoretical studies of perceptual learning.

HEBEPHRENIA
Schizophrenic psychosis in which the main symptoms are absurd and inappropriate behavior. Delusions, hallucinations and infantile behavior are also common.

HEDONISM
A philosophy that holds that the main purpose or goal in life is to seek pleasure and avoid pain.

HELIOPHOBIA
An abnormal fear of light or sunshine.

Zip Art

Camera Press

The mind minders

So you've a mind to be a trick cyclist and peddle panaceas. But has your _ego_ got what _id_ takes?

There are so many kinds of psycho-therapy around that many people are confused about who does what. Glancing through a directory tells you very little; even professionals find it difficult to keep up-to-date with current developments. But there are some basic differences between practitioners of psychotherapy.

Professional Prejudice

Psychiatrists need medical qualifi-cations before they specialize in the treatment of mental illness, then usu-ally take further training in a mental institution. They often use psycho-therapeutic techniques, but may also use other physical treatment. Only a qualified doctor can prescribe drugs.

Psychoanalysts are psychothera-pists who have taken special training in the theory and practice of psycho-analysis. They may be basically Freud-

ian, Adlerian or Jungian in approach. Part of their training is to undergo analysis themselves.

Lay analysts are not trained in medi-cine either, but usually have degrees in another subject and train under an established analyst. Although they very often work with children, there is sometimes a professional prejudice against lay analysts working with adults. Two of the most famous are Anna Freud and Erik Erikson.

Clinical psychologists are thera-pists or research workers with a doc-tor's degree. They take their first degree in psychology, then a one-year predoctoral or postdoctoral internship in psychotherapy and psychological assessment. Their work is done under the guidance of a psychiatrist.

Counselors usually have a master's degree or doctorate in counseling psychology. They often work in

Above: Junkies on a drug cure air their grievances and help each other get through the treatment.

schools and colleges, where they are available for help with personal prob-lems. If the problem is serious, they refer the client to a psychiatrist.

Psychiatric social workers take a graduate degree in psychiatric social work. They have supervised practical training, together with two years of courses in psychology. Usually, they are attached to hospitals.

Whether based on a medical degree, or qualification in psychology or other subject, some principles are the same for any kind of therapy. Of course, there are many people who operate as therapists without any formal quali-fications at all. You have probably done so yourself. If a friend comes to you with some personal problem, he places you in the position of a therapist. Clergymen and medical doctors frequently find themselves in this situation. So do teachers, or indeed anyone with a sympathetic disposition. There is a lot of evidence, for example in W. Schonfield's book *Psychotherapy, The Purchase of Friendship*, that ordinary people can be as successful in helping others as those purposely trained to do so.

Basic requirements for therapists, whatever school of therapy is conducting the training program, all acknowledge the need for practice in the complex interpersonal skills. The trainee therapist will observe an experienced therapist at work, either directly or by means of two-way mirrors and taped sessions (with the permission of the patients). In a group, he will "sit in" as an observer with an experienced leader. He will attend a training seminar at least once a week and discuss his work.

Practical Experience

Self-understanding is essential. Many analysts prefer to train someone who has had mildly neurotic symptoms but has been cured himself, rather than someone with no self-doubt or apparent problems. If a trainee shows himself to be rigid, oversubjective or self-protective, his training is designed to change him. Going through the same sorts of experience as his clients can give him greater empathy.

In addition to practical experience and self-awareness, any therapist must have some theoretical knowledge of human nature. Training for this will vary according to the kind of therapy in which he is specializing.

A group therapist also needs special knowledge of group dynamics. An experienced therapist who has trained many young psychiatrists boils down training objectives for group therapists into certain basic skills: sensitivity to his own emotional responses, and the series of reactions he has to events in the group; awareness of how his responses relate to what is taking place in the group; increased capacity to understand the patients in the group; and ability to react with empathy to the patients.

So far, these social skills are exactly what a client would also hope to get from a group. The new therapist learns in the same way as his

A marriage under strain may be saved by exploring the problems with a therapist. The London Centre for Psychotherapy is a charity which provides low-cost, expert treatment.

eventual clients: from his training group, which closely resembles any therapy group. After training, he then retraces the newly discovered steps to self-awareness with his clients.

The next objectives are somewhat different. It is the task of the client not only to get in touch with his feelings, and to come to understand the others better, but to make his feelings clear to them. The client undertakes to be as open and honest about his feelings and reactions as he can, so the therapist must also be in touch with his own emotions, being careful to use them in ways which are helpful to his clients. Essentially the therapist wants

to use his feelings, in a controlled way, to help his clients understand what he and they are jointly experiencing. To do this, he should be aware of the interpersonal processes within the group and be able to control his own reactions.

Good Vibrations

In addition to heightened sensitivity and the ability to use feelings constructively, the therapist needs to know how and when to guide the group. At one extreme, the analytical group therapist very rarely intervenes; at the other, the transaction analyst frequently stops the group talk to point out just what has been going on. When he does break the stream of group activity, the leader must be able to deal with group members' reactions to his interventions and, more generally, to his presence in the group. Just as vital as this, he must have the ability to deal with harmful group interactions and to promote good interactions among his clients.

Like any other students, trainee therapists tend to look to their teacher for guidance and instruction. In the training seminar, however, they find themselves the victims of the same procedure they practice on their patients. Most leaders do not immediately

embark on instruction, but let the burden of discussion fall on the trainees. In the seminar, each trainee reports his own experience with his clients and hears about the work of the others. The supervisor intervenes only if he thinks that his help is needed or that he has a useful contribution to make. At first, the trainees tend to hang back except when talking about their own work; gradually, the discussion becomes more cooperative. Other trainees might point out that one of them constantly made reference to the problems of one person in his group, to the exclusion of the others. This trainee himself might never have

noticed his bias, but when it is pointed out to him, he might go back and try to be more objective. His training group would follow up the problem, making sure that he tried to behave more fairly.

A therapist is only a human being, so he very often behaves in the unproductive ways that we can all fall into. Events in the therapy group may be emotionally threatening to him, so, instead of admitting to the training group what has happened, he will be tempted to talk about safe issues, like the implementation of research or some other intellectual topic. But the other trainees can be depended upon not to let him go away with such avoidance strategies. A good supervisor will leave the members of his group to make their own judgments so far as possible; not only do they learn faster, but critical comments are often less damaging when they come from those we regard as equals.

Transaction Analysis

Another common source of resistance is the trainee's inability to recognize the existence of group processes, so that he concentrates entirely on individuals (this sometimes shows itself as leader-centered behavior in the training group). He may also be unwilling to deal with fantasy or symbolic material in the group discussion.

Becoming a therapist is a tough business. It demands flexibility, balance, maturity, sensitivity, integrity—not that every therapist has these qualities, or that other people do not. Some particular kinds of therapy make the job easier by providing a theoretical framework to help the therapist interpret what his clients say and do. One of the most influential recent systems is *transaction analysis*.

TA, as it is known, grew out of weekly therapists' meetings with Eric Berne (who wrote *Games People Play*) in the fifties and sixties. Their purpose was to devise a kind of therapy which would be easier to understand, faster and more effective than the traditional sorts. They kept to ordinary language, and committed themselves to a therapy for the people. Transactions are interchanges between people, which Berne has analyzed on the simple basis of three possible "characters" or egostates, which we all have—the child, the adult, and the parent. This

Gered Mankowitz

Unrealistic expectations of life may lead to such frustration and depression that a person's full potential is never realized. Relief can be found in psychotherapy.

has its roots in psychoanalysis, but it is a far cry from the mystifying jargon so often found.

We all start out as the child who takes in from his environment messages that grow into a coherent system of thoughts and feelings. Depending on our experience, the child can be timid or bold, fawning or independent, crushed or creative. According to Berne, we transact in order to exchange "strokes," or units of recognition. The child needs physical strokes to survive, but no one gets through childhood without some negative "strokes" as well as positive ones, however loving his parents. Because he needs stroking for survival, the child ego-state may prefer negative

strokes to none at all. He may even go searching for the kinds of negative stroke he got in his real childhood. Someone brought up with blows (however figurative) and disapproval may continue to crave them.

Parent and Child

Every Child incorporates into himself attitudes and values from his parents and the significant adults around him. At his most impressionable, he cannot judge how reasonable his parents' rules and prohibitions may be; he takes them on trust. This builds up the second ego-state, that of the Parent. This is not an exact representation of the actual parents the child had, nor is it what he be-

comes when he is a parent. It is a system of thoughts and feelings derived from the real parent *as the child saw them.*

It is not usually until after the age of 12 that we develop the Adult—the reasonable, reality-oriented part of ourselves. The Adult is not motivated by feelings of his own, but can be activated by the Child or Parent. Berne's system is based on neurological studies which indicate that

Trying to analyze your own hang-ups may give you a distorted view of yourself (left). But talking things over with a sympathetic friend (right) might be more helpful in putting together the pieces.

memories are stored in a very complete way; even though we do not always have access to them, early "programs" continue to dictate our behavior long after we have grown up.

All three systems operate, often in rapid succession, in our everyday exchanges. Once you know what they are, you can often *choose* to operate out of a particular ego-state. You may, at work, become the placating, charming Child, to bring out the Parent in your colleague. Tone of voice, gesture, facial expression, and choice of words can give clues to identifying ego-states. Try to analyze your next exchange using this pattern. (Like everything else, it is often easier to recognize other people's states than your own.) Suppose you are reading this and your husband or wife tells you that supper is ready. The dialogue could go like this:

"Supper's ready."

"Just let me finish this page."

"Why do you always have to be doing something else just when supper's ready?"

"Why do you always have to nag?"

Wooden Leg

The simple statement about the meal being ready *could* be an Adult-to-Adult communication; or, depending on the tone of voice, it might be a Parent-to-Child communication—a disguised order. "Just let me finish this page" *could* be the Adult speaking, but the use of the word "let" suggests the Child. The last two are Parent-Child and Child-Parent exchanges, or possibly the last comment is a switch over to the critical Parent.

The TA therapist listens to transactions in the group, then presents the members with an analysis of their communications. Some patterns become habitual; Berne has labeled them amusingly. "What Do You Expect From a Man With a Wooden Leg?" is a "game" which uses disability, real or imaginary, to get out of demanding situations. "If It Wasn't For Him/Her" is a favorite ploy of people who are too afraid of failure to avoid being put to the test. *Games People Play* is full of funny, but serious, examples. The emphasis in TA is on present patterns of transaction, but TA often stimulates recall of early experience. One of the basic principles is that however "sick" or maladapted the client may be, his Adult can be reached for a realistic treatment contract. There is at present an extensive training program for TA professionals and an expanding network of teaching groups that train people to use TA in their own lives and work.

The tendency of TA to put responsibility on the client for his own improvement, which contrasts with classical psychoanalysis and its emphasis on the transfer to the analyst with its accompanying dependence, owes something to Carl Rogers' client-centered therapy. Here, the therapist has to start from a position of unconditional positive regard for the client. He has also to bring into the therapy an empathetic understanding of his client. Rogers assumes that people are innately good and that, given the chance, they will respond positively in the process of self-actualization.

The Rogerian therapist tries to reduce conflicts in the client by mirroring to him what his feelings are. In a context of regard and acceptance, the client comes to accept his own feelings, as they are shown to him. Special techniques are unnecessary. What counts is the sensitivity and warmth of the therapist. In common with other new forms of therapy, this can be faster than the traditional process; usually, client-centered therapy takes less than forty weekly visits. Because the client assumes responsibility for his treatment, the process of self-actualization can go on after therapy is concluded.

You may hear more about "reality therapy" in the future. It combines the emphasis on the responsibility of the client with a behavioral approach. It is conducted in individual sessions rather than in groups. Most therapists avoid making decisions for their clients, which often annoys the client who is asking for help of a very definite kind. William Glasser, the "founder of reality therapy," believes in encouraging the client to make a plan aimed at a desired goal, then asking him to commit himself to the goal. The past is forbidden ground—"History will kill you," Glasser says. The present and the future are all that really matter.

Positive Picture

If the client cannot stick to his plan, he is asked to make no excuses; and the therapist assures him that he will not be punished or rejected. The goals then become truly the individual's— he does not need to "please" the therapist. As in Rogerian therapy, the therapist has to concentrate on the good and productive aspects of the client's life and build up a positive picture for him. But the reality therapist never asks *why*; no attempt is made to give insight, but simply to examine behavior and to make clear to the client that he has a choice of action open to him. Anything which encourages failure identity is avoided. Training in reality therapy involves different goals and procedures from ordinary therapy; the Institute for Reality Therapy has been established to provide this training to psychiatrists.

Anyone can claim to administer psychotherapy. Most people provide therapeutic contact on an informal basis when someone they know is in trouble. But if therapy is to be on a prolonged basis, most of us would be happier if some professional standards were met. Encounter groups can provide intense, meaningful experiences, but also destructive ones, if the leader is not competent.

Consumer Demand

The American Psychological Association has established a standing committee to study the ethical implications of group sensitivity training. The National Training Laboratories have publicized a set of standards to ensure that leaders, and those who train them, are responsible and well-qualified. The ethos of the Esalen groups, which sprang up in California, and of Fritz Perls' Gestalt therapy, is that the client can do what he wants with the experience—even damage himself if that is what he wants to do. This seems to imply little need for training; but it is likely that if the newer forms of therapy are to continue, formal training will become absolutely essential.

In the last twenty years, new approaches to psychotherapy have mushroomed as dissatisfaction with traditional methods increased. Analysis was found to be too long, too expensive, too uncertain in result. Behavior therapy challenged the need to look for causes of maladaptive responses in the past history of patients. More people sought self-awareness and fulfillment rather than total release from neurotic symptoms, and therapies grew up to suit consumer demand.

It is still too early to know which systems will survive and prove their worth; but already traditional therapy has started to borrow the more effective techniques of the new wave. Most therapists who are also psychiatrists are eclectic—that is, they are not necessarily committed to one particular doctrine of therapy, but use the techniques that seem best with an individual client or with a particular group. In this freer atmosphere, we should see developments leading to faster and more effective therapy.

David Godfrey

Child of the times

Put behind bars at an early age, are our children fettered by society's harsh requirements?

Today, the rights of children—adequate food, clothing, medical and psychological care, education and training, protection against exploitation, cruelty and neglect, against exposure to moral or physical danger— are recognized and safeguarded by statute. Children are the most valuable assets of the state. The historian Clarke Hall wrote, ''Of all the assets of which the state stands possessed, none are more valuable than the children, but of all its assets, the state has been in the past of none so wasteful or heedless.''

Changes in society's attitude towards children are reflected in legislation to protect children from abuse by others and, indeed, from the consequences of their own immaturity and inexperience. Before the nineteenth century, society virtually ignored the statutory protection of children; this resulted in untold abuses of and suffering for children, at the hands of both their parents and their employers.

We have little direct evidence of how prehistoric man treated his children, although a few bone toys have been found. But by observing primitive communities that still exist it is possible to get a fairly accurate picture of the child's place in past societies.

Firstly, children are integrated into the tribe or group much more closely and much earlier than in more advanced societies. Because life was often at a subsistence level and was, therefore, a constant struggle for survival, the child, both in present and past primitive societies, had a definite and immediately significant function in the community.

Very soon in life he would be taught the skills and crafts of the community, specified generally by its needs: fishing skills in a fishing community, hunting techniques and crafts for a forest people, and agricultural knowhow for a farming community. He would have little or no choice in the matter, and the period of irresponsible childhood was likely to be quickly and abruptly ended, so that his training and contribution to the community could begin.

The child was likely to be groomed along very rigid lines for a predetermined role in the kinship system, as an heir of the family and of a tradition which had evolved in the way it had because of its success in ensuring the survival of the social group.

The modern child does not fit so well into the system. Because of the highly complex nature of the dawning industrial society of nineteenth-century Europe and America, there was little room in the work situation for the child because he did not possess the necessary skills to work beside his father. But this did not stop employers from using children for unskilled work in mines and factories.

Another marked difference between primitive and present-day families is that, in primitive societies, the modern idea of individual parenthood is rather vague. For example, in the polygamous compound family a man lives with his several wives and children; in the polyandrous compound, as found among the Toda of southern India, a woman lives with her several husbands and children. Where children are indiscriminately suckled by all mothers and communally fed by all men, the idea of a personal and individual mother and father does not signify very much. Roles are blurred, consequently, and the gulf between generations does not seem so great.

Small World

Today of course, with what Westerners would regard as a more humane philosophy of childhood, the whole process of the child's upbringing emphasizes, for a longer period of time, the difference between childhood and adulthood. Most of his day is occupied with play. Up to the age of about four or five, the young child is left in his mother's care. His father may see very little of him, if he has the ordinary kind of nine-to-five, five-day-a-week office or factory job. For most of the year his older brothers and sisters will be in school. If he does not go to a play group he may see few children his own age. His world during this period is a very narrow one in which his mother is the central figure. His existence centers very much around the home, unless, as is becoming more common, the mother goes out to work and places him in a day nursery, where he will, perhaps, "grow up" a little more quickly.

In primitive societies, the transition

Mary Evans

from boyhood to manhood is of profound importance, accompanied by initiation ceremonies (like circumcision when a boy reaches puberty) which are calculated to impress upon the boy the significance of his new status. In nearly all cases such ceremonies involve suffering and sometimes acute and prolonged pain. Initiation ceremonies are usually painful and sometimes dangerous, but neither the sufferer nor the wounder regards them as cruel. In fact, cruelty to children is not so much repugnant as totally alien to the primitive mind. The Sioux, a North American Indian tribe who inflicted the most barbarous tortures on their enemies, were horrified and baffled when they saw white settlers slapping their children. After initiation the male child is accepted as a full member of the group or tribe —he is automatically a man. This is very different from the prolonged and ambiguous period between childhood and adulthood we call adolescence.

Changes in society's attitude towards children are reflected, in part, by its evolving child legislation. In earlier social systems, the law concerned itself with the child as little as possible, and in rather the same way as it dealt with the married woman: as an adjunct to, and as the property of, the male. Yet who more than a child needs protection? After all, a child is physically weak, emotionally and sexually immature, intellectually untrained and inexperienced, and somewhat unstable in behavior.

The first laws relating specifically to children were typically adult-centered in the sense that they protected the parents' or owner's interest in the child's "market value" for marriage or employment. An early Roman father

Selling children to work as chimney sweeps was a horrifying practice condemned by moralists but virtually ignored in a "practical" society.

had complete power over his children throughout their life. This applied to sons and daughters, but in the case of a daughter only until she passed into the "manus" of her husband.

A father could sell his children and even inflict the death penalty upon them, and he could take their wages from them quite automatically. Their status, in fact, was little better than a slave's. Children were the absolute property of their parents and could be treated as though they had no natural rights at all for many centuries after the Roman Empire had vanished.

This was especially true of child marriages which were inevitably business arrangements involving inheritance or land. Stories have been told of both partners bursting into tears at being told they must marry each other and of little girls playing with their dolls at their weddings.

Miniature Adults

In the past, adult life for European children began as soon as they were old and strong enough to act as animated scarecrows—frightening birds from crops or gleaning a few ears of corn. From then on they were workers like anyone else in the family. The books and pictures produced before the fourteenth century give the impression that childhood hardly existed. Children were considered to have adult emotions and moral attitudes fixed in their mind at birth. There was, unfortunately, the disadvantage of their ignorance and helplessness.

Until the end of the eighteenth cen-

Children seven years of age and older were considered adults and were judicially murdered for minor crimes. In England, up to 1780, the penalty of death by hanging for over two hundred offenses was exacted with chilling regularity. Many children, like the little girl of seven hanged in the marketplace at Norwich for stealing a petticoat, were executed for trivial offenses, which nowadays would entail no more than probation. On one day alone in February, 1814, at the Old Bailey Sessions, five children were condemned to death for petty larceny. In 1748, when a ten-year-old English boy was hanged for killing a five-year-old girl, the sentencing judge stated that leniency might lead "to the very dangerous consequence to have it thought that children might commit such atrocious crimes with impunity."

Child Labor

Probably the great majority of parents have always loved their children, but the way of showing this affection has been, in the past, different from ours today. Then, life was rough and hard for all, not only for children. Children were expected to share the common hardships and responsibilities of the adults at an early age. After all, they were "little adults" and often bore the brunt of the hard times they lived in.

The eighteenth century statistics on infant mortality in England and Wales are awesome. In the first half of that century, the odds were three-to-one against a child completing five years of life, and in the second half of the century children born in London had a fifty-fifty chance of surviving until their fifth birthday. According to the London Bills of Mortality, of 1,178,346 deaths between 1730 and 1779, a total of 526,973 were those of children under five years of age.

From the late seventeenth century onwards, poor children were expected to help support themselves, and child labor became the accepted pattern. Yet, though existence for the children of agricultural Britain was hard and grinding, it was not degrading and brutalizing. The Industrial Revolution soon changed all that. As the mills and factories arose in Birmingham, Manchester, Bradford, and Leeds, the lives of the children who were forced to work in them became bestial. The argument used by the overseers was that punishments for arriving late in the morning had to be cruel enough to overcome the temptation for children to stay more than three or four

Cruelty to children was an all-too-common feature following the Industrial Revolution. The law was slow to punish the offenders.

tury, and to a lesser extent in the nineteenth century, it was a common practice to abandon unwanted children—either offspring of unmarried mothers or of parents who considered their family already overlarge—in the streets and lanes of the cities or the countryside. Frequently these children died before being discovered.

Medieval citizens had a simple remedy for incapacitated and poverty-stricken children: young beggars were whipped out of town with their parents, and even the church offered only sporadic charity. By the Elizabethan Age, a system of parish poor

law had been established so that paupers would not literally starve to death before the eyes of their neighbors. But many children "on the parish" died.

Spurred on by these conditions, Thomas Coram opened a foundling hospital in England in 1745, where abandoned children were brought up and apprenticed to a trade. But this was really only skimming the surface, and for another century deserted children either died or went to the parish workhouse. In the mid-eighteenth century, for every three births registered in Paris, one was a foundling. Sometimes the waifs were discovered by beggars who would mutilate them to arouse pity among the public and would also lease them to other beggars for the night.

Factory owners were keen to employ child labor since it was cheap and children could do work in cramped conditions where adults could not go. Child mortality was very high, but money talked louder than those who cared, a far cry from the love and attention we lavish on our children today.

hours in bed. Unknown numbers of boys were being sold to chimney-sweepers as climbing boys, while other children were traded to beggars. The law offered little protection against these abuses. When Anne Martin was accused of mutilating the bodies of children with whom she went begging about the country, the punishment she received for putting out their eyes was a mere two years' imprisonment.

It was only as recently as 1868, the date of the last public execution in Britain, that children were spared from witnessing such events as a practical warning against crime. Within the family, too, punishments were frequent and savage. Children were flogged and beaten with straps and whips, thought to be necessary aids to discipline. Some of the contemporary religious views, for example those of early Calvinists, positively encouraged harsh treatment of children. They believed that all children were by nature evil and that, since they had nothing but this natural evil to guide them, pious and prudent parents must check their naughty passions. Wesley himself would not suffer his children to play any games, saying that a child who played when he was young would also play when he was a man.

The philosopher Jean Jacques Rousseau had considerable influence in changing society's attitudes towards children. In 1762 he published *Emile*, a treatise on education that gave some revolutionary advice. ''Men, see human beings; this is your first duty. . . . Love childhood, indulge its games, its pleasures, and its lovable nature. Who has not looked back with regret on an age when laughter is always on the lips and when the spirit is always at peace? . . . Why fill with bitterness

Perhaps modern parents have overdone it. Too much coddling and that child is spoiled.

and sorrow these first swift years which will never return for them any more than they can return for you."

No one of Rousseau's stature and influence had ever before written of children in this way. The effect was felt so profoundly that before the end of the century over two hundred responses to *Emile* had been written in England alone.

Another great reforming writer, Charles Dickens, leaves us in no doubt about the prevalence of cruelty to children during the complacent and rather pious Victorian years that reaped the riches of the Industrial Revolution. Both cottage industries and factories used child labor extensively until the mid-nineteenth century. Handling bobbins in lace making,

straw plaiting, picking up cotton waste, creeping under unguarded machines where adults could not go, working in underground mines as trappers, opening and shutting doors which controlled the ventilation of mines, filling carriages with coal and pushing the racks—these were the types of jobs children were forced to do.

Even children under five years of age were employed; older children labored in mines and factories for more than 15 hours a day under appalling conditions often enforced by fear and brutality. Children in the workhouse were made to toil in dangerous places. If they refused they were committed to prison. Dickens described graphically the shocking conditions of that era in his book *Hard Times*. The indifference and fatalistic attitude with which people viewed the high rate of infant mortality and the demoralization of children in industry may be

staggering to a modern parent.

But we have to bear in mind that these people lacked the medical knowledge which we possess today to understand—still less to cure—the diseases which ravaged successive generations of underfed children. They were also ignorant of the minimal standards in working conditions and childbearing and had no inkling of the modern concepts of child welfare.

As recently as the nineteenth century, 80 percent of illegitimate children put out to nurse in London died during their first year of life because the nurses collected their fee and then did away with the infant. Parents, as a rule, felt quite self-righteous about extremely harsh discipline, believing that one of their responsibilities was to "break the will" of their children. They seemed unaware that children could be socialized by anything other than cruelty.

Mary Evans

Music to my ears

"Music oft hath such charm to make bad good, and good provoke to harm."

If it is suggested that music is a magical force—a gift from the gods, a creation of occult powers, a means of communication between man and his deities or devils, a supernatural language of spirits and demons—it is bound to raise an eyebrow. Yet, it is, in a sense, true. Whether we ourselves believe in such divine forces is immaterial because there were once people who did, and it was their belief which shaped the musical traditions which we have inherited.

Such a notion clashes resoundingly with the ideas of modern times and is not easily equated with what we con-

sider to be the right and proper place of music in our society. It is available to us at the flick of a switch from radios, record players, and juke-boxes. It is so abundant that we scarcely notice most of it, let alone credit it with deep mystical significance. It serves only as an incidental background.

Even in the concert hall, where we allow ourselves to be "carried away" by music, it does not give us what we would call a religious experience. To us the concert hall seems a perfectly natural setting for a musical event yet, if our earliest ancestors or even a

pygmy or bushman were to see us sitting in rows, poker-faced and motionless, soaking up the music without batting an eyelid, they would not believe their eyes.

Don't Just Listen

To them music was never an art form merely to be enjoyed. It was a living force to be used. It provided a spur to action in the realms of religion, politics, and society. It was the highest form of personal and collective self-expression. Music was never just to be listened to; it was to become involved in. It evoked a response in

1991

every fiber of body and soul, awakening man's emotions and instincts, giving him spiritual uplift, and stirring him to live life to the full—to sing, to dance, hunt, fight, work, let off steam, to make love, and to praise his gods for the miracle of life.

It has always been man's instinctive tendency to attribute any natural phenomenon which is beyond his understanding to supernatural divinities. No exception was his discovery that wind whistles, that missiles sing as they fly through the air, that a staff whines as he waves it around his head, or that hollow objects produce a resonant note on impact with others. There was no accounting for such distinctive musical sounds; they seemed to come from nowhere, as if by magic. They must therefore be the voices of the gods. One music historian wrote, "Music is the only particle of the divine essence which men have been able to capture, and this has enabled them, by means of prescribed rites, to identify themselves with the gods and exercise control over them."

Talking to God

Needless to say, when man found that he could reproduce these mysterious and pure sounds by blowing through reeds, banging hollow logs, or striking shells, he thought he had found the means of communicating with the gods. From then on it was a question of learning the language. The gods spoke to man through nature and it seemed to be man's bounden duty to harness nature to make music and, with singing and dancing, to dedicate all creation to the worship and service of the creators.

But for all his efforts he still failed to master his environment, and he logically attributed the hostility of nature to the presence of malevolent, supernatural forces—evil spirits and demons—who, he believed, might be appeased and driven out by song. Music could be used as an offensive or defensive weapon. The incantations of witchdoctors would drive away the spirits which brought ill-fortune; the battle cries of tribal warriors would summon the aid of deities and imbue them with superhuman powers.

Music became an essential ingredient of rainmaking ritual, funeral and fertility rites, harvest observances. Every phase of life and death deserving the attention of the gods had its musical accompaniment. It was so integral to man's battle for survival that music spilled over into all areas of human endeavor and assumed a place preeminent in his culture.

For all his ignorance of the physics of sound, of air vibration, of harmonic sequence, and of musical theory as we know it, primitive man realized that music had some structure and form. He noted that particular sounds could be relied upon to evoke invariable emotional and instinctive responses in himself and his fellows. The creation of pleasing or agonizing sounds and the arousal of their related feelings need not be left to chance, but could be effected at will. By trial and error he explored the relationship, and various patterns began to emerge.

Although musical styles are as many and varied as the gods men once worshiped, they share a good deal of common ground. All music makes the clear distinction between the moods of excitement and repose. High notes and fast rhythms are identified with frenzy, vitality, and joy; low notes and slow rhythms with lethargy, inertia, relaxation, and sorrow. These are universal, because the inflections of the voice and the natural rhythms of the body—heartbeat, breathing, and movement of limbs—on which they are so obviously based are also universal.

Another common feature is that the human ear is attuned to the "natural octave." This has nothing to do with our eight-note scale but is an appreciation of the affinity between two notes apart. Although the instruments of the Arunta tribe in Australia are incapable of sounding octaves, their songs follow the pitch relationships of our musical system. They must have arrived at it intuitively, since they are too isolated to have borrowed from any outside musical tradition.

Cross-fertilization

Out of this common ground grew a profusion of musical styles—European, Indian, Chinese, African—each developing in its own way. Hearing them today in their modern form, they sound so vastly different that it is hard to imagine that they could have evolved from common roots. There are no fixed stages of evolution through which music must progress. All styles are, in their own way, as structured, sophisticated, and valid as any other. To our ears Indian music sounds primitive, yet its theory and technique are immeasurably more complex and organized than ours. Over the years there has been much interbreeding and cross-fertilization of styles, and our kind of music is colored by influences from many other traditions.

A good example of this is the development of jazz in the space of little more than a hundred years. When the

simple and primitive chants of Negro slaves—their blues and cotton-field work songs—latched on to the Western musical form, they took a new lease on life. Played on more versatile instruments, embellished and ornamented in the classical tradition, they provided the basis for a new and highly sophisticated art form which has preserved many of the elements of its primitive beginnings. It revolutionized popular music and even invaded the "arty" scene.

As primitive man discovered more about music, its shape and logic, and unraveled its mysteries, he did not separate it in his mind from the supernatural world. The more he knew about it, and applied his knowledge, the greater would be his power over the gods, the elements, nature, and his enemies. He often attributed his discoveries to divine intervention.

Music at the Forge

For instance, the story of the origin of the Chinese scale dates back to the third century B.C., and probably circulated much earlier. Realizing that music ought to have some pattern of fixed notes, the Emperor Huang-ti sent his master of music in search of it. The story goes that in a secluded valley he cut a stem from a bamboo tree and blew into it, producing a note, whereupon a male and a female phoenix settled in a nearby tree and burst into song. Each sang six notes which the musician was able to reproduce by cutting eleven more bamboo stems, which he then presented to the emperor, his mission accomplished. Most mythologies provide some such account of the origins of musical form.

Often regarded as the father of musical theory is Pythagoras, who investigated music in relation to the other two subjects for which he is better known—mathematics and philosophy. He elevated music to a scientific level. Legend has it that one day he was passing a forge where four blacksmiths were striking anvils of different sizes and producing different notes. Noting the relative weights of the anvils he went home and suspended four weights of equivalent proportions on strings stretched from the ceiling. When he plucked the strings he found they produced the same four notes he had originally heard.

He began to experiment with the lyre and found that there was a mathematical relationship between notes which, when played together, produced pleasing harmonies. He started to think that numerical and mathematical secrets were behind the harmony

of all creation, and thereafter music was given a prominent place in Greek philosophy. Plato also ranked music highly in his scheme of things, regarding it as the embodiment of all the order and harmony.

Superhuman Powers

This objective and intellectual study of music disclosed that music was the artifact of man; it had perfectly logical and rational explanations, and had no connection with the supernatural world whatever. Yet there was no gainsaying its power over people, which was still a mystery, and hence perpetuated the belief in its ethereal source. Because he applied his know-

ledge of music, Pythagoras was considered to be a magician. An occasion is recorded when he subdued a rabble of drunken sailors who, excited by rumbustious music, had "forced the door of an honest woman." Pythagoras persuaded the flutist to play a slow solemn dirge. As a result of the change in tempo, calm was restored. The onlookers were astonished. They thought they had seen superhuman powers at work. Ancient writings abound with stories of the power of music—of Orpheus taming wild beasts or Amphion building the walls of Thebes to the strains of the lyre.

There are also many stories in religious scriptures, history and mytho-

Top left: Music and dance play a vital role in Zulu ritual. Top right: The ancient Greeks regarded music as the embodiment of order and harmony. Above: Music and religion once went hand in hand; an angelic orchestra plays in Fra Angelico's *Christ Glorified in the Court of Heaven.*

logy attesting to the healing power of music. In primitive thinking disease was the work of malevolent spirits which could be exorcised by music. The surgical implements of the primeval medicine man included an assortment of musical instruments, and a repertoire of incantations was part of his stock in trade. Even as late as

1641, a priest published a score of music specially written as a cure for tarantula bites. Remarkable cures for mental and bodily disorders have been claimed, and we have no reason to doubt many of them, knowing what we do about mind-over-matter psychology. The attitude of the patient is a decisive factor in recovery; if he believes profoundly that music will cure him, it probably will.

It is interesting that the man with a melodious cure for tarantula bites should have been a Christian priest, since a belief in the power of music over the deity was not part of the faith. But music played an important part in the rituals of worship, and still does. Its liturgical purpose was to serve as the finest vehicle in man's power for the glorification of God, and to arouse religious ecstasy or induce a meditative composure in his people. The early church produced some of the most magnificent music ever written. At one time the churches were the only places where music could be heard, and certainly the only institutions which provided for the full-time pursuit of musical interests. Early composers were almost all on the church's payroll. Although Christian music owed much to the Syrian, Alexandrian, Greek and Jewish styles which had gone before, it is to the early church that we trace the origins of our musical traditions.

Religious Symbolism

But in a sense it was a pity that music came under the exclusive supervision of the church. Apart from imposing limits on its free development, it set it apart from other areas of life in which it was so effective and enriching in primitive communities. It lost some of its variety, its spontaneity, and appeal to the basic human instincts. Within the framework of the liturgy it had to be majestic, dignified, or solemn, and, of course, dancing as a form of worship or religious self-expression was taboo. Nor, one suspects, was it considered proper to enjoy the music for its own sake.

Although music was now breaking away from its primitive roots, it retained some of its original characteristics. Its power to facilitate communion with the deity was one, its symbolism another. St. Augustine regarded the stretched parchment of the

The emotional power of music is well employed by the amorous gentleman in Watteau's *Le Gamme d'Amour*. Military marches also have a stirring effect, making us feel patriotic.

tympanum as representing the body of Christ crucified. Another idea held that the ten strings of the psaltery represented the Ten Commandments. Even as late as the seventeenth century an idea had survived that the organ symbolized the Holy Trinity: the player (the Father), the blower (the Son) and the wind (the Holy Spirit) —the pipes were the angelic hosts.

A primitive parallel is found in the beliefs of the Dogon tribesmen of the Sudan. For them, the drum is the embodiment of the four elements: the

parchment from which it is made is originally moist (water) and is dried in the sun (fire) to be stretched over wooden frames (earth) to produce sound vibrations (air).

We had to wait till the eleventh century for the arrival of secular music, which was an offshoot of the religious traditions. It borrowed its forms and notation from religious music and used it to ennoble temporal affairs. Madrigals, lays, ballads, laments, folk songs and dances drew their inspiration from social customs, chivalrous

exploits, courtly love, ancient legends, and military campaigns; extolling love, virtue and morality, they were played and sung for the sheer fun of it.

Religious music continued to develop in its own fashion; eventually it found its way out of the churches and into the concert halls where works written on religious themes could be heard and enjoyed for themselves and were regarded as adjuncts to worship. Although music was not free from the domination of the church, it was still a long time before it could develop freely along any course which the creative imagination of the composer cared to take it. It now had to serve a new master, the patron.

The courts of kings and the households of the nobility provided an alternative setting for full-time musical activity. Just as he once had to praise God, the musician now had to direct his adulation towards his earthly lords and masters—extolling their virtues, their wisdom, courage, and justice, and giving musical expression to their exploits and ambitions.

Duty Bound

The musician was a retainer and was not particularly esteemed in high society. His first duty was to please his patron, and this could be done only by honoring the musical traditions of the time and reflecting the distilled emotions of the court in which he was billeted. The creation of music was now becoming a specialist job.

Although the musician was becoming separate from his audience, his individual rights as a creative artist were not yet acknowledged. Creative imagination was not encouraged if that meant breaking lose from traditional musical structures for the sake of self-expression. The composer Haydn accepted his place in society and fulfilled his public duties. Mozart did not. Early in his career he fell out with Haydn because he refused to be bound by the conventions of the period; he stuck to his guns and suffered for his obstinacy. The courts abandoned him and allowed him to die a pauper. Beethoven was the first composer who reckoned he owed the world nothing, and won respect for the idea that the artist's first duty was to himself and his own imagination.

The Romantic composers who followed, Chopin in particular, pursued their own lights and broke new ground. They were not so bound by form and structure as their predecessors. Under earlier influences, music had been sticking too rigidly to its own theory, which inhibited full and free expression of emotions and basic instincts. The Romantics presided over its liberation, drawing their inspiration from their own deepest souls, from nature, from religion and mythology, from their own national and cultural traditions, legend, and folklore. They set music on its return journey to its primeval roots and revived the idea of music as a life force.

Emotional Response

To say that this trend set in motion by the Romantics has continued till the present day is not to imply that we all believe again in music's divine origins and supernatural powers. Yet we know that music does appear to have strange powers to do things to us, and its effect is much the same as it was on our ancestors who did hold such beliefs. In their absence, we must look to psychology for an explanation of music's power over us and of why music has survived as an integral part of present-day ritual.

When we hear a military band approaching and the tramp of marching feet, our instinct might be to rush out, chests puffed up with national pride, and fall into step. When we enter a cathedral or monastery and hear an organ fugue or monks intoning a plainsong chant, we feel subdued, reverent, and meditative. When we hear a Strauss waltz or a jazz stomp we are swept onto our feet and want to dance. The music has aroused some kind of emotional response and provided a spur to an appropriate action.

But equally possible is that the military band will provoke feelings of disgust and revulsion in the pacifist, that the church organ will incite the fanatical atheist to acts of violent sacrilege, or that the dance music will sicken the musical highbrow. Our response to music obviously depends on our own psychological predisposition. The sounds are open to a variety of interpretations, but we go along with the music only insofar as we go along with the ideas associated with it.

For practical purposes, association is enough to account for music's "control" of our behavior. There is nothing inherently powerful about music itself. We have either been conditioned to react to certain kinds of music in prescribed ways, or else the music calls forth memories of past experiences in the presence of, say, the organ or the military band, which reawakens the emotions which we felt at the time.

Many of us are capable of summoning up prescribed emotions on demand and music often makes such a demand. If we speculate about why a lullaby sends us to sleep, we see that there might be three reasons. Do we nod off because the lullaby has infallible powers to make us drowsy, or because we *know* it's a lullaby and feel we ought to go to sleep, or because we are sleepy anyway?

Music has only such powers as we ascribe to it. Whether we are worshiping God or gardening, music can help create the right atmosphere and provide a fitting accompaniment to the deed if it carries the right associations with it. The effect of the military band is to inspire the spirit of heroism and feelings of regimental solidarity. It is the modern equivalent of the intoned war cries of the ancient warrior. The psychological effect is today's counterpart of the witchdoctor whose incantations drove away the devils which possessed an afflicted soul. The music played to factory workers to increase their productivity has its precedent in traditional work songs which both set the pace of the body's movements for specific tasks and called on the gods to bless the harvest. It seems that the ritual function of music has not changed a bit.

Magic Moments

But several factors in today's music seem pitted against such a movement. One is that the glut of instant canned music dulls the senses, so that it ceases to play upon our emotions and feelings. Music is not reserved for "magic moments" or ritualistic purposes. We have developed a capacity to take it or leave it, to switch on and off at will.

Yet there is evidence that we still have something in common with the instinctive responses of our forebears. Some years ago the police were called to the Olympia music hall in Paris when a concert audience had become so excited by the music they had ripped up all the seats and smashed all the mirrors. This incident was one of the first wave of such events which, particularly in rock and pop, have become prevalent.

Such incidents are followed by public condemnation and disgust. A typical reaction would be for someone to shake his head and say, "What are people today coming to?" A more pertinent question might be, "What have people today come from?" Recent musical trends, even in the most advanced societies, suggest we might be going back there, that through music we might regain contact with our most primitive instincts, and regard it once again, if not as a supernatural endowment, as a life force.

Robin Clifford

Run up to run down

Three score years and ten is not so long to live. And for some, middle age means panic—the fear that nothing's been achieved. The signs of wear and tear are plain for all to see. But if the wrinkles rankle, maybe it's time to grow up. You cannot beat the clock.

Few people like to admit they are middle-aged. It is a slightly disparaging and at the same time rather woolly term reserved more for an outmoded frame of mind than a tiring body. But middle age has been used to describe the period of life between youth and old age since the late seventeenth century, so at least it has sound enough historical associations.

Of course, life in those days was rather compressed, and middle age probably meant the brief spell between the twenties, when manhood and womanhood began, and the fifties, when the shadow of a not too far distant mortality hovered. Those who managed to survive the biblical three score years and ten were in the minority until the turn of this century.

Whether it is possible to look upon middle age as a scientific entity or not is perhaps only of academic interest. Once you decide exactly which

Above: One of the most striking signs of aging is a sagging posture.

age group you are talking about the actual title you give it is immaterial, but for the sake of analysis, the age group of 44 to 64 seems a reasonable spread, particularly as statistical surveys tend to group these two decades.

Exactly what happens to us during these years depends primarily on sex. If it is male, the chance of dying at age 64 will be nearly three times as great as it was at 44. But if fate is not on the male side, fertility certainly is, for men can normally father a child well into their eighties if they happen to be around as long as that. Women after these two decades have only half as much likelihood of being called to meet their maker as men. But by the time they are halfway through middle age they will have lost one of the badges of femininity, their fertility.

Crisis Years

Another curious sexually orientated characteristic of middle age is a very sharp decline in wage earners among womenfolk, particularly during the second decade of middle age. Recent figures in Britain show that there is very little drop in the number of men out at work over the five consecutive four-year periods that make up the middle-aged years. But although roughly as many women as men are out at work between age 44 and 54, there is a sharp decline after this, and women usually spend the last decade of middle age in the home.

The notion of the so-called middle age "crisis" probably grew out of some work done by H. C. Lehman over thirty years ago. In essence it still remains valid even today. Some of our most cherished beliefs about the "wisdom" of the older man certainly fall by the wayside when you start to look at statistics. In fact, the middle-aged have an edge on youth in only two areas: holding high government office and earning a lot of money.

The "brainy" scientist in the movies is usually depicted as a middle-aged absentminded professor, but in reality the 24-to-44 age group wins hands down on such achievements. When inventors and chess champions are considered, again youth leads the field. In the world of books, traditionally a field where wisdom may be expected to pay dividends, it is sad to realize that an author is only half as likely to write a "best-seller" during the years between 45 and 50 as he was during the previous five years. Even the founders of religious movements are more likely to be under 45 than past it. "Life begins at 40" seems to have a rather hollow ring.

There are, however, compensations. You are, for instance, much less likely to suffer from schizophrenia during these later years. And on the whole you are not so likely to be admitted to a psychiatric hospital, if a bit of an early surge in mental deterioration that starts at 55 in women and 65 in men is ignored. But for many of the middle-aged, life is a happy time, especially if ambitions have been reasonably well fulfilled, when family cares or worries recede and the individual begins to live a life that is more his own than it has been for years previously. And of course the extra money that comes along in the middle years makes everything easier.

Exactly what does happen to our bodies and our lives generally, during these years is worth exploring in a little detail, if only because of the many health hazards of middle age that can be foreseen and avoided. These can be grouped together as mainly physical, psychological and behavioral. There is a considerable amount of evidence that the so-called middle-age crisis, in both sexes, in this day and age of sophisticated medicine, is very much a man-made affair from the physical point of view. In other words, it is more to do with a self-inflicted destructive environment than the inevitable effects of aging.

Hazards of Smoking

One of the things we all enjoy about youth and deplore about middle age is that during the former years illness is a novelty. But once you are well on into the forties getting ill is regarded as just part of getting older. But a quick glance at a few medical details of health problems in middle age will show the error of such a dismal philosophy, and perhaps the most easy factor to consider on this score is the effect on middle-aged man of that ever-popular and soothing panacea of our day, the cigarette.

It is one of the most curious phenomena of modern life that, although the effects of tobacco smoking on the human body are so well known, an era that admires youth so profoundly and dreads the infirmities of middle age still blindly continues to ignore the facts. Oddly, perhaps, statistics make little or no impact on this state of affairs. Maybe this is because we think that usually only "older" people die of cancer. Next along this line of reasoning comes the somewhat reticent acceptance that "you've got to die of something, sometime, haven't you?" And the ultimate rationalization that sums it all up says, "Why not

smoke then? It makes life more enjoyable and rewarding. Anyway, if you're going to get cancer, why not cancer of the lungs?"

Although a ten-year-old with a grasp of the facts could shoot holes through this train of argument there are none so blind as those who do not want to see. Smoking is tied up not only with cancer, but with all sorts of diseases of the middle years. It is one of the greatest single factors likely to be involved in a middle-age health crisis.

Soul-Searching

Taking a man who smokes upwards of 20 cigarettes a day, here are the increases in mortality he is liable to experience over the nonsmoker during middle age. His overall death rate is seven times that of the nonsmoker. He is twenty times more likely to develop lung cancer or a fatal disease of his leg arteries. The smoker is nine times more likely to succumb to bronchitis, and three times more likely to be killed by a stroke or a coronary thrombosis. Now it must be stressed that these are mortality figures. For everyone who ultimately dies of such an illness there are many more who suffer and are disabled, and the large majority feel this disability biting hard into an otherwise healthy time of life. Heavy smoking is one of the avoidable factors in the middle-age crisis that nobody really seems to bother about.

Another thing that worries many men and women as they approach middle age, and which contributes to the anxiety and soul-searching at this time, is a change in appearance. While it is impossible to argue against the inevitability of gradual aging of the body, much of what is assumed to be middle-aged "deterioration" is in fact a question of physical mismanagement of the body. Appearance is determined by a combination of several factors. The body skeleton, with its muscles and connective tissues, contributes to general bearing, and so do the skin and the subcutaneous fat that lies beneath it.

The skeleton itself changes very little during the middle years of life, although later there is a tendency for bones to become more brittle and for stature to decrease slightly due to a gradual shrinking of the little elastic disks between the bones of the spinal column. But these effects are not noticeable to any extent just yet.

Neither does muscle tissue change much during the middle years. We reach muscular perfection around the age of 30, and after this there is a small but gradual diminution of speed and power of contraction. There are, however, great individual differences in muscular function and efficiency. But again, much depends on the use the muscle is put to rather than the muscles themselves. Exercises can improve muscles that have fallen into disuse; tests have proved that it is possible to increase muscular bulk and improve muscles well on into the fifties. There are few changes in well-trained muscles that would affect the speed of muscular reflexes or the usual repetitive movements that make up middle-aged muscular activity.

Loss of Elasticity

Probably the only significant change in middle age is within the connective tissue which supports, binds and generally connects our various organs and body tissues. One of the most important factors in the biology of connective tissue is a substance called collagen, a complex protein substance whose most characteristic quality is elasticity. Collagen changes with aging, and generally speaking the most notable change is a gradual loss of this elasticity. This means that, once stretched, the "elastic" no longer returns to its former length. One of the changes that characterizes the deterioration in collagen function is delay in wound healing, and this is because the collagen that appears in a scar in an elderly person is only "lightly bound," and is relatively inefficient. But surgeons will confirm, however, that wound healing is very nearly as quick and efficient in middle age as it is in youth, and so much of the "collagen aging" of middle age may well be a result of other factors, many of which are, once again, self-inflicted.

Perhaps the most easily demonstrated of these is seen in what is sometimes referred to as the "elastosis" syndrome in women. This so called "disease" of middle age is what sends so many women in their forties and fifties to the plastic surgeon for a "face lift" operation of one sort or another. Doctors have recognized for many years what causes this particular aspect of the middle-aged crisis. It is much more common in places like Australia and California, where summers are long and sunny, than it is in Scandinavian countries or even Britain. Now, as a result of the "sunshine" vacation, so long believed to be healthful, more and more people are being affected.

Elastosis of middle age, with the characteristic baggy appearance of the eyelids and drooping cheeks and jowls, is really simply a secondary effect of exposure to ultraviolet light of high intensity. This produces collagen damage, loss of elasticity, stretching of the skin's connective tissue and ultimately sagging of the tissues. If anyone doubts that this is possible, all he needs to do is to compare the skin on the inside of his arm, for instance, with that of his face.

Another thing that is laid at the door of middle age is a loss of a youthful posture. But once again it is possible to remedy the distortions that mark the difference between a young-looking figure and a neglected middle-aged one. First there is a tendency to hold the head forward, which destroys the normal youthful set of the neck on the shoulders. The convex spinal curve at the middle of the chest also tends to be accentuated. This "rounds" the back, while the lumbar curve is stressed in the opposite direction. The knees tend to turn inwards in walking and there is a distinct flattening of the normal foot arches. In a nutshell, the whole process is a gravity-induced compression of the figure, referred to as "full frontal sag."

Gravity Effects

But it is not only gravity that produces this type of middle-aged sagging of the tissues—overweight comes into it too. Bones, joints, muscles and tendons, connective tissues, and the skin have been designed to withstand very definite stress loads. But modern life and, perhaps even more important, modern dietary practice alter our metabolic processes, and too much fat builds up in vital organs. This constantly overloads the frame leading all too often to the sort of figure that is part and parcel of the middle-aged "look."

Clearly a reasonably well-planned system of exercises, especially those in which the "gravity effects" of the passing years are warded off, can reduce many of the postural defects that creep into middle age. We should always remember the value of regular swimming as an exercise. We evolved from aquatic creatures many millions of years ago, and our body instantly responds to the weightlessness of swimming. Not only does the instant release from gravity allow us to enjoy a fuller range of movements than we have for quite a while, but the tonic effect of cold water on skin and circulation is always beneficial.

Dietary discretion is extremely important in middle age if obesity is not to ruin looks, spoil body function and make a reasonable personal image an impossibility. In weight watching, an ounce of prevention is worth a pound of cure, and a little attention to planning meals around an adequate basis of protein while regulating carbohydrates, will pay handsome health dividends. A highly refined carbohydrate, like white sugar, is particularly liable to be converted to fat on the body. But it seems the knowledge that calories do not always work by numbers alone is probably one of the most carefully hidden "secrets" of human nutrition.

Those who would preserve their frame in a healthy middle life must learn some of the basic facts of nutrition, especially about carbohydrates and the place they occupy in a balanced diet. The very word carbohydrate has been debased in the language of popular science until to some people it has just become a synonym for sugar. Thus a low-carbohydrate diet means, to them, no sugar in tea or coffee and perhaps, strangely, no potatoes.

Most foodstuffs are, however, a combination of the three basic building bricks—carbohydrate, protein and fat—all of which are essential to good health at all ages, but especially in the middle years it is necessary to get the balance right. It is usually better to talk of foods rather than the basic nutritional elements they contain. The reason highly refined foods have led us into bad nutritional habits is that in their refined state they have often been shorn of their basic health-giving qualities. All that is left of them in their highly processed state is a filling and fattening quality that spells disaster to the middle-aged person in terms of health and body image.

Receding Hairline

A few other current myths about middle age should be scotched for all time. First, baldness. This, when it occurs in young men, is often viewed with horror as a sign of approaching middle age and degeneration. In fact, nothing could be farther from the truth. Baldness is very rarely associated with illness, but far more often it is a constitutional, inherited characteristic. The common type of baldness, in which the hair recedes symmetrically from the hairline and a distinct bald patch occurs on the back of the head, is a strictly masculine trait and has, with little justification, actually been said to be a sign of virility. It can start in the twenties, with the amount of hair loss proceeding gradually throughout the middle years. There is another type of baldness that is associated with aging and is sometimes called senile baldness. This is characterized by a general thinning of the hair which also becomes very fine and brittle. Similarly, graying of the hair, although associated with aging, has nothing to do with a deterioration of the body. Once again, it can occur from the twenties onward and should be dissociated from anything akin to a middle-age crisis.

Another physical change that depresses many middle-aged people is deterioration of their eyesight. Wearing glasses is still, to many, a signal that senility is just around the corner. In fact, the age at which you must wear glasses is a matter of luck, not aging. Probably the only thing that tends to age in the eye is the little internal lens—and this ages at a constant rate throughout the whole of life in all people. How is it, therefore,

that some people need glasses to read or see a number on a bus at 30 when others can do quite well without spectacles at 70? The answer is simple and has nothing to do with middle age: it simply depends on the size of eyeball you were born with.

Eyes, like feet, come in all sizes. The lens acts as a fine-adjustment device for focusing. If you have a medium-sized eyeball of ideal length, from the optical point of view, the lens has very little work to do. If, however, your eye is on the long or short side, an efficient lens is a must and, as it tires with use, glasses are needed to help focusing. Some people believe that if they do not wear glasses when they have focusing problems they will strain their eyes and damage them. In fact you can no more strain eyes than

you can ears, and whether or not you wear glasses in middle age depends on how clearly you want to see.

A worry of middle-aged men that has its roots more firmly set in folk-lore than fact concerns the penis. This is not remarkable, because the male reproductive organ has a fantastic mystery woven around it. The phallic symbol is much involved with primitive religion as well as early decorative art of mystical significance, and so it is of no small wonder that "penis fears" dominate many men's lives in middle age. Perhaps the most common dread is that the penis is shrinking or wasting away. It is a medical fact that, although there are tremendous variations in natural penis size (which bear little relation to body size, incidentally), there is no evidence that the penis shrinks in middle age, or is any less efficient as an organ.

Finally, alcohol can become an important factor in middle age, taking a severe toll on the physical frame and possibly destroying a man or a woman. It is important to realize that there is more to alcoholism than a hangover, and most people drink too much at some time during their lives. The majority of us, however, learn by our mistakes. Some do not, for a curious variety of reasons. Sometimes the constant availability of alcohol is too seductive to be resisted. Some people have to drink as part of their life-style, and giving up alcohol would mean a reorganization of the whole fabric of their lives. There are different patterns of drinking, and even the medical profession does not always agree on the definition of alcoholism. A good working definition is that if you have to take a drink to face up to a difficult situation in life then you are at risk.

Alcohol destroys life in the middle years in all sorts of ways. Most people believe that cirrhosis of the liver is the main danger. But although this disease does kill many alcoholics and heavy drinkers, other factors are probably more damaging to the human body. Death or severe incapacitating injury due to acute alcoholic intoxication, accidental death due to drug or drink situations, and depression leading to suicide are frequent complications of alcoholism, preventing people who could have had a productive, fulfilled middle age from ever surviving into old age.

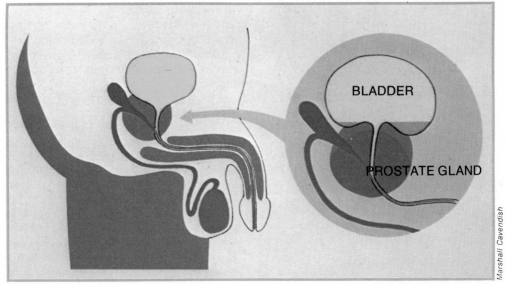

Marshall Cavendish

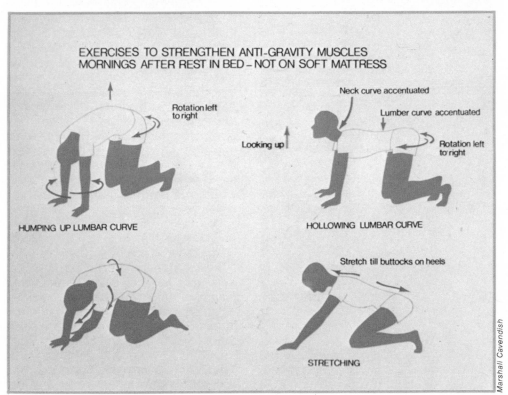

EXERCISES TO STRENGTHEN ANTI-GRAVITY MUSCLES
MORNINGS AFTER REST IN BED – NOT ON SOFT MATTRESS

Rotation left to right

HUMPING UP LUMBAR CURVE

Looking up

Neck curve accentuated

Lumber curve accentuated

Rotation left to right

HOLLOWING LUMBAR CURVE

Stretch till buttocks on heels

STRETCHING

Marshall Cavendish

Top left: Enlargement of the prostate —one of the male sex glands—can occur in late middle age. Left: Anti-gravity exercises help ward off a middle-age posture.

The seven year itch

Seven years on and what have you got? A mate, some kids and a dinner that's hot. But where's the excitement, the glamor galore? You call that a marriage—it's really a bore.

As a Roman Catholic priest recently observed, "more sins have been committed in the name of love than almost anything else." And his point is supported by the number of divorces and separations that occur each year. When a couple fall passionately in love and decide to marry they do so primarily because they are in love; and when they decide to part some years later, as often as not it is because they have fallen wildly in love with someone else.

But of course not all love affairs and marriages end in divorce or separation, though few fail to sustain some nasty shocks along the way. Marriage is, after all, something of a gamble. In what other circumstances would a person promise, witnessed by a state official, to remain in a binding situation for the duration of his life? Such irreversible deeds are reserved usually only for religious men taking final vows or people totally dedicated to a particular cause—and even in these circumstances the promises occasionally get broken.

Bursting Bubbles

The cynic would say that most marriages are motivated by other causes than love alone: social and parental constraints, money, security among others. They would also say that marriage is not finally a binding contract because in most countries it can be annulled or broken, officially. Nevertheless, couples continue to opt for marriage—the official contract—rather than the unofficial alliance made by living together. And most of these couples believe they are genuinely in love when they take the big step.

Two people who are completely in love with each other cannot countenance—even though reason warns them that it is a possibility—that one day in the future they will fall *out* of love with each other, however temporarily. Infatuation does not admit any alternative: bubbles *do* burst. But the fact remains that many marriages are rocked, sometimes irrevocably, when one partner is afflicted by "the seven year itch."

The reason the number seven was invoked as the crucial figure is not clear; seven is after all, mythologically, a lucky number, and the disruption of a marriage, however momentarily pleasant, could hardly be called a fortunate happening. One possible explanation may stem from the traditional seven stages of man (and

Kim Sayer/Bob Fowlke

Where is that beautiful dreamworld he promised me seven years ago?

2000

woman): infancy, childhood, adolescence, first maturity, middle age, old age and senility. It has been suggested that the seven year itch occurs at the end of one of these "stages"—usually as a man or woman enters middle age, but sometimes also at the transition from middle to old age. But these categories are quite arbitrary, for we all age differently and at varying rates. A second, more plausible explanation for the derivation of the seven year syndrome is that statistics have shown that at *about* this time in a marriage things do seem to become less stable for many reasons.

Outside Contact

While accepting that there is in reality no such thing as an "average" couple, in the same way that people do not have the average 2.2 children, figures show trends in people's behavior. It is "typical," for example, for two people to marry in their early twenties and have several children within the first three years.

Penny and Sam fit this pattern, and both have every reason to believe in the existence of the seven year itch, as Sam explains: "Penny was 22 and I was 23 when we married. We had been engaged for two years and had saved our money. We both wanted children—in fact Penny was just pregnant when we married, but I wouldn't call it a shotgun wedding because we had set the date months before. Our little girl was born eight months after we married and our son just two years later. For the first five years we were pretty happy. We worked hard to get a nice home together and felt we were making a proper family situation. But life was getting more expensive all the time, and by the time the children were three and five we could no longer afford even our weekly outing together. I found myself refusing even an occasional drink with my friends in the evening because I knew that even one round would affect the family budget. Until you are forced to spend all your time together you don't realize how important outside contact is.

"Looking back I can see that it was certainly worse for Penny; I at least got out of the house for a few hours every day. By the time both children were at school our finances were a bit healthier, and suddenly Penny had time on her hands during the day. But we had fallen into the habit of not going out together already. It was six months before I found out that Penny was having an affair, and I discovered it only because one of

her so-called 'friends' told me. The guy was a teacher at our son's nursery school and lived near us. I was dumbfounded—and furious—and especially so because I had been fighting the temptation to go to bed with one of the girls at the office who was after me, and free as a bird. I did in fact have a brief fling with her later, after Penny's affair had finished.

"Things really blew up almost exactly seven years after we married, but I believe it has nothing to do with a seven year period. It's just that we had lots of problems, mostly stemming from financial strain, which we did not work out together. We were fairly poor, bored, and had lost touch with each other. I hadn't realized either how worrying the age problem was to Penny. She felt that she was nearing 30 and all she stood for was a wife and mother with only the prospect of the children growing up and away, when she would be left with nothing. Luckily we managed to patch our marriage up—but it was touch and go. Now we always tell each other if something is eating us, and we go out together once a week—and each have a 'bachelor' night with friends. It means we have had to economize in other areas—we go on vacation to my parents' place in the country, for instance, rather than something expensive—but if we hadn't insisted on some kind of outside, independent life away from the children, the marriage would have collapsed."

Someone's Property

The identity crisis that many "captive" wives and mothers experience is often responsible for the seven year itch. One professional woman who resumed a career when her son was of school age six years after she had married said, "I fell for the man who made me feel that I was worth something as an individual, that I could work, and work well—in my case, writing. He could have had two heads and I would still have been attracted to him. For me, and I suspect for many women, love starts not in the pit of the stomach but in the head. A man who gives you enormous confidence again when you have been feeling that you are nothing but a washing and feeding machine stands in real danger of becoming your Svengali. So many husbands just do not realize how important it is to feel that you are something more than his, and your children's, property. I fell madly in love with the editor who did this for me. I did sleep with him once, and it was a disaster, but I'm eternally

grateful to him for turning me into a self-confident woman again."

It is not only women who are victims of identity crises. Men also feel trapped by the institution of marriage, even if they love their wives and offspring. They may feel that their only useful role is that of breadwinner, and watch dismayed as the pretty girls they married turn into busy mothers and tired wives. The husband may know that it is no one's fault that the family situation is largely a humdrum affair, and he may feel guilty, but this does not prevent him from looking wistfully at the beautiful, unburdened girls he meets outside his home. Because women have been reared on the notion that man is the strong partner, the supporter, they may miss completely the fact that he too needs reassurance and support, wants to feel that he is an attractive individual and not just a bank balance.

Suet Dumpling

"I had been looking at girls more and more lustfully for several years before I finally took the plunge and had an affair. It wasn't that I didn't love my wife, but she had changed a lot since we married. When I met her she was a beautiful, well-groomed publicity girl. After three children and seven years she was a terribly competent, unglamorous wife. Money was no problem: I earn a good salary as an accountant—always have—and she has never really had to want for anything important, including clothes for herself. But she was totally wrapped up in the children. She always looked clean and neat, but about as sexy as a suet dumpling. And it made me mad —she had help in the home, and money, but didn't seem to care to do anything to pretty herself up.

"It may sound awful, but I think it was her complacency that drove me away finally. She couldn't believe that I could possibly find another person —let alone woman—of any interest, even though her own conversation was limited exclusively to plans for the children. She wasn't at all interested in sex, but 'submitted' reluctantly on occasion, always giving the impression that it had to be done quickly, like a three-minute egg. What started as a guilty resentment grew to be an enormous irritation, and after seven years of it the itch was so virulent it had to be scratched. After the first affair, the rest were easy. I made the classic excuse of having a lot of work at the office, which she accepted without question. I think it was this apparent lack of any need of me as a person that finally drove me away from her completely.

"When I told her I wanted out she was surprised and tried to dissuade me as though I were a small boy asking for sticky candy. In the end she had to accept the situation because I just upped and left. I support her and the children—and see them every Sunday—but apart from that have no contact with her as a wife at all. We haven't divorced because there seems no point. I am certainly not anxious to marry again, and I imagine the chances of her doing so are remote.

"I have heard a number of my friends bemoan the fact that their wives have changed a lot over the years—and it isn't, in spite of what women think, the physical changes of age that really count. The biggest single complaint is that they seem to take everything for granted and never want to alter the status quo. I wish they would understand that a man wants a companion, a partner, and not just a housekeeper; if they did I think there would be far fewer separations and divorces."

This man's experience might not be typical, but his comments are disturbing nonetheless, for they indicate what some married couples know for certain, and many suspect: that it is routine, acceptance and boredom that threaten many a relationship. Women have long been exhorted through the media to "keep young and beautiful" if they really want to be loved. But perhaps the advice should include an exhortation to keep lively, whatever the cost. Yet this is easier said than done, especially if through circumstances, or even choice, they do not have outlets for expressing their personalities outside the home. As one young mother said, "It is hard to fascinate your husband when he comes home after a hard day at the office if your day has been one long round of cooking, cleaning, and talking to children." And it is a fact that boredom breeds boredom; that once on the familiar treadmill of everyday routine, however pleasant, it is hard to get off; and the more one feels resentful, or is resented, the more difficult it becomes to break the pattern.

Root Causes

There is another aspect of the seven year itch, however, that cannot be explained as the result of a boring or bad relationship. The marriage which is basically a stable, happy one can also be the breeding ground for the "itch," just because it *is* secure. If a man is certain of his wife's love, sure that whatever happens his relationship with her will withstand it, then he may well feel free to dally a little—to chase butterflies, catch them even; the secure wife may feel the same.

One very beautiful French woman in her late fifties who is still eminently desirable and adored by her husband believes that the art of keeping a mate interested relies on two special aptitudes. "First, a woman must let a man know that she finds him good—fascinating, sexy, whatever—and when I talk about a woman I believe that the same rules apply to a man. She must make him feel needed,

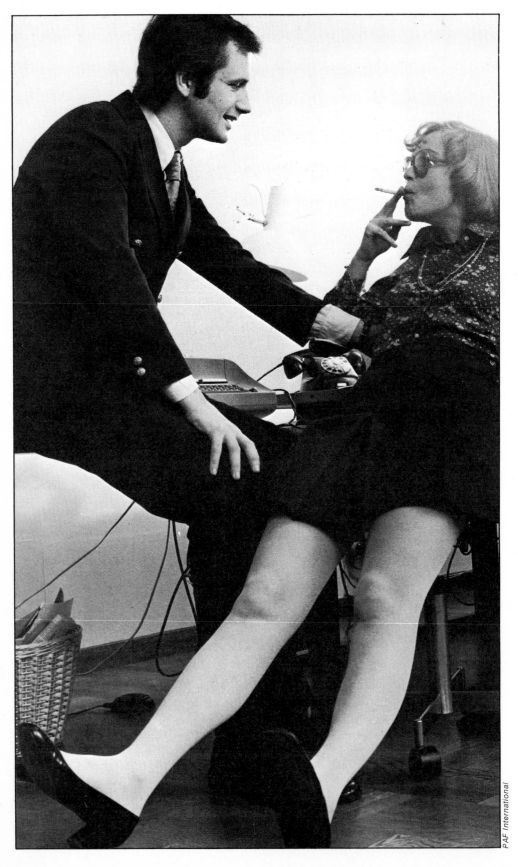

There's nearly always someone at the office ready to help a married man scratch his itchy feet.

wanted, desired (with the proviso that she does love him, of course), and in this way she will never be alone. The old French maxim about being chef in the kitchen, lady in the drawing room, and whore in bed is one of the best pieces of advice ever given. And, secondly, she—or he— must accept that predictability, routine, and jealousy are the archenemies of a good relationship.

"If my husband looks covetously at a young, pretty girl, my reaction might be to create a scene, or to sulk. That is stupid. Why shouldn't he enjoy looking at—and even desiring—something beautiful? I have no copyright on his eyesight or his inmost feelings. But on the other hand I am a woman and I love him. I do not want him to prefer her finally to me. If I am very strong, very noble, I might turn a blind eye and let him indulge his fancy —I have done this on several occasions—but I think it far better on the whole to show him how good I am,

to tell him I love him, prove I want him, to please him. And then if I can show him by a little carefully timed flirtation that I too am desired by other men, I stand a good chance of winning!''

As a Frenchwoman with an indubitable track record, her advice has to be listened to, even if some might accuse her of pandering to the unfair advantage that men have always had over women. They may not agree with her beliefs, but in one respect at least her theories are relevant to the problem of the seven year itch. She has recognized what many people—both women and men—refuse to admit: that just because you have made a unique contract with one person, you have no right to expect that the contractual duties extend into a person's mind. At a more obvious level, if *you* were physically attracted to your husband, you are unreasonable in expecting that no one else will be. You have a right to expect that he will not carry

She doesn't need to read between the lines to know he finds the newspaper more stimulating than her.

through from thought to deed, but if he does it will question the fundamental strength of your relationship.

Where one woman—or man—could accept that the seven year itch is what it appears to be, a tickling sensation that needs to be relieved, another might be broken by the discovery of infidelity. There are many things that the sensitive man or woman can do to prevent a partner from straying, and they all center on caring for your spouse and also making the most of your own assets— looks, personality, self-esteem.

There has never been a good marriage that has not undergone trials of some kind, including often the desire on one or both sides to seek new sexual pleasures, but the marriage will disintegrate only if the itch is a symptom of a worse disease.

ENCYCLOPEDIA OF HUMAN BEHAVIOR

HELIOTROPISM
An automatic tendency on the part of some organisms to turn themselves towards a light source.

HELMHOLTZ, HERMANN VON (1821-1894)
A German physicist who was deeply interested in psychology and made some remarkable contributions to our understanding of the mechanisms of sight and hearing.

HEMIANESTHESIA
Loss of sensation in one half of the body.

HEMIANOPIA
Loss of vision in one half of the visual field. It is most commonly due to brain damage of some kind.

HEMIOPHOBIA
An abnormal fear of blood.

HEMIPLEGIA
Paralysis of one half of the body.

HEMISPHERE
One of the two halves of the brain which are joined deep inside the skull by the bundle of nerve cells known as the *corpus callosum.*

HEMISPHERICAL DOMINANCE
The tendency for one side of the brain to control body movements and hence produce right- or left-handedness.

HEPATIC
Relating to the liver.

HEREDITY
The collection of characteristics which are transmitted from parent to child through the reproductive mechanism. The important information is carried in tiny structures, within all living cells, known as the *genes* and *chromosomes.* All living cells, with the exception of the sperm and ovum, contain complete sets of chromosomes, and these minute structures are used as reliable copying devices by the cells to build and repair body tissue. As sperm and ovum cells contain only half the normal complement of chromosome material, when conception takes place the fertilized cell consists precisely of 50 percent of the hereditary material from the father and 50 percent from the mother. The exact process by which the copying of the hereditary material takes place is still unknown, but it is believed that molecules of the substance known as deoxyribonucleic acid (DNA) are somehow involved.

HEREDITY-ENVIRONMENT CONTROVERSY
The question of how much of an individual's personality and even social behavior is determined by what he has inherited from his parents and how much depends upon his life experiences. The argument involves such questions as whether a disposition towards alcoholism, cancer, or criminality can be inherited.

HERMAPHRODITE
Someone who is both male and female; in physiological terms someone with male and female sex organs more or less equally developed. This term is occasionally used in psychology to refer to a person with bisexual tendencies.

HEROIN
A drug derived from the narcotic morphine, and even more highly addictive.

HERPES ZOSTER
A virus disease sometimes known as *shingles* involving a skin eruption caused by the inflammation of sensory nerves. It is often precipitated by psychological stress.

HERTZ
A term recently introduced by international agreement to refer to a frequency of one cycle per second.

HETERODOX
Beliefs which differ from or are opposite to those normally accepted *(orthodox).*

HETEROGENEOUS
Mixed; showing many different characteristics.

HETEROSEXUALITY
Attraction to members of the opposite sex.

HETEROTROPIA
Medical term for *strabismus*, or being cross-eyed.

HEURISTIC THOUGHT
Thinking which is devoted to original approaches towards problem solving; creative thinking.

HIBERNATION
A prolonged sleeplike state which certain animals adopt during the winter period. Body temperature falls and the heart rate is reduced to the barest minimum for survival. This state has little in common with sleep however, and its function is to preserve an animal's energy during a period when food supply is short or nonexistent.

HIGHER BRAIN CENTERS
Those parts of the cerebral cortex which handle imagination, thinking, memory and other thought processes.

HIGH-GRADE DEFECTIVE
Someone with an IQ considerably lower than the average—say between 60 and 70—who is nonetheless capable of doing useful, if routine, work, provided that he has a certain amount of supervision.

HINDBRAIN
The back part of the brain which contains the structures known as the *cerebellum,* the *pons,* and the *medulla.*

HIPPOANTHROPY
The belief that one is a horse or could change into a horse at will.

HIPPOCAMPUS
A tiny structure in the brain which looks rather like a seahorse and from which its name is derived. It is believed to have some function connected with memory.

HISTOGRAM
A plot of scores or values on a graph, more commonly known as a *bar chart*.

HISTOLOGY
The study of the structure of body tissue.

HODOPHOBIA
An abnormal fear of traveling.

HOLERGASIA
A very severe form of psychosis in which there is a totally and generally irreversible breakdown in personality.

HOLISM
The approach to psychology or biology which states that it is impossible to get a true understanding of animal behavior without looking at the creature as a whole. No matter how precisely a creature can be described in terms of the activity and function of different nerve cells, hormones or biochemical actions, this will never give the complete picture. The whole is more than the sum of its parts.

HOMEOPATHY
Once fashionable—but now somewhat discredited—approach to medicine in which it was believed that illnesses could be cured with minute doses of substances which produced symptoms similar to the disease itself.

HOMEOSTASIS
The principle by which an organism maintains itself in a stable, balanced, physical condition. This is achieved by a complex series of what are known as *feedback mechanisms*. To give the simplest example, when the blood sugar level becomes low—due to a deficiency in nutrients—messages are sent to a particular part of the brain which in turn causes stomach contractions. These are accompanied by a feeling of hunger, and a search for food automatically begins. When enough food has been eaten, stomach contractions cease, a switch is thrown in the appropriate center of the brain, and hunger stops. Throughout the course of life, organisms strive to achieve balanced states of this kind. The science of developing machines built on homeostatic principles is known as *cybernetics*.

HOMING
The desire and the capacity of an animal to return to its home when removed from it for one reason or another. The desire is not difficult to understand, but the ability that some animals have to "home" (when they have been removed experimentally to great distances and over territory which they have had no opportunity to explore before) is quite remarkable. Pigeons have been known to home successfully over hundreds of miles, even after they have been carried in a sealed box from their home to the point of release. Dogs and cats also show some evidence of this ability, though perhaps on a lesser scale. Homing powers were once thought to be related to extrasensory perception, but this explanation has now been modified in favor of the suggestion that some of these animals may have in their brains an "absolute directional sense," a kind of internal compass. It is also known that many birds navigate by using the stars and the sun, and it is certainly true that pigeons become disoriented when released in a fog or under very cloudy skies.

HOMOGENEOUS
The same; showing generally similar characteristics.

HOMOSEXUALITY
Sexual intercourse with (or sexual feelings for) someone of the same sex. There is both male and female homosexuality.

HORIZONTAL-VERTICAL ILLUSION
A striking illusion in which a vertical line bisecting a horizontal line of equivalent length, appears to be significantly longer.

HORMIC PSYCHOLOGY
An early psychological theory put forward by William McDougall, based on the belief that every organism has an essential "will to live."

HORMONE
A chemical substance produced by an organ in the body. Its function is to send a message to another part of the body and set in motion (or switch off) a particular sequence of behavior. The hormones are literally chemical messengers carried around in the bloodstream, and they serve as a backup function to the messages sent through the nervous system.

HOROSCOPE
A chart which gives the relative positions of planets and stars at particular times and dates and which is used to predict future events. It forms an important part of the pseudoscience of *astrology*.

HUE
Color as it is perceived. Technically, *colored* light means light of a particular wavelength; after the brain has perceived it as being, say, red it is then *hue*.

HULL, CLARK (1884-1952)
The American psychologist who attempted to develop a mathematical theory for animal behavior. He was immensely influential for a period until it was realized that his equations were far too simple to describe the complexities of the brain and behavior.

HUMANISTIC PSYCHOLOGY
A recent movement within psychology which aims to make the science less concerned with the academic study of behavior for its own sake, and concentrates more on its application to human, social, and world problems.

HUMOR
Originally a liquid or fluid of some kind, but has now come to mean a pleasant emotional state. The emotions were related to the so-called elements—earth, fire, air and water—and were supposed to have equivalent characteristics.

HUNGER
A desire for food, induced by contractions of the empty stomach.

HYBRID
The offspring of parents who come from different species of animals. Since there is only one human species, there are technically no human hybrids. Lion-tiger crossings (sometimes known as tigons) are hybrids, as are mules (horse-donkey crossings). Most hybrids are sterile.

HYDROCEPHALOUS
Disorder in which cerebrospinal fluid is produced in excessive quantities causing enlargement of the skull. This occurs in infants and results in severe mental retardation.

HYDROPHOBIA
Technically, an abnormal fear of water; but the word also now refers to the condition known as *rabies*.

HYDROTHERAPY
Treatment of physical or mental illnesses by water. In psychology it tends to refer to the practice of giving agitated or depressed patients prolonged hot baths.

HYPERACTIVE
Excessively active or overactive.

HYPERACUSIA
Unusual sensitivity of hearing, developed by many blind people as partial compensation for their loss of vision.

HYPERALGESIA
Extreme sensitivity to pain.

HYPERESTHESIA
Extreme heightening of all the senses.

HYPERGENITALISM
Abnormal development of the genital organs.

HYPERGLYCEMIA
Excessive sugar in the blood, generally caused by *diabetes*.

HYPERKINESIS
A tendency to move around in an excited and agitated way. This is a relatively common condition in childhood when the hyperkinetic child may have sleep problems or disciplinary trouble at school.

HYPERTHYROIDISM
Excessive activity of the thyroid gland which causes extreme restlessness and excitability.

HYPNAGOGIC IMAGE
Vivid, seemingly real experience of a hallucinatory kind which sometimes occurs in the transitional state between sleeping and waking. This is probably due to the fact that one part of the brain is still asleep and dreaming while consciousness has been aroused and is able to inspect the dream as though it were a real event in the outside world. These images are often accompanied by a temporary paralysis and may be very frightening, especially to children.

HYPNOANALYSIS
An approach to psychotherapy or psychoanalysis in which the patient is first hypnotized and then questioned in an attempt to track down the source of his unconscious conflicts or anxieties.

HYPNOBAT
Someone who walks in his sleep.

HYPNOGENIC
Producing sleep or hypnosis.

HYPNOID
Similar to sleep or the hypnotic state.

HYPNOPEDIA
A technical term for teaching or learning during sleep. The evidence that the brain can store information during sleep is not good, but some psychologists believe that they have demonstrated that in certain semiconscious states on the borderline between waking and sleeping some learning can take place.

HYPNOPHOBIA
An abnormal fear of falling asleep.

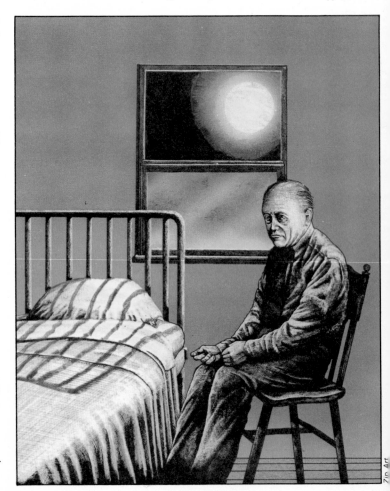

HYPNOSIS

A strange trancelike state in which the subject appears to be detached from the surrounding world and capable of attending and responding to the presence and commands of only one individual—the hypnotist. The curious phenomena associated with hypnotism were first studied systematically in Paris in the late nineteenth century by the Austrian doctor Franz Mesmer. Mesmer at first believed that the trancelike states were brought about by some natural invisible force in human beings which he called *animal magnetism*, but the phenomena soon became named after him, as *mesmerism*. Many years later the name was changed to hypnosis because of the sleeplike characteristics of the hypnotized subject. When it was found that hypnotized patients were apparently resistant to pain, the technique was used as an aid to surgery, though the arrival of general anesthetics in the middle of the nineteenth century replaced it. At one time, hypnosis was considered to induce certain changes in the human brain, but recent experiments suggest that it is a less dramatic and less useful phenomenon than was once believed. The electrical activity of the brain of a person in "hypnotic sleep," for example, bears no relationship to that of normal sleep and is apparently in no way different from the signals emitted from the waking brain.

HYPNOTHERAPY

Psychotherapy using hypnosis to overcome the patient's resistance to unconscious thoughts.

HYPNOTIC

Something, usually a drug, which induces sleep.

HYPO-

The opposite of *hyper-*. This prefix means "greatly reduced or less than"; for example, *hypo*somnia means a *decreased* need for sleep.

HYPOCHONDRIA

A neurotic condition in which the individual is unusually concerned with his health and may be convinced that he is suffering from a severe illness when he is, in fact, not physically ill at all.

HYPOTHALAMUS

A relatively small but very important part of the brain, believed to play an important role in emotional and motivational states.

HYPOXIA

A severe deficiency of oxygen.

HYSTERIA

The ancient name for a neurotic condition characterized by a great variety of symptoms which may vary from persistent aches and pains, which have no obvious organic cause, to paralysis of large parts of the body. The word was coined by the Greek physician Hippocrates, from the word *hysteron*, which means "uterus." It was once assumed that all hysterical conditions were due to disorders of the uterus.

ICHTHYOPHOBIA

An abnormal fear of fish.

ICTUS

A stroke or epileptic fit.

ID

A term coined by Freud to denote one of the three major divisions of human personality according to his theory. The mind as a whole is composed of three, slightly separate, entities—the *ego* (the conscious self), the *superego* (broadly speaking the "conscience") and the *id*, which is the sum total of instinctive, unconscious drives and wishes which we inherit and which form part of our basically animal nature. According to Freud, the id is the dominant force in early life, so that babies and young children are almost totally devoted to satisfying the basic instinctive needs. Gradually the world and other people begin to modify the personality, and the ego and superego take shape. Id forces remain strong throughout life, however, and many neuroses are due to unconscious conflicts between the id and the superego.

IDEA

A mental concept not specifically concerned with any recent experience of the senses.

IDEATION

The formation of ideas.

IDEATIONAL LEARNING

A term used to refer to learning in which there is the maximum use of constructive thought and a conscious grasp of the nature of the problem. It contrasts with *rote learning*, which is the more or less meaningless repetition of words or phrases.

IDÉE FIXE

A rigid point of view or obsessive idea.

IDENTICAL TWINS

Twin babies whose genetic or inherited constitutions are identical. They are caused when the fertilized ovum for some reason splits and forms two precisely similar eggs. Identical twins are always of the same sex, and any differences in personality that occur in them arise only as the result of their experiences in the outside world. They are also known as *monozygotic twins*.

IDENTIFICATION

The process of allying oneself in an intellectual, idealistic or emotional way with some other person or cause. This is a natural and healthy response in the normal individual. Identification is also important in the enjoyment of any work of fiction, from a novel to a movie plot, because it allows the observer to feel engrossed and absorbed in an otherwise unreal world by immersing himself in the personality of one or more of the characters.

IDEOGRAM

A symbol which allows a complicated idea to be expressed in an exceedingly simple form. For example, a skull and crossbones could be used to denote all kinds of danger from poison to armed banditry.

IDEOLOGY

An integrated system of beliefs, such as republicanism, communism, or catholicism.

IDEOMOTOR RESPONSE

A purposeful action—that is, a physical movement set in motion by an idea.

IDIOLALIA

Extremely slow or meaningless speech associated with low intelligence.

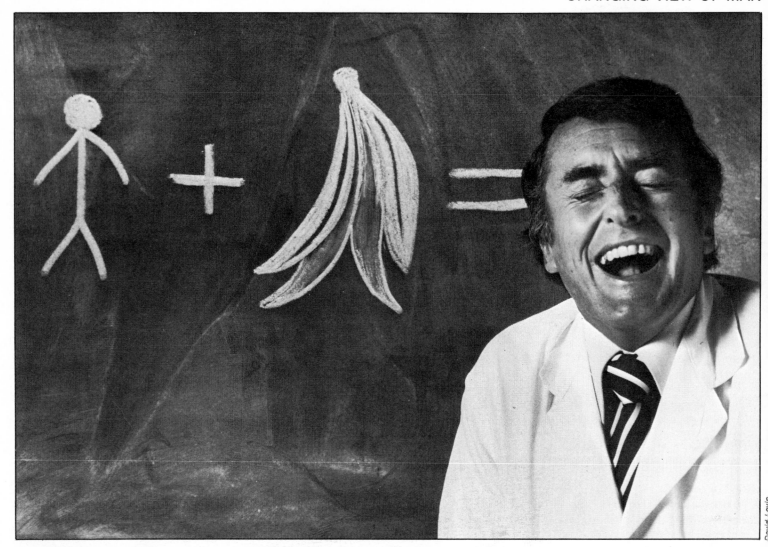

Only when I laugh

Even when life is no joke, a touch of humor can work wonders in dispelling the gloom. The ability to say the wrong thing at the right time is surely a gift from the great joker in the sky.

Humor is an ingredient of life which has no place or value except as part of the total recipe; it is capable of enriching the mixture, but equally of souring the whole concoction.

Most jokes, or the retelling of a comic situation, involve an attempt to revive and draw us into a set of circumstances without which the humor introduced by the "punchline" or "payoff" would not be recognized as funny. If it is not reconstructed it is because it does not need to be, either because we are already part of the situation, or because the "setup" is already understood.

Here is one of the shortest jokes on record: The *Titanic* is unsinkagurgle. This is probably the least funny rendering this joke will ever have. Its purpose here, though, is to make an

academic point—*not* to make someone laugh. In the first place, it is a gag which should be listened to, not read. In the second place, it is out of context, and notable more for what it leaves out than for what it states.

Ho! Ho! Ho!

Even in its correct context, the humorous impact depends on the listener having that assumed knowledge and filling in the missing facts for himself. They are that 1) the *Titanic* was a liner which was said to be unsinkable; 2) it sank on its maiden voyage; 3) the words are uttered by somebody with an unshakable faith in the liner's invincibility; 4) he is on it; 5) the liner is sinking; 6) they are his last words which prove to be inaccurate until the last two sylla-

bles when . . . 7) he drowns. If the listener can instantly connect all this with the words he has heard, he will laugh. Next time he hears them he will not, because the "gurgle" will not come as a surprise. And there will be people who will not laugh. After all, the *Titanic* disaster really happened.

This touches on the other serious side of humor and laughter which is far more sinister and all-pervasive than you might expect. It can be derisory, vicious, and cruel. To tell the *Titanic* joke to the widow of a man drowned in the disaster has the opposite effect to the one intended (unless you wanted to upset her), even though the joke remains the same.

Any comedian or humorist will tell you that making people laugh is a serious, heartrending, sometimes soul-destroying business. And psychologists who have tried to discover the secret of laughter have found the task both tormenting and perplexing. Philosophers since Aristotle and Plato have tended to focus their attention on laughter's most depressing aspects. Poets, authors, scriptwriters, and other practitioners of humor have shied away from investigating the phenomenon too deeply, for fear that it might stem the free flow of funny ideas, like the centipede which, after being asked in what order it moved its legs, was never able to walk again. For these people, laughter has become divorced from the pleasure and enjoyment which, in the experience of the rest of us, appear to give rise to it.

Harsh Reality

In a drab and wretched world we regard laughter as an indication that in spite of adversity there remains something inherently good, joyful, and indomitable about the human spirit. It seems to be the manifestation of all that is good in us. This is far from the truth. In fact, it is more often than not the exhibition of the very worst in us—the expression of the most cruel, malicious, and malevolent instincts of which human nature is capable, a reflection of the general human predicament.

We live in a humorless world. It is ruthlessly competitive and harsh. Our behavior is tempered and ordered by rules of etiquette and by social custom, even our freest everyday speech is subject to rules of syntax and grammar. Underlying all human life are natural or self-imposed regulations springing from the biological urge and the social necessity of creating order out of chaos. We are creatures of habit, and so natural does it seem to conduct our lives within a well-structured framework that we are scarcely aware of it. What we are aware of, however, is any deviation from the normal pattern of life. Such departures are the basis of all humor, comedy, and wit—anything which makes us laugh.

A list of the things we laugh at illustrates this point—oddity, novelty, deformity, small misfortunes, indecency, out-of-placeness, affectation, pretense, ignorance, awkwardness, ineptitude, absurdity. Many writers have produced more detailed lists of objects of laughter which fit into those categories. Max Beerbohm's is as good as any: "Mothers-in-law, henpecked husbands, twins, old maids, certain other races, fatness, thinness,

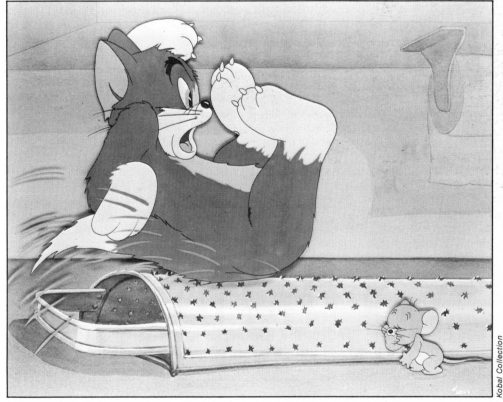

long hair worn by men, baldness, seasickness, stuttering, bad cheese, shooting the moon (which means leaving a hotel without paying the bill)!" It is a curious list to which we can add from our own experience —the sucker, the miser, the cuckold, and any other of the countless joke subjects which are the foodstuffs of humor. Each involves a departure from the norm and each deviation has

Top: One of the all-time great comedians, Charlie Chaplin. Above: The painful humor of the cartoon.

its own characteristics. In word play, puns, malapropisms ("I have difficulty in *reprehending* the meanings of words"), or spoonerisms ("Let us drink to the queer old dean"), the departure is from the norms of spelling, pronunciation, syntax, or grammar.

Kobal Collection

These are all the clichés of humor and comedy. There are also a number of stock situations which can usually be relied upon to get a laugh: the absentminded professor putting his watch in the saucepan and timing its boiling with his egg; the schoolmaster entering the classroom with the bucket of water balanced above the slightly opened door; the man slipping on the banana skin. These situations are all diversions from the norm.

But to recognize that our sense of humor is tickled when life makes off along bizarre tributaries does not explain why such deviations make us laugh. Laughter is not the expression of any inner satisfaction they give us. It is interesting to note that the activities which give us the deepest contentment—eating, sex, religious meditation—are not accompanied by laughter. Nor is a display of brilliant wit or repartee, which we know is funny and find intensely satisfying, but which elicits at the most a faint smile of appreciation.

Think of all the occasions when we laugh: when we are tickled; when we are embarrassed; when we are stuck for conversation; when we need to recover from a faux pas. We laugh in disbelief, or as a gesture of defiance in the face of danger and extreme adversity, and then again when they have passed. The nervous giggle is an expression of insecurity; the polite chuckle can escalate into uncontrollable convulsions once we have caught the laughter infection from other people. And then again, we sometimes laugh for no apparent reason whatsoever.

Reflex Action

Laughter is a unique reflex action. Unlike other reflexes, such as withdrawing the hand from a scorching fire or sneezing, it does not appear to have a purpose related to the stimulus which prompted it. Why should these extraordinary contortions of the face and body be sparked off by something we hear, see, or read.

The author Arthur Koestler provides an explanation: we laugh to discharge surplus emotional energy. The narrative of a joke or the reconstruction of a situation builds up an emotional charge inside us. Its momentum is increased as we assimilate the account by thought. What happens when the punchline comes is that our thoughts suddenly switch to a new plane of ideas, when we are suddenly made aware of a contrast, a deviation, a twist of logic, or an association of ideas which before seemed unconnected.

Thought is very agile. One can transfer thoughts from one idea to another very quickly. But emotions are not so nimble. They tend to persist along a single plane and change more gradually. When the thought latches on to the new idea, it detaches itself from the emotions, which are too sluggish to go with it. They are left high and dry, but are carried forward by the momentum which has been building up. Deserted by the thought, the emotional charge cannot be sustained and must then be released. Laughter is the discharge of the emotional content of the story or situation which becomes suddenly superfluous and redundant. It is rather like an emergency stop in a car—the brake is applied, but the car continues to move forward.

Emotional Explosion

We can apply this idea to the "banana skin" situation. Just like a narrative, normal life carries an emotional charge; the mind suddenly perceives a man slipping on a banana skin, but the emotions are not ready for it since they are primed for normal activity. This emotional charge has to be detonated before they can adapt to the new situation. Laughter is that necessary explosion.

It is impossible to avoid mentioning the impact of the banana skin again, even though time has worn it thin. It illustrates more than any other situation the two-sided character of humor and laughter, although a closer examination of our list of funny subjects will prove the same point. The sight of the fat man flat on his back on the pavement with his legs in the air may be funny, but it is also pathetic. The man who fell is certainly not amused. But, to the passing schoolboy, who likes to see pomposity punctured, the spectacle is hysterical. His laughter is derisory, unsympathetic, and heartless.

From the "sublime" of the ordinary course of life we have come to the ridiculous. From there, it is but a short step to the tragic. If laughter is thought to be born of a joyful heart it may be as well to consider what makes it so. Is it a feeling of superiority, of delight in another person's humiliation or suffering, or of triumph in finding an outlet for tensions, pent-up aggression, or latent sadism or sexuality, which society decrees we should keep in check? Another look at our list of humorous "targets" will confirm that most humor is usually at the expense of someone else.

While we can laugh *with* someone, we can also laugh *at* him, thereby hurting his pride, injuring his feelings,

and reducing him to absurd and humiliating proportions. In Hogarth's time, it was fashionable to visit lunatic asylums and laugh at the inmates. It is probably no coincidence that the physical manifestations of amusement—the contorted face, the reddening cheeks, the tears in the eyes, the muscular tension, the staccato breathing—bear a striking resemblance to the expression of pain and suffering—sobbing, or hysterical screaming.

Only up to a point can laughter be good-humored and pleasurable, unsullied by more sinister feelings. There comes a time when deviations from the norm go beyond the pale of mild eccentricity, where peculiarity, nonconformity, or deformity become too severe to be laughable. If the laughter continues it is aggressive, mocking, and malicious. The blind man walking into a lamp post is no joke. The practical joke that gets out of hand and begins to cause unreasonable agony to its victim suddenly turns nasty, and the laughter dies as the emotions which originally produced it are abruptly checked by other sensations—fear, sympathy, pity, or disgust.

Writers on humor from Aristotle to Freud are agreed that it contains a predominant strain of aggression. It is a weapon which can be effectively used to humiliate and repel, to cut people down to size, to topple governments, to cause great suffering, and at the same time to strengthen our own position. We all have aggression in us and harbor malevolent thoughts. And we would all agree that people are imperfect and that the world is not a very funny place. But the existence of laughter and humor indicates that we have accepted life for what it is.

Verbal Sparring

One of the best things about laughter is that it provides a safety valve for the outlet of aggressive feelings. It is better to laugh at someone than hit him, which is what our emotions would ultimately force us to do if they had not already been sublimated in laughter. It is a socially acceptable means of releasing tensions, airing inhibitions and anxieties, and gratifying hidden wishes in a harmless way. Moreover, by wrapping up "attack" in a humorous form, we do not run the risk of physical repercussions, except from somebody without the wit to retaliate in a similar vein. There is more violence in "verbal sparring" than meets the eye.

There is a story of a confrontation between Lord Queensberry and Oscar

Wilde which illustrates the power of laughter. According to the film of Wilde's life, Queensberry had dreamed up a novel way of expressing his contempt for Wilde's relationship with Lord Alfred Douglas (Queensberry's son). As the playwright left the theater and was receiving bouquets of flowers from his adoring public, Queensberry stepped out of the crowd and presented him with a "spray" of rotten cabbages. The unruffled Wilde accepted it with the same good grace as he had received the others, adding, ". . . And every time I smell them, I shall think of you." Queensberry's gesture had backfired, and the ensuing laughter proclaimed a win on points for Wilde and a resounding defeat for Queensberry, who scurried away in utter misery. Wit and cruelty went hand in hand.

Under Attack

But what was the laughter all about? Was it an expression of scorn and derision for Queensberry, or of admiration for Wilde, or of enjoyment of the joke, or just relief that what might have been an uglier scene was nobly concluded. One thing is certain; it was not the laughter of pure joy or happiness. The situation's appeal to Wilde himself was not to his sense of humor, but to his aggression, arrogance, and sense of superiority.

This incident will also shed light on one of the most asked questions about humor: Why is it that one person finds something funny and another person does not? It is obvious why Queensberry was not amused. In other circumstances the remark might have amused him well enough. But thinking of all humor in terms of an attack, it is evident that our ability to laugh depends very much on which side of the assault we are on—whether we are the assailant or the butt. If, as it appears, all jokes have a cutting edge, should we find ourselves on the receiving end, we would rise to our own defense. This involves summoning up protective emotions which override those which might have produced laughter.

The target of a joke is not always so clear as it is in, say, racial stories or yarns about baldness or obesity. In some cases we may not realize that it is *us* that the story is getting at. Remembering that laughter is the product of an emotional charge, it is possible that a narrative can unhinge an impulse which is deep-seated in our psyche, enough for us to respond jocularly but without recognizing that it is just this element of our personality which is under attack. Perhaps it is the tendency to bury their emotions and not allow them to be touched which is behind the renowned capacity of the British to "laugh at themselves."

Different senses of humor are judged on a person's ability to laugh and to say or do funny things. The first depends on the nature of the emotional charge and the extent to which it is suppressed or liberated by other feelings, which explains why even the most humorous person is sometimes "Not in the mood for jokes." The second comes from having a particularly distorted view of the world and having the intellectual or physical technique of expressing it.

What a person considers funny is also determined by their framework or "terms of reference." Many British television viewers will probably remember Bob Hope's goof at a Royal Command Performance some years ago, when he told of a conversation he once had with a grasshopper.

Hope: We've got a drink named after you.

Grasshopper: Really? A drink called Irving?

The joke was lost on British audiences, because few people were familiar with a drink called Grasshopper. Although most people could work out the association on which the joke was based fairly quickly, it did not get the instant recognition and instinctive identification which are essential to spontaneous laughter.

A scientist can regale other scientists with splendid witticisms about chemical formulae, but they would fall flat before an audience of laymen. The humor was there, but it was not recognizable. The point is that different people have different areas of knowledge and a variety of life-styles and interests, which they pursue to the exclusion of others. In order to be able to identify with a joke or a reconstruction of a comic event, its subject matter has to be within our own experience or knowledge.

Slapstick Comedy

There is, however, a body of experience which is common to us all, but even within its range senses of humor are not uniform. We are all familiar with mothers-in-law and traveling salesmen, which is why jokes based on them have the best circulation.

By this token, visual humor should be universally acceptable. Yet slapstick is perhaps the form of comedy on which opinions are most divided. Ask the people who hate it why they do, and they will probably say that it is not credible. Implied in this answer is that what they really want to see are actors with *real* daggers stuck through them and actually hurting themselves falling off ladders into buckets. In view of what we know about aggression and humor, there may be some truth in this. But the reality they are looking for is missing because slapstick is not a mirror to their own lives. Slapstick is an attempt to abstract humor from its real-life setting.

Hidden Aggression

Alternatively, the will to laugh is stifled by other emotions. The archetypal man who slipped on the banana-skin had the schoolboy laughing, but he also may have had an old lady running to his assistance. She is sympathetic because she knows how he feels. She has lived long enough to have come adrift on a few banana-skins herself, or had some similar falls from grace. It is not the man who has suffered, it is she, herself. When the television announcer says, "And now, comedy—sit back and watch . . ." he means precisely the opposite: he wants you to "be drawn in and share . . ." Only when the show has elicited a sense of identification from us are we prepared to laugh.

It is a curious thing, and a constant headache to many comedians, that if their performances fail to amuse, their audiences are not prepared to remain neutral. They are positively outraged. The reminiscences of most comics include stories of early disasters, when they were booed or driven off the stage in a hail of missiles.

Those whose careers take them to the top may find they have the opposite experience. Gone are the days when they had to "fight" for a laugh (and, incidentally, show-business terms are riddled with aggression: "punchline," "knock-out," "go out there and slay 'em," "brought the house down"). Now they do nothing at all and people all around them are at once helpless with laughter. A TV star's reputation goes before him, and familiarity with it makes people laugh because they somehow expect to. It shows how much of humor is in the mind of the beholder, and how little need be contributed by a recognizable source. In his book *The Anatomy of Laughter*, Richard Boston devotes several pages to a character called Sydney Smith, a parson with a wide reputation for sharp wit and persistent good humor. On one occasion he had a gathering of dinner guests in hysterics simply by saying grace, which

Camera Press

parate elements of thought which are unexpectedly brought together and explode into a third which is greater than the sum of its parts. Much the same is the notion that humor and wit arise when two incompatible ideas are suddenly brought together and seen to have a hitherto unobserved connection. Their collision, according to Koestler, gives us fresh insight into the nature and order of things which we take for granted. It offers us a momentary escape from the one-dimensional plane on which we habitually think.

Old Chestnuts

The examples these two writers use to illustrate their ideas are not among the funniest jokes, but their theories can be applied to almost any joke in current circulation. Among them might be this banality:

Q: What did the bra say to the hat?
A: You go on ahead, and I'll give these two a lift.

The first line introduces two subjects which are unconnected. The second brings them together unexpectedly, and their alliance explodes into the third idea, which relates to a car journey. Here is another example:

When God said, "The Earth must be flooded,"
The Sun looked down from the sky
And said to the Sea,
"Well, there's just you and me—
Tell you what—*you* wash, and I'll dry!"

The formula is the same. The verse is about the Great Flood until the last line. Suddenly our thoughts switch to doing the dishes, which has no connection until we see that "washing" and "drying" are the legitimate functions of sea and sun. Added to that we instantly recognize the common colloquialism which occurs in the last line. If we do not associate the last line with washing dishes and our thoughts remain on the one plane, the verse still makes sense, but is without humor.

A last example is an old chestnut, which we shall spare dissection, except to say that it contains in it all the elements of humor, both pleasurable and sinister. "Two explorers are hacking their way through the jungle when they are ambushed by natives. One of them makes towards the attackers and is immediately impaled by numerous spears and arrows, until he begins to look like a pin cushion. His companion rushes to his aid and is surprised to find his friend shows no signs of being in pain. 'But doesn't it hurt?' he asks. 'Oh, no,' says the dying man. 'Only when I laugh!'"

he did with no less than appropriate piety. Most of us know someone like him, and our expectation that he will be funny helps to make him so.

Yet equally true is that if a person with a reputation for dullness ventures a funny comment or antic he causes equal hilarity, which is a reaction to its very *un*expectedness. The ease with which politicians or eminent people from other walks of life get their laughs must be the envy of many a professional humorist.

In a book of British royal wit an incident is recorded in which a former Prince of Wales happened to pass a group of workmen digging a hole in the road, to whom he quipped, "Hot

Humor doesn't need a ticket to ride from culture to culture. The best funnies often use no words.

work, eh?" causing great mirth. The only grain of amusement in this sally is that such an inanity should ever have found its way into a compendium of royal wit. The laughter stemmed from shock that a member of the royal family was capable of uttering anything so mundane. With Queen Victoria on the throne, royal wit was not at its peak, though its standard has risen since then.

But what is wit? Freud's definition of a joke provides something of an answer. A joke consists of two dis-

David Kinefield

Foreign bodies

One man's pretty flower is another man's poison—if he is allergic to its pollen.

The word allergy comes from two Greek words meaning "different reaction" and is used to describe a special sensitivity and response that many people have to quite harmless substances. There is an enormous variety of substances which can cause allergies, ranging from pollens to detergents, from food to cosmetics, from pets to perfume. And there is a wide variety of allergic response, from hay fever to eczema, dyspepsia to asthma, nettle rash to headache.

Tilting at Windmills

The allergic reaction arises from the body's disease-fighting defense mechanisms working, unnecessarily, overtime. It has been described as a "biological tilting at windmills"; the inbuilt defense systems, particularly those that give rise to inflammation, are brought into action to attack "foreign invaders" which the allergic person's body identifies, wrongly, as extremely dangerous.

In the normal course of events, one of the most important disease-fighting processes possessed by the body is a system known as immunity. When microbes enter the body they stimulate the production of substances in the blood called *antibodies*, which combine with the disease-carrying organisms, or with the poisons released by them, and inactivate them. Each different type of antibody in the blood is made in response to a specific infection. The immune system "recognizes" the presence of a characteristic chemical—called an *antigen*—in the invading microbe and produces a specific antibody. Antibodies against one type of infection will not in general be effective against another's antigens: a mumps antibody, for example, will not inactivate a cold virus.

When an infection first enters the body, it usually takes a few days for the immune system to produce antibodies tailormade to combat it, so when we are first infected by a

disease like, say, measles, the germs can take hold and multiply until the antibodies are mobilized against them. Until this happens we suffer the symptoms of the disease.

Once antibodies have been formed, however, they remain in the bloodstream for long periods, often for a lifetime. If the same infection enters again, the specific antibodies are immediately brought into play to inactivate the microbes before they can settle and multiply, so the disease fails to take hold: we have become *immune* to the infection.

Both antigens and antibodies are proteins—and the "immune response" is actually a reaction of the body to foreign protein. Of course, many foreign proteins which enter the body —such as in food, for example—are absolutely harmless, and the immune system normally does not bother to produce antibodies against them. People who are allergic, however, have an abnormal immune response to some foreign proteins, called *allergens,* the antigens of allergy.

Just to make life a little more complicated, not all allergens are proteins. An allergic response can be produced by drugs or other chemicals and even by basic chemical elements, such as metals. What seems to occur in such cases is that the substances—called *haptens*—combine with proteins already in the body to make other "foreign" proteins against which antibodies are made.

When an allergen first enters the body, there is no obvious response to it, for by itself it does not cause disease. But in an allergic person the immune system gets busy producing antibodies. This process is known as *sensitization,* for the next time that the allergen comes into contact with the body, the antigens and antibodies will combine to produce the symptoms of allergy.

When we are fighting an infection, the symptoms of this antigen-antibody reaction are quite acceptable for they are far better than letting the disease catch hold. Common symptoms are fever, inflammation and, in the infections of nose and breathing passages, overproduction of mucus.

In the allergic disease, similar symptoms occur, but they are annoying and unacceptable because they are not doing any good. The antibodies connected with allergy tend to associate themselves with particular types of body tissue—and the symptoms of allergy depend on the site where they meet the allergen. If it is in the nose, for example, hay fever will be produced; if the skin is affected, symptoms may be eczema or a rash.

Expanding Blood Vessels

Aside from this automatic mechanism, there are some other factors involved in allergic reactions. First is the role of a substance called *histamine,* released when body tissues are damaged, such as during the antibody-antigen reaction. Histamine sets up inflammation by causing minute blood vessels to expand and also by allowing fluid to seep from the blood into the tissue. This is an important first step in the process of healing.

Nettle rash—a red, itching skin rash, for example—is due to the release of histamine; hay fever is due to histamine-induced inflammation of the mucous membranes in the nose. Histamine release also causes a tightening up of the air passages in the lungs, the classic asthma symptom, and overactivity of the stomach and intestines. We now have a range of drugs which inhibit the release of histamine, called, not unnaturally, *antihistamines,* and these are very important in controlling symptoms.

The second factor to be taken into account is the psychological one. In a number of cases, it seems, the "allergen" is not some chemical compound but a physical reaction of the body to some sort of emotional stress. We do not fully understand the processes by which this response occurs but it is an important factor in many allergic diseases, notably asthma.

Hereditary Basis

When you consider the enormous number of foreign proteins that do come into contact with our bodies, the small number of people who develop allergies is really quite surprising. Overall, only about one person in ten ever shows signs of allergic response. It is quite possible that many more people do have some sort of allergy, but the symptoms are so minor that they are ignored.

Just why this percentage of the population should be abnormally sensitive is unknown, but we do know that there is a strong hereditary basis for a tendency to allergy. In other words, children born to people with allergies are more likely themselves to develop allergies. But specific allergies are not inherited. A child of a hay fever sufferer, for example, is not especially prone to that condition, but he is more liable to develop *some* form of allergy, whether it is asthma or simply getting a rash from eating shellfish. Again, we are very much in the dark about this inherited tendency.

Another feature of allergies is that people who suffer from one kind of allergic reaction are more likely than average to suffer from others as well. Childhood eczema and asthma are closely linked, for example. The common allergies are hay fever, asthma, various skin diseases, and abnormal reactions to certain foods.

Strictly speaking, hay fever should apply to abnormal sensitivity to grass pollens, but today it is generally taken to include any allergic reaction occurring in the nose, eye or upper respiratory tract. The mucous membrane lining of these organs is irritated and inflamed, and the common symptoms are intense itching in the nose and eyes, violent sneezing, and watering eyes, caused because the tear ducts draining into the nose are blocked. Hay fever sufferers may also get headaches and stomach upsets, and, occasionally, insomnia and depression are accompaniment.

The cause of trouble is usually pollen from trees, flowering shrubs and grasses, although anything in the dust in the air we breathe can set up an attack in a sensitive person. Hay fever is generally a seasonal complaint, occurring as different species of plants pollenate. In spring, hay fever is almost always due to tree pollens; oak, elm, birch, maple and cottonwood are the worst offenders. In summer the grasses take over, and a species known as timothy grass is particularly troublesome. In Europe, hay fever generally dies out in the fall, although pollen from some of the daisy family does affect some sufferers. In the United States, however, fall is often a bad time, for it is then that members of the ragweed, amaranth and sage families are pollenating.

Many places now run regular "pollen counts" to give suffers early warning of the hazards they face each day. Ideally the sufferer ought to avoid going out when the pollen count is really high. They should also move to areas, such as the seaside, where the higher humidity keeps the pollen levels down. But for most people, of course, such steps are not practical: they want something to stop the reaction, not just ways to avoid pollen.

Sleepy Side Effects

Many people tend to laugh at hay fever sufferers, but in severe cases the allergy can be really crippling, keeping the afflicted from going out to enjoy themselves and even occasionally preventing them from working. It can be a major problem for some schoolchildren too, interfering with their studies and often, since important examinations seem to take place at the height of the hay fever season, impeding their scholastic progress.

Antihistamine drugs are often prescribed and are generally very successful in relieving symptoms. Unfortunately a frequent side effect is that they cause drowsiness, sometimes to such a degree that the sufferer just cannot live and work normally if he is taking them.

For such people, or for really intractable cases of hay fever, the best approach is a process known as *desensitization* (or *hyposensitization*)—removing or lowering the reaction to an allergen. This technique is used for other allergies such as asthma.

First the allergen causing the trouble has to be identified. This is done by making a series of light scratches, usually on the patient's forearm, but sometimes on the back, and applying a few drops of solutions containing

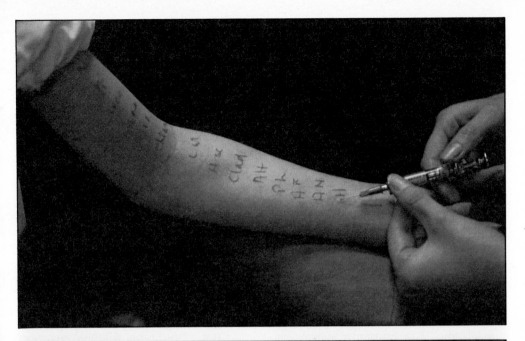

Marshall Cavendish

during the difficult high-pollen months. New vaccines, however, have been developed which require far fewer injections.

Another approach that has been tried is to use a "cocktail" vaccine containing thirty or so different allergens. But often they failed to work adequately because the allergens causing the trouble in any particular patient were not present in sufficient quantities to produce enough antibodies. Today allergists prefer to identify the cause of the trouble and then make a vaccine specifically for the individual patient's needs. If you are a sufferer from hay fever it is well worthwhile seeking your doctor's help and advice: there is no longer any need to suffer every summer.

One form of hay fever does not seem to have any seasonal variations but produces the stuffy nose, sneezing and watery eyes all year. Almost invariably this type of hay fever is due to tiny living organisms which are found in house dust.

Sneezing and Wheezing

It was only in 1967 that these microscopic creatures—known as the house dust mite or *Dermatophagoides pteronyssinus*—were shown to be one of the principal allergens in house dust, which from ancient times has been known to cause sneezing and wheezing. But more important still, they have now been identified as the principal cause in many cases of asthma.

Bronchial asthma is a temporary narrowing of the branched breathing passages (the *bronchi*) in the lungs which results in difficulty in breathing, usually accompanied by wheezing noises. The triggering factor of an asthmatic attack is an involuntary contraction (spasm) of the muscles around the bronchi. There are many different causes of asthma and often several factors may be at work in any one sufferer, but an allergic response is implicated in the majority of cases.

The allergens cause release of histamine, which leads to a swelling of the mucous membrane in the bronchi and constriction of the muscle, almost blocking the air passages. Attacks started in this way are known as *extrinsic asthma*, because they have an external triggering agent. In those cases where there is no obvious allergen at work, the condition is known as *intrinsic asthma* (arising from some as yet unknown internal process).

The house dust mite feeds on tiny scales of dry skin. It is so small (about 0.3 millimeters long and 0.2 millimeters wide) that it is easily breathed

many of the different substances known to cause allergies. (The allergist will already have a few clues, from the patient's symptoms, as to which substances are most likely to be involved.) Allergens to which the subject is especially sensitive will produce a red "flare" around the scratch.

Once the allergen has been identified, it is made up into a special vaccine which is injected into the patient over a series of weeks. At first, the dose given is so small that it causes no ill effects, and it is gradually built up until eventually the patient can tolerate a dose that would previously have caused severe symptoms.

What seems to happen is that the vaccine causes antibodies to be pro-

Top: The cause of an allergy can be found by injecting various allergen solutions. Above: Asthma offenders.

duced which circulate in the blood and do not congregate in specific tissues, like ordinary allergy antibodies. So when the naturally occurring allergens attack, they are inactivated in the bloodstream *before* they reach the sensitive tissues.

Desensitization has to be done well before the hay fever season starts. The general pattern up until very recently has been to begin the course about two months before the hay fever season, gradually building up the dose at two-week intervals. Lower doses are then given, again every two weeks in. It causes a similar allergic response to pollens. Mites like dusty, humid surfaces in which to live and they particularly like mattresses and, to a lesser extent, carpets and soft furnishings. Anything that stirs up the dust in a home, like bed making or carpet beating, can easily bring on an attack in sensitive asthmatics.

In the summer months, pollens can set off asthmatic attacks, and there are also many other airborne invaders—including dusts from industrial processes and mold spores (which are released mainly in the fall). Household pets can be a problem too: hair from cats and dogs can be particularly irritating. Other pets like caged birds or rabbits can also trigger an attack.

Triggered Off

Certain foods to which a person has become sensitized may also be the precipitating factor in some young asthmatics. In fact asthma, which begins in early infancy, is often attributed to a child's allergy to cow's milk, used in bottle feeding.

Infection seems to play a much more important role in asthma cases which develop later in life, particularly in people over forty. Bacteria can cause inflammation of the bronchi (called bronchitis) and can also set off attacks of asthma. In a curious way, however, the bacteria seem often to act as allergens rather than infective agents. In other words, the asthmatic may have an allergic response to certain bacteria, even though not infected.

Emotional stress can trigger off an asthmatic attack. This is not really surprising since emotion does have a physical effect on the heart, the blood vessels and internal muscles. So anyone susceptible to asthma may have an attack precipitated when an emotional situation affects blood vessels and muscles around the bronchi.

The treatment of asthma is a matter for experts, and if you or your children suffer any wheezing attacks or difficulty in breathing you should immediately seek your doctor's advice. There are many drugs which can prevent or control asthmatic attacks, and if specific allergens can be identified, a course of desensitizing injections may be given. We now have, for example, a vaccine against the house dust mite which has proved effective in many cases. But because emotional factors do so often play a role in asthma, treatment may require a long period of counseling to help the patient overcome his unwanted response to psychological stimuli.

Symptoms rather similar to asthma can occur from a variety of bacterial infections, but it is often very difficult to make a distinction between infection and allergic response. Among the diseases that are now generally regarded as allergic are "farmer's lung," caused by breathing in spores from fungi in rotting hay, grain or vegetable produce. As well as causing breathing difficulties, farmer's lung also causes fever and muscular pains. "Bird fancier's lung" is a similar complaint, caused by breathing in particles of dust from the feathers of caged house birds and pigeons. There is also byssinosis, caused by the inhalation of cotton dust, and bagassosis, from the fibers of sugar cane.

One man's meat *is* very often another man's poison: there is a wide range of food to which many people are allergic. The common symptoms are violent stomach upsets and, often, an accompanying rash. Sometimes what appear to be food allergies may in fact be food poisoning due to bacteria, or food "intolerance" caused because the suffer is deficient in enzymes needed to digest certain foods.

Nonetheless, more than fifty different diseases and symptoms have been attributed to food allergies. Among the commonest are allergies to eggs, milk, wheat, shellfish, nuts, chocolate, vegetables, and fruit (especially strawberries). Often such allergies develop early in childhood and they are frequently associated with other allergic conditions, like eczema and asthma.

In many cases, of course, the offending foods may simply be avoided, but in cases where this is impractical a course of desensitizing injections may be given. Again, if your child shows any signs of these allergies, he should be taken to a doctor for expert diagnosis, treatment and advice.

Itchy Blotches

Drugs, notably penicillin, barbiturates and serums used for immunization, can also invoke an allergic response in some people. So, too, can some vaccines which have an albumen (egg white) base. If you have become allergic to any drug you should always tell your doctor before he treats you for any illness, so he will be able to select alternative drugs which do not provoke your allergic response.

Food allergies are probably the most frequent cause of urticaria (nettle rash or hives). Nettles release histamine and some other poisonous substances, which cause the tiny capillary blood vessels to leak fluid into surrounding tissues, bringing on an itching or burning sensation. The name nettle rash is used because a similar process occurs in an allergic reaction, with similar accompanying itchy blotches on the skin. In severe cases, antihistamines may be used to stop the symptoms, and there are also one or two other drugs which doctors can prescribe to damp down the allergic response and the inflammation.

Many other skin problems are caused by allergies. Dermatitis simply means inflammation of the skin, which could be caused by a variety of factors, such as a wound or an infection, but nowadays the term is more generally used for a wide range of skin troubles which seem to be mainly allergic in origin. There are two types of dermatitis; atopic and contact dermatitis.

Allergic to Yourself

In the atopic type, the skin reaction is not due to any direct contact of irritating substance with the skin but to something swallowed or breathed in. It generally produces patchy irregular itching blotches. The cause may be a food, animal scurf, pollen or dust. Very often atopic dermatitis is associated with other allergic diseases like hay fever and asthma. Sometimes a similar skin disease occurs very early in infancy (infantile eczema), and if this is the case the child very often "grows out" of it by the time he reaches his teens. But again, you should seek expert advice if your child suffers so that the cause of the trouble may be identified and avoided.

Contact dermatitis is the commonest of all skin diseases and is the result of the direct application of some irritating substance to the skin.

Cosmetics, jewelry, plants (especially primula and ragweed), woods, metals (particularly nickel and chromium), lubricants and synthetic resins have all been implicated. Such substances may not evoke an immediate response: their action is usually delayed and cumulative.

Cure is largely a matter of identifying and avoiding the offending substances, although this may be easier said than done, particularly if it is something that the sufferer comes into contact with at work.

Much still remains to be learned about allergic diseases but although there are still a great many unanswered questions, there is no longer any need for the allergic person to suffer in silence. Allergens can often be identified and avoided or the sufferer desensitized—and doctors now have many drugs available that can control, prevent and relieve the worst of the symptoms.

Kim Sayer

The son also rises

The lands of the rising sun still preserve ancient oriental ways of education.

What are the essential differences, if any, between children brought up in the West and East? The term "Western child" is so broad as almost to defy any attempt at definition. He could be an inhabitant of the United States, the United Kingdom, Western Europe, Canada or—going as far as the Southern hemisphere—Australia or New Zealand. Although Europe, North America and Australia are geographically far apart, they share a similar culture. A child growing up in Christchurch, New Zealand, probably has far more in common with a youngster in Minneapolis than with his geographically closer counterpart in Tokyo.

But then again, who is the Eastern child? Do we typify him by taking him

from a rural setting in India or China, simply because these countries still have huge countryside-based peasant communities, many of whom still cling proudly to traditional ways? Why not take an urban Indonesian youngster and a rural French child to represent the East and West respectively?

In the end the choice has to be somewhat arbitrary. Nevertheless, modern technology in the West has succeeded in breaking down the barriers of nationalism to a great extent. And although the child growing up in London will not have exactly the same kind of upbringing as the child in Melbourne or Paris, there are certain characteristics which apply to all so-called "Western" peoples.

The same may be said of "Eastern" communities. The ways of a traditional rural life are still pervasive, even in a highly developed industrial society like Japan. Eastern countries have resisted radical changes in the nature of family life and child rearing more successfully than Western nations.

Some of the main features of urbanization in the West—like high density of population, great residential mobility, and rapid communication through public and private transport, television, radio and the press—have led to a decline in physical isolation. At the same time there is a certain impersonality about the modern town.

When a husband and his wife set up home in a new suburb, it is quite likely that many of their closest friends will not be living there and even more probable that none of their relations will be very close at hand. This is not so even in a highly urbanized Eastern country like Japan.

Where the Western child's parents function as a small isolated unit relatively free from the constraints that would be imposed in a small community or clan, the Japanese or Chinese child is constantly made aware of the obligations he has towards the group. These are the people who have helped in his upbringing and who figure in his duties to uphold the honor and traditions of the group. The formal groups of which the child in the urban, industrialized West is aware are too diverse and often too remote for him to feel any special obligation towards them, except through ties of affection and common experience. The pressures with which he becomes familiar are not those of tradition and conformity but of rapid change and bewildering diversity.

Legal Protection

In early childhood at least, the child is cushioned from these confusing influences by a system which places him in a separate world. The day-to-day separation of adults and children is characteristic of the Western way of life. Children are urged to play among themselves, relatively isolated from the grown-ups. And as the various age groups share fewer activities, the "generation gap" widens.

Much of the emphasis in bringing up Western children has shifted from custom and tradition to a legal framework, and the law now reflects great changes in the value placed on children in the family and society at large. After his birth, modern law uses many different methods to protect a child's interests. In a child's early years, the law looks to the parents or guardian to care for it: a legal duty is imposed upon them to provide food, medical aid, and shelter. If they fail in this duty, they will be guilty of criminal neglect. With illegitimate children, the mother alone is the legal guardian

and the father usually has no rights in bringing up the child.

A parent may usually determine the religion in which the child will be brought up. In cases of dispute, after a divorce or death of the parents, it may fall to the court to determine this issue along with the manner in which the child will be educated.

A sign of modern society's regard for children, both in their own right and in the sense of being precious

resources, is the provisions made for training young ones. A good education is of such importance in most countries that the law ensures that a child receives one.

Happy Childhood

In law and everyday practice, the world of the Western child is very much his oyster, to which psychologists and educationists have devoted a great deal of research and writ-

Duty to family and forebears pervades the Eastern child's upbringing. Right: Making offerings at the family shrine. Opposite page: The Shinto initiation ceremony (below) impresses on the child his loyalty to the emperor; school in China is no playgroup (top left) — even six-year-olds feel it their duty to do well; youngsters work the soil on a Chinese commune (top right).

ing. It is a world from which the cares and responsibilities of adult life are excluded. Toys and books for children are now a flourishing industry in Europe and North America, and the consumer industries, especially the food manufacturers, are paying more attention to the growing child market. Candies and cool drinks are designed with the child in mind rather than his parents. But with this, the storm and stress of adolescence in the West is

symptomatic of the rigid dichotomy between childhood and adulthood.

The early life of the Cantonese child living in Hong Kong or a Japanese child living in a village illustrates some basic points about the character of a child's social life in the Far East. Through their training these children find it easy to adapt to the grown-up world. From the age of two a child is expected to develop as fast as possible. From the early years the

customs of child rearing differ from those in the West. The parents treat their child of two or three years as parents in Western countries would treat a child or ten or so. Outwardly, the relationship between parents and child may not be as intimate and affectionate as between European children and their parents. But in the relationship there is indeed great love coupled with a mutual feeling of respect. What is particularly distinctive

is a definite sense of belonging to a group larger than the family circle.

Children in more traditional Eastern families are instructed in the laws, ethics and religious practices of the community, and the importance of traditional beliefs are stressed very strongly. These matters are conveyed rather haphazardly to many Western children. Eastern youngsters are informed that if they fail to perform the religious rituals correctly they will displease the ancestral spirits to whom the ceremonies are dedicated. In the West an attitude of disinterest and irreverence to the old and traditional is only too common.

Stages of Development

A child in a Western society lacks the many common standards to which the Eastern youngster can refer. If his parents are practicing Catholics, Anglicans or Jews, he will probably make his first Communion or celebrate his Bar Mitzvah. Both ceremonies are comparable to an initiation rite in a more traditional society. Such events announce the child's new status to other members of the group (in this case church or temple) and give him a sense of identity with those who have undergone the experience.

Yet it is hard to find ceremonies in our largely secular Western society which are so generally recognized, perhaps because of the diverse nature of the society itself. In an urbanized society there remain few rituals or ceremonies which are generally recognized by the whole community as special marks of the various stages in a child's development.

On the other hand, in isolated rural or peasant communities and societies such as still exist in India and other Eastern countries, formal rites are a principal means of demonstrating to the community and the child himself that he is socially as well as physically accepted as an adult. These rites have a traditional order. They may have gone on for generations with little change, conveying a clear meaning to all the members of the community.

In many Eastern countries, the child's most important religious experiences are in the home and are often directly related to the rites surrounding shrines dedicated to the family's ancestors. In Japan even the most "progressive" family may well have a shrine in the home and make daily offerings to it. It is at these observances that the child is made doubly aware of his debt to both the living and the dead. When he is six he is taken to the local Shinto shrine. The priest stresses loyalty to the emperor and presents a book of ethics.

This sort of thing must seem rather alien to the industrialized societies of Western Europe and the United States, where a striking feature of life is the diversity of social, ethnic and religious groups. Class differences, occupational and kinship groupings cut across each other, often resulting in a confusion of roles.

In the Japanese (and Chinese) customs of child rearing, there is something of a reversal of the Western approach. The Western child probably experiences most parental discipline in his earlier years. He is surrounded by all sorts of constraints on his behavior, especially with respect to physical functions. It is his parents' expectation that, as he grows older, he will become less dependent on his parents and gradually be free of his family's influence.

In the East the pattern is reversed. The young child is given a great deal of freedom, but as he grows older, he will become increasingly aware of a debt to his family and of his allegiance to them and a duty to behave correctly in the eyes of the world. With age comes, not independence, but dependence and responsibility to others, not to oneself. The son is expected to take his father's place in the future, carrying on the family name and its traditions—a kind of trustee.

Obscene Games

Great emphasis is laid upon filial piety in Japan. The child has a debt to his forebears because of the life he has been given. This is called *giri* and includes all duties to one's family. The *giri* must be repaid and it may be a burden very hard to bear. In the Japanese home the father is shown extreme deference and his demands are complied with immediately. The young boy can, however, express his feelings against his mother with relative immunity.

There are conventions for teaching the child the necessary physical skills, including such matters as sleeping and sitting positions. Girls are allowed less freedom than boys. From their early years they are taught that their role in life is obedience to father and mother, tending to small children and later to a husband. The situation of the young girl is less well-defined than that of the boy.

In their preschool groups, Japanese children are very free with each other. Many of their games are unabashedly obscene from the Westerner's point of view. Living in such close quarters with adults, they know the facts of life from an early age. Masturbation is not regarded as dangerous.

Children of this age boast and criticize each others' homes. This individuality is a great contrast to the self-abnegation in their parents' talk. But gradually the child's individualistic aims are subdued as he learns society's attitude to such matters.

Teaching by Teasing

Lying behind these self-abnegating characteristics are the ideas of shame and loss of face. Both of these still remain strong motivational forces in Japanese (and non-Communist Chinese) society. Generally speaking, shame is a group phenomenon, whereas the Christian concept of guilt—pervasive in the West—is a personal feeling. To have lost face means that you have lowered yourself before the group; the parents of the Japanese child will tell him that he will be laughed at if he is naughty or cannot control himself physically.

There is a constant process of literally teasing the child into good behavior. It begins when the mother has another baby. The older child is immediately weaned. The suddenness of the little "king's" forced abdication must come as a terrible affront, and the result is usually several weeks of temper tantrums. The mother teases the child when he tries to nurse and calls him a baby: "That little boy is laughing at you because you're a boy and still want to nurse." She may also put pepper on her nipple.

This teasing is not confined to weaning. If a child cries or is naughty, the mother will fondle a visiting child and say, "I am going to adopt this baby. I want a nice, good child." This causes furious rage in her own child, and if it is a boy he may vent his rage by pummeling her. Another disciplinary method is to ask a male visitor to take the child away. The man acts his part and when the baby has had a major tantrum, screaming to its mother for rescue, she will take it back, having extracted a promise to be good.

The panic such teasing occasions in the two- to five-year-old child is all the greater because home is really a haven of safety and indulgence. These and other experiences cultivate the fear of ridicule and of ostracism which is so marked in the Japanese adult.

For many Oriental children education became a serious matter from quite an early age. Ancient adult rituals were often complex, and a child needed much training in order

to conduct himself properly. Many Japanese parents still waste little time on "baby talk" with their child. Instead, as soon as the child starts to show signs of being able to imitate words, they make him repeat the appropriate phrases of respect, making sure that his grammar is correct. The process develops into a kind of game which both parents and child enjoy, but it has a serious purpose behind it. Even the process of learning the ideographic writing requires much patience and hard work.

Honor of the Family

After the Shinto initiation service at age six the Japanese child goes to coeducational primary school for another six years, where he will meet children of all classes. Many lifelong friendships are made at school: always the importance of the individual is played down and harmonious relations are emphasized. Most local communities give vigorous support to the schools. Classroom activity may seem rather regimented, without the free play periods which are commonly found in a Western primary school. No attempt is made to teach the child to think critically; unquestioning acceptance is the rule.

If the teacher gives a child a bad report the family name is disgraced and they will turn against him; indeed sometimes his schoolmates may ostracize him. A lowering of status is communicated to the growing boy by a new and serious extension of the pattern of babyhood teasing, and he learns to avoid embarrassing situations. The central idea in this character training is to gradually inculcate

the fear of ridicule. The child must learn to subordinate his will to the ever-increasing duties to neighbors, family and community.

Next comes a five-year secondary school. After years of cooperation, the fierce rivalry of the entrance exam comes as a shock. The custom at this period is for older boys to mortify and torture new boys. The humiliations are insults to *giri* (this concept of family duty begins to strengthen at age ten) and must be repaid. Grievances are nursed and opportunities to revenge insults (even sometimes into adult life) are sought.

Females do not have this code. They are disciplined by their parents' calm, unswerving expectation that they will do their duty. Excluded from male play groups at nine and ten years of age, they begin to interest themselves in essentially feminine things. Although of a lower status than boys, girls have had up to then a relatively free time. But when the sexes are segregated, the boys make a great show of male superiority, and often girls become sullen and uncooperative. For them, childish fun is over.

Enjoyment of Sex

The pattern of inequality of the sexes is started in the home. Although arranged marriages and tyrannical mothers-in-law are becoming a thing of the past, a girl may still find that her roles are confused. She may be expected to do well at school and university; yet at the same time she is expected to submit to her family's refusal to allow her to leave home.

Adolescence awakens a boy's interest in the opposite sex, though they

When all is said and done, kids are kids — East or West — and a beach is a beach — a whole lot of fun.

learn and master the techniques of courting with much embarrassment. The man is given the impression that sex is something removed from the serious business of life. It is something to be enjoyed. Premarital intercourse appears to be fairly common.

In many Oriental households today conflicts of roles and ideals may occur when traditional standards of upbringing come into opposition with the social requirements and uncertainties of a fast-moving, industrialized environment. Emerging from a close-knit family background, a young person has to take his or her place in a society that has become in many ways as competitive as the most advanced Western industrial society.

Notions of honor and family loyalty have to be reconciled with those of loyalty to the "firm." The individual can no longer count completely on his family to provide backing for his career: promotion depends on his allegiance and success with the company. But a greater problem arises from the loyalty towards their own generation which many young people develop along with new freedoms.

In March, 1970, nine Japanese students, followers of an extreme left-wing political group, hijacked a jet airplane. Yet, they were armed with the traditional swords of their ancestors. Today the Eastern child is faced with the task of reconciling centuries-old cultures with the most unsettling new developments which the twentieth century presents.

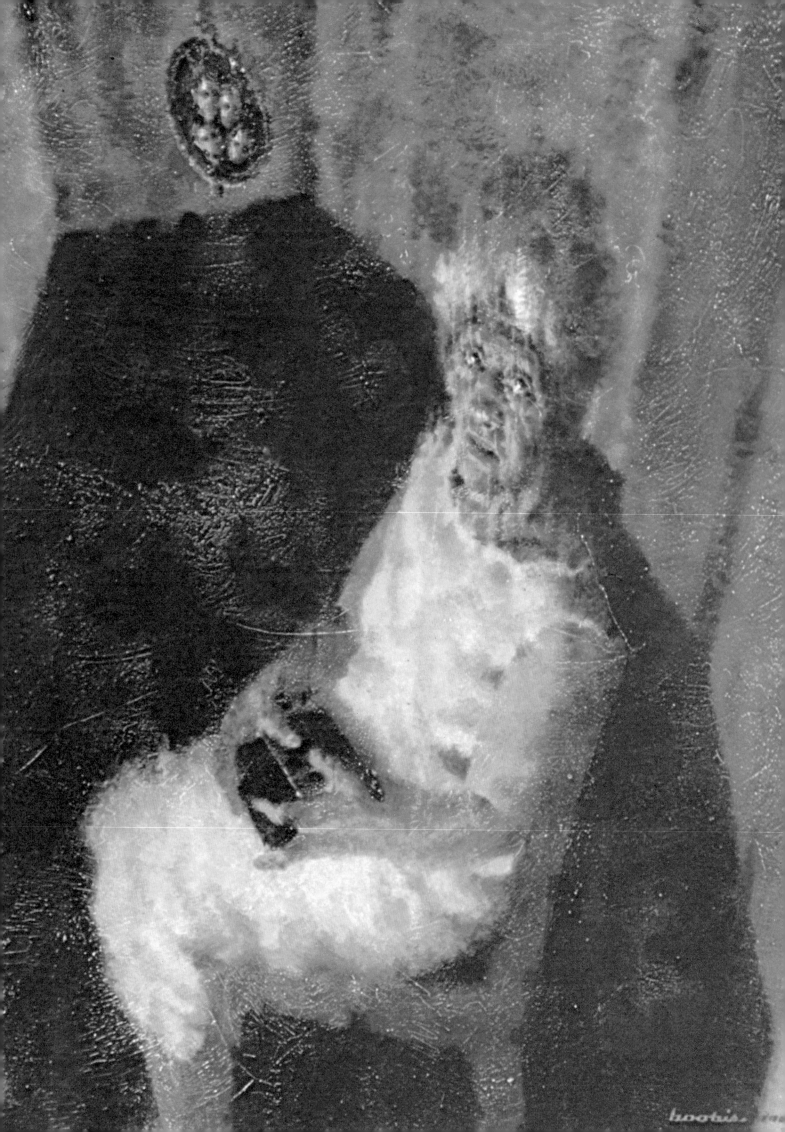

Decade decay

By middle age, man is beginning to show signs of the wear and tear of modern times.

When man falls prey to physical, psychological or social pressures, it is intriguing to try to sort out exactly what has gone wrong. There are always faults in the person himself and this is often referred to as the human internal factor in illness.

It is becoming increasingly evident in medical research, however, that outside environmental and social factors are becoming more important than ever in the development of illness, especially those involved in the so-called middle-age crisis.

During the last two or three decades we have concentrated on trying to improve mankind's physical environment. Thus the effects of hot and cold have been examined, and health standards with regard to the temperature of factories, shops and offices have evolved. The effects of excessive noise are being minimized, but still traumatic noise-induced deafness has added its small but concrete contribution to the middle-age crisis in a fair number of people. Poor illumination, with its concomitant high accident rate, has also been greatly reduced except perhaps in the home, and so a middle age marred because of an avoidable accident has become less likely today.

The Air We Breathe

Although constant vigilance is required to prevent the chemical and radiation hazards that are always potentially a risk in organized society, by and large mankind has been lucky, although a few workers in a wide variety of industries have had their expectation of a healthy and happy middle age ruined by this problem.

Lastly, perhaps, we have come to value as something precious the purity of the air we breathe. Nevertheless it is little more than 20 years since the last killer fog over 500 feet deep covered the whole of the London area for several days and led to the death of around 4,000 people. The lessons to be gained from controls applied to the

air we breathe have been relatively recently learned. There does, however, exist one vast area of human activity in which we have not been able to make much impact, so far as preventing a middle-age crisis and this involves stress in the environment. Indeed our working and social life is becoming more and more dominated by mechanization, automation, business organization systems, and production processes which add to our level of daily stress.

A tendency exists to consider stress-induced illness to be the prerogative of the highly paid executive class. Nothing could be further from the truth. Production processes are being more and more split into isolated fragments. Assembly-line work, with its constant pressure and timed production schedules, can be as stressful as a top executive's efforts to remain in command.

It is, of course, impossible to live without stress in the same way as it is impossible to live without anxiety. Anxiety, however, is a built-in factor so far as the human animal is concerned, and serves in very many of its

Left: The advancing years promise little for those in industrialized societies where family ties have broken down. Right: Change is a powerful stress-inducing factor.

LIFE CHANGE UNITS SCALE	
EVENT	STRESS VALUE
Death of Spouse	100
Divorce	73
Marital separation	65
Jail term	63
Death of close family member	63
Personal injury or illness	53
Marriage	50
Fired at work	47
Marital reconciliation	45
Retirement	45
Change in health of family member	44
Pregnancy	40
Sex difficulties	39
Gain of a new family member	39
Business readjustment	39
Change in financial state	38
Death of close friend	37
Change to different line of work	36
Change in number of arguments with spouse	35
Large mortgage	31
Foreclosure of mortgage or loan	30
Change in responsibilities at work	29
Son or daughter leaving home	29
Trouble with in-laws	28
Outstanding personal achievement	26
Wife begins or stops work	26
Begin or end college	25
Change in living conditions	24
Revision of personal habits	23
Trouble with boss	20
Change in work hours or conditions	20
Change in residence	20
Change in college	19
Change in recreation	19
Change in church activities	18
Change in social activities	17
Small mortgage	17
Change in sleeping habits	16
Change in number of family get-togethers	15

connotations, as a protection. Indeed, the concept of anxiety is intimately connected with the "old" adaptation patterns around which we have evolved and is concerned primarily with preparing the whole organism either for "fight or flight"—overcoming an adversary or escaping from him. Stress may not have the same survival function, but it is impossible to eliminate it totally from our life today, and it continues to make increasing inroads into the personality during middle age.

Stress Situation

It is usually quite impracticable to fly from stress, although many behavior patterns have evolved with just this in mind. For instance, there is flight into alcohol, or flight into drugs. Some see aggression as a reaction to a stress situation, and there is a certain amount of animal experimentation that backs this hypothesis. Similar arguments, all plausible in their way, have been put forward in an attempt to explain how stress in modern society has engendered novel and worrying concepts of modern living and sexual mores, and even the development of new religions.

Stress seems to hit hardest at middle age. By the time we reach the later years, we feel we should live in a way acceptable to our neighbors, friends and acquaintances. We also feel the need to find spiritual nourishment from what we do, and that by now we should be in a position to have the means to satisfy our various emotional yearnings. All too often, however, middle age refuses us these satisfactions. The natural reaction then is to "press on" and use our unquenchable human appetite for power in an attempt to better our position. Any more disappointments along this sad road, of course, generate still more stress.

Thus we experience in middle age a curious paradox. In many ways we have a better control of our future at this time than mankind has ever experienced. Illnesses related to microbes have become a thing of the past; the external environment has been largely brought under control.

But, somewhere along the line, the *internal* environment of man has become deranged. The first person to make measurements scientifically of this derangement was Dr. Thomas Holmes, professor of psychiatry at the University of Washington in Seattle.

For some time it has been accepted that changes of life-style are associated with disease, from pneumonia to an attack of shingles. Often, the change seems to work along nervous pathways, and what has changed in a person's way of living shows up in blood pressure or perhaps in skin or stomach trouble. But changes in life-style can affect such basic things as immunity against infection.

The Phobic Years

It is important to realize that Dr. Holmes and his researchers did not base their assessment of pressures in middle age solely on difficulties, worries and tragedies, but included happy events and joyous happenings as well. He devised a scale for calculating an individual's stress quotient—called a Life Change Units Scale—based on a study of thousands of people throughout the United States.

Having produced this table the next thing to do was to test it in action. This was done, as it happened, on a series of 3,000 men serving in the U.S. Navy. Computerized results eventually showed that the man in the top 10 percent of life-style change units suffered twice as much illness as those in the bottom 10 percent, and the higher the score the more severe the character of the illness sustained.

In other words, the more complex and difficult life becomes (and the peak of complexity naturally falls within the middle years), the more stress affects the human frame. The exact impact depends on many things, including the sex of the individual.

In women, stress affects menstrual function profoundly and often influences fertility. Phobias, best described as exaggerated fears of a particular happening or situation, are a common stress feature in women. Thus in middle age we often find women who are afraid to go out (agarophobia: literally fear of the market place), or those who suffer from claustrophobia, the fear of being closed up. In the first case they cannot do the shopping or even go on a pleasant social outing; in the second they fear being "trapped" in buildings, cars, trains or aircraft.

The pressure of high-speed living is enough to make you blow a gasket.

Dennis Waugh

Dennis Waugh

PAF International

Another frequent stress illness in middle-aged women is a disease called conversion hysteria. In this case, the patient feels generally anxious about the environment and may not focus on any particular area. Stress and anxiety are both difficult to talk about and express in words. The inner pain they give the psyche, therefore, is often transformed by the process called conversion into a more easily voiced symptom like backache, headache, tiredness and indigestion.

Anxiety Crisis

Middle-aged men also suffer stress-induced illnesses. Two physical conditions that affect men particularly—cancer of the lung and coronary thrombosis—have definite physical or environmental causes, but they also involve a stress factor. Indeed, a body of medical opinion holds that high blood pressure, dietary habits, smoking and blood abnormalities are involved in only about 25 percent of all cases of coronary heart disease and that the patient's personality and the way he works, with the stress factors he encounters each day, are the main factors involved.

Sufferers from heart disease, in other words, tend to fall into a distinct personality type. The ambitious

—those with an inner driving force who try to achieve higher and higher goals—are the potential victims and, of course, it is in middle age that most of this stressful striving takes place. Oddly, too, some investigators find that those with high stress scores are more liable to fall victim to cancer of the lung than those with low stress scores. Even when the smoking factor is excluded, the lung cancer sufferer can be shown to be a person who tends to "absorb" anxiety factors rather than to react to them.

Perhaps the disease that shows the greatest effect of stress, particularly during the middle years, is ulcerative colitis. This is a disease of the large bowel, in which shallow indolent ulcers develop that lead to diarrhea, loss of blood, general weakness, and, unless the disease is adequately treated, even death. Usually the illness runs a chronic course throughout middle age, sometimes getting a bit better, sometimes a bit worse. Although the ultimate cause of ulcerative colitis is unknown, it is generally accepted that relapses and exacerbations of the disease occur with stress.

Clearly it is impossible to protect the middle-aged from an occasional stress crisis. But much can be gained from an intelligent appraisal of cir-

Were man meant to live in huge skyscrapers and breathe in smog, nature would have provided chimneys instead of flowers and trees.

cumstances during the middle years, be they at work or at home, as well as constant guard against too many stress-producing changes in a given time. The human body has evolved with stress at its elbow since the beginning of time. It is when we try to take on too much stress within too little time that the system falls and an often avoidable crisis spoils our life.

No Longer Desirable

There is one more major contributor to the middle-age crisis, and that is sex. Middle age is hedged around by all sorts of half-truths and superstitions so far as sex is concerned. For instance, women lose their fertility during middle age and many of them find themselves in a crisis situation because they secretly believe they will also lose their attractiveness, sexual desire and even their sexual function at this time.

In actual fact, all that finally happens to a woman at the menopause is that she stops menstruating and becomes infertile. This is basically due to a decrease in her ovarian hormone production and not, as some believe, a drying up of all her sex hormones. Sex hormones in women are produced in appreciable levels for many years after the change of life, and in any case there is no real evidence that the more emotional qualities of human sexuality are in any way linked with sex hormone production. Admittedly, there are a few women who experience hormone changes of a magnitude sufficient to produce very definite bodily changes

To spend the later years of life confined to an armchair watching TV may be comfortable, but is it a waste of precious time?

that can cause anxiety in the middle years. The important thing to remember, however, is that these can always be treated medically before any unwanted sexual problems develop. Indeed for many middle-aged women the loss of the possibility of an unwanted pregnancy improves their sexual appetite and enjoyment.

The middle-aged man too often fears a male "climacteric," and, for some, impotence and all it stands for hangs like a sword of Damocles over their virility. There are many causes for this, some of which are, interestingly enough, produced by women. As a result of middle-age stresses, many men go through a period of sexual

doldrums, and one unfortunate incident can render them temporarily impotent. The way the spouse reacts to this small particle of total sexual experience is very important to the couple's sexual functioning.

If the woman is strongly critical of the man's failure and expresses her disappointment in him with some vehemence, then there is every likelihood that the next coital attempt will end in failure, and perhaps the third one, too. Sexual confidence in men is very easily undermined in this way, and soon a condition emerges in which he does, in fact, become impotent. He is suffering, however, from psychic impotence not organic.

This is not to say that organic impotence is not a possibility in middle age. Impotence in middle-aged men can follow gonorrhea or infections of the urinary tract, particularly chronic prostatitis. There is a condition involving fibrous distortion of the penis, called Peyrories disease after the surgeon who first described it, which is usually followed by impotence. A number of hormonal disturbances may also cause impotence in middle-aged men, particularly those secondary to thyroid disease. In some cases of hardening of the arteries, the vessels that supply the testes become "furred up," and the blood supply to these organs becomes poor. Perhaps the commonest physical illness associated with impotence in the middle-aged man is diabetes, though probably the commonest "organic" cause of impotence in men is drink.

Keep At It

Alcohol has been shown to produce significantly greater destructive changes in the testes than it does in the liver, and the chronic alcoholic, or heavy drinker is at risk in this way unless he mends his ways. Certain drugs that are used medically for the treatment of high blood pressure are known to produce secondary organic impotence, a point always weighed carefully by the doctor before he prescribes them. Addictive drugs are also liable to produce secondary organic impotence, especially opiates and their derivatives, like heroin.

It seems highly likely, however, that psychic impotence is by far the most likely to produce a middle-age crisis than all the other causes of organic impotence put together. Sexual fitness is like all other forms of physical and mental fitness during middle age: it has to be attended to regularly. As a well-known community physician put it, "If you don't want to lose it, use it."

ENCYCLOPEDIA OF HUMAN BEHAVIOR

IDIORETINAL LIGHT
The vague gray color seen even with eyes closed in complete darkness. This is due to minor, low-level activity in the retina which occurs even in the absence of light.

IDIOSYNCRASY
A personal peculiarity of some kind.

IDIOT
Someone scoring less than 20 on an IQ scale. This, in intellectual terms, represents the lowest grade of humanity. Idiots are more or less incapable of learning and cannot speak or look after themselves in any way.

IDIOT SAVANT
A phrase used to refer to a person with basically low intelligence who nonetheless shows superior but peculiar abilities, normally of one specific kind. The most common examples are people who can hardly read or write and yet can apparently perform remarkable feats of arithmetical calculation in their heads.

IGNIS FATUUS
Will-o'-the-wisp or "wandering light." Now identified as phosphorescent marsh gas, it was once mistaken for ghosts or spirits.

ILLITERATE
Someone over the age of ten who cannot read or write as the result of inadequate education rather than mental deficiency.

ILLUSION
A perceptual mistake. In the classic case, as with visual illusions, information reaching the eye and being passed on to the brain is misinterpreted in some odd way by the brain's recognition mechanism. Illusions are of particular interest to psychologists because they appear to give an insight into the structure of the brain's recognition system.

IMAGE
At the most basic level, the pattern of light and shade projected onto the retina through the lens of the eye. At a less concrete level, it is a kind of thought process in which a person seems to see or hear, in the brain, a trace of some visual or auditory experience of the past.

IMAGINATION
Creative or inventive thought, generally of a purposeful kind as in *daydreaming*.

IMBECILE
A person with an IQ of between 20 and 50. Imbeciles can do simple tasks but are incapable of looking after themselves.

IMMORAL
Violating accepted social, moral or ethical codes.

IMMUNIZATION
The process of making a person resistant to a disease, most commonly by giving him small doses of the disease and thus "training" the body's defenses to ward off any major infection at a later date.

IMPLICIT BEHAVIOR
Activity of some kind which cannot be observed or studied without special measuring instruments. This might include muscular or glandular responses to emotive situations.

IMPOSSIBLE OBJECTS
The name given to a class of cleverly designed patterns which fool the brain's perceptual processes and create an object which is impossible to see "as a whole." The trick involves making one part of the object lead to expectations which conflict with the features of another part.

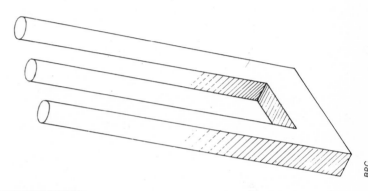

BPC

IMPOTENCE
Literally powerlessness, but connoting mostly the inability to perform a complete or satisfactory sex act. This term refers to males only and is not to be confused with *sterility*.

IMPRINTING
Remarkably rapid or even instantaneous learning observed in young animals at critical periods after birth or hatching. In the most spectacular cases, young chicks or ducks will accept as "mother" more or less the first moving object they see on emerging from the egg. Once imprinted, the fixation cannot be unlearned, and young animals have been experimentally and permanently attached to "mothers" from totally different species, or even human beings and clockwork toys. Imprinting presumably has biological survival value inasmuch as it provides an instant bond between the young and its parent.

IMPULSIVE NEUROSIS
A tendency to thoughtless behavior and making snap judgments which overrides normal rational behavior. This disturbs the individual's personal and social equilibrium.

INADEQUACY
A feeling of inferiority or incapacity to act or make decisions. *Inadequate personality* is a term used by psychologists to refer to social misfits of various kinds.

INBREEDING
Mating between blood relatives. Taboos against this practice are common throughout the world.

INCEST
Mating between close blood relations—in Western societies between brothers and sisters, mothers and sons. Some societies consider mating between first cousins incestuous.

INCEST DREAM
A relatively common dream of having sex with a close blood

relation. Freud believed that such dreams reflected unconscious wishes, typically of the kind which make up the so-called *Oedipus Complex.* Psychologists do not consider these dreams indicate any basic sexual perversions.

INCOMPATIBLE
Not capable of working or living together peacefully.

INCONTINENCE
The inability to control urination or defecation, though this does not usually refer to young children in the pretraining stage. It is often associated with mental disorder or senility.

INCUBATION
The process of "hatching an idea." This is often a period when no conscious thinking seems to be taking place but from which the solution to a problem finally emerges.

INCUBUS
A demon or evil spirit who visits humans during sleep.

INCUS
One of the tiny bones that make up the hearing apparatus of the middle ear.

INDECENCY
Behavior, generally of a sexual kind, which offends social morality.

INDEPENDENT VARIABLE
Also called the *experimental variable,* the facet of an experiment which is controlled by the experimenter and whose effect on some other factor is then studied. In an experiment to see whether a drug affects the human memory, the independent variable is the drug and the subject's score on a memory test is called the *dependent variable.*

INDIFFERENCE POINT
A no-man's-land between two extremes of experience: for example, the point at which tickling ceases to be a pleasant experience but before it becomes definitely unpleasant.

INDIFFERENT STIMULUS
A stimulus or sensation which does not have any psychological effect on a person or animal.

INDIRECT VISION
A visual sensation which occurs when the image of an object is thrown outside the central portion of the retina. Indirect vision is blurry and incomplete and causes an automatic reflex movement to bring the subject into central fixation.

INDIVIDUALISM
A tendency to extreme self-dependence, occasionally coupled with lack of concern for other people's needs.

INDIVIDUAL PSYCHOLOGY
The approach to psychology developed by Alfred Adler, a former disciple of Freud. Adler's main quarrel with Freud was over the latter's insistence that the basic human motivation was the libido or "sex drive." Adler believed that a drive for power was by far the most important force controlling human personality, that human beings went through life developing and preserving a positive self-image, and that neuroses were devices by which the individual protected himself from loss of self-esteem. He coined the term *inferiority complex* to refer to the drive which led inadequate people to bolster their self-image in a search for power.

INDUCED COLOR
A change in the apparent quality of a color when some other color is placed alongside it.

INDUSTRIAL PSYCHOLOGY
The branch of psychology that tries to discover what laws of human behavior can be applied to solving problems arising in business, industry, and economic affairs. Industrial psychology began to come into its own when the first reliable intelligence and personality tests were devised.

INERTIA
The tendency for something to remain in one place unless some definite force is applied to it. It is a concept drawn from physics but can be used in psychology to refer to a particularly static and inflexible state of mind.

INFANCY
The first period of life after birth, generally supposed to end when a child has acquired simple language skills and is no longer totally dependent upon its parents.

INFANTILE AMNESIA
Lack of memory of events in the first few years of life. Psychoanalysts believe this is largely due to repression, but most psychologists assume that memories are not easily recalled because the child was without language at the time.

INFANTILE BIRTH THEORIES
The various peculiar ideas that children form about the mechanics of birth—for instance, that babies emerge from the navel or the anus.

INFANTILE SEXUALITY
A concept first developed by Freud which was considered to be very shocking at the time, but which merely pointed out what we now hold to be rather obvious—that young children are capable of experiencing sexual pleasure. This does not of course mean that children understand the nature of the pleasure, but merely that they can experience it.

INFANTILISM
A tendency on the part of a child, or even an adult, to retreat when under stress into infantile forms of behavior. Thumb sucking and nail biting are obvious common examples.

INFERENCE
Coming to a conclusion about something on the basis of previous knowledge or experience, rather than by making direct observation of the facts.

INFERIOR
A term used in physiology to refer to the parts of an organ which are physically beneath other parts.

INFERIORITY COMPLEX
A fundamental idea put forward by psychologist Alfred Adler to account for the way in which inadequate people—for example, on a physical level, those who are very short in stature—seek power to preserve their self-esteem.

INFORMATION THEORY
A development from the engineering sciences which attempts to produce theories of communication and the transmission of information from one point to another. Its most important use is among telephone engineers and those involved in the design of computers. Physiologists and psychologists have also taken it up, however, in the hope

that some of its principles could be applied to understanding the complex communications network—the nervous system.

INGESTION
The process by which an organism takes in food.

INHERENT
Something built in to an organism at birth.

INHERIT
To receive a characteristic of some kind from one's parents through the genetic mechanism.

INHIBITION
In physiology, a process of blocking an ongoing action by some other bodily mechanism—the firing of some nerves, for example, can be interrupted by the firing of other special inhibitory nerves. In psychology, it refers to a mental block of some kind, particularly the prevention of undesirable unconscious thoughts from reaching consciousness.

INITIATION RITE
A ritual or ceremony common in many nonindustrial societies which is performed on members of a social group when they reach some important transitional state—typically adolescence. In some cases there may be mutilation or scarring of the face or body. Initiation rites appear from time to time in Western societies, as in college fraternities.

INKBLOT TEST
One of a large number of so-called projection tests designed to assess personality. The patient is shown an inkblot smeared on a paper and is invited to make up a story about its shape. As the blot itself rarely has any meaningful form, the patient is obliged to manufacture a story for it, and the theme is supposed to indicate his personality problems.

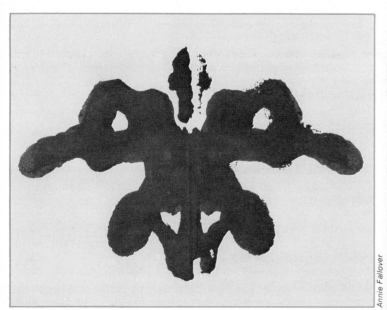
Annie Fallover

INNATE
Something present at birth in an organism. It may refer to the potential which is present: one speaks of "innate intelligence," which refers not so much to the IQ at birth but rather to the person's maximum possible development.

INNER EAR
The deepest section of the ear, which includes the cochlea and the semicircular canals. The latter, incidentally, regulate balance and have very little to do with hearing.

INNERVATION
The triggering or firing of a muscle by other nerves.

INSANITY
A legal, not a psychological, term for a disturbed mental condition in which the individual is not responsible for his actions.

INSIGHT
A process of sudden understanding in which a novel solution to a problem appears apparently "out of the blue." It was once assumed to be a faculty of humans only, but psychologists now accept that many of the higher animals, including monkeys and even some rodents, are capable of insight. In psychoanalysis the word is used to refer to the moment, often a dramatic one, when a patient receives the first deep awareness of the origin and nature of his problems.

INSIGHT THERAPY
An approach to psychoanalysis, currently very fashionable in the United States, in which the treatment is devoted to leading the patient to gain insights into his illness.

INSOMNIA
Chronic—that is, long-term—difficulty in sleeping. It is most commonly caused by worry or anxiety and is often a forerunner of mental disturbance of some kind.

INSPIRATION
In physiology, the act of drawing air into the lungs, as contrasted with expiration. In psychology, it is something which leads to a moment of *insight* or sudden understanding.

INSTABILITY
A tendency to abrupt changes in emotional behavior.

INSTINCT
An inherited pattern of behavior common to all members of

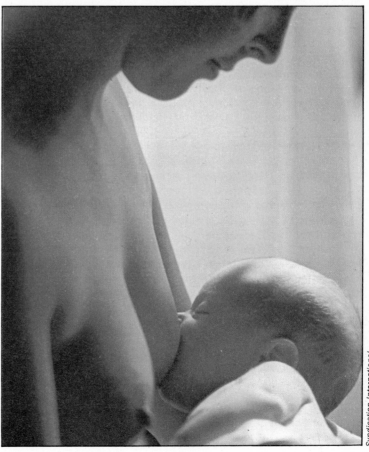
Syndication International

a particular species. If behavior patterns are inherited by a group of animals only and not by all others in the species, the inherited behavior is not technically instinctive. Instincts include the sucking reflex, in which an infant will suck on any object placed in its mouth, and, in the case of birds, fear responses in which members of a species will take flight when shown the silhouette of certain birds of prey. Another important characteristic of instincts is that they are almost impossible to "unlearn" or eradicate by training.

INSTRUCTION
Teaching in a systematic and preplanned fashion.

INSTRUMENTAL LEARNING
A type of learning in which the subject achieves its reward or goal by making some specific movement—for example, an animal pushing a lever to open a door to a food box.

INSULIN
An important hormone created in the pancreas. Its main function is in breaking down carbohydrates in the body.

INSULIN SHOCK THERAPY
An obsolete approach to inducing a coma for therapeutic purposes by giving a patient an overdose of insulin. The coma is short-lived but, as with electroconvulsive therapy, acts to lift depression and relieve anxiety by some means not fully understood.

INTEGRATED PERSONALITY
A personality at peace with itself, in which unconscious and conscious forces work in harmony and neurotic conflicts do not occur. The integrated personality represents an ideal state which is probably never permanently present in any single human being.

INTELLECT
All mental processes which come under the heading of thinking, judging and "knowing."

INTELLECTUALIZATION
A term used in psychoanalysis to refer to the way in which some people attempt to look at all problems, including deeply emotional ones, in purely intellectual terms. Because this approach tends to deny emotion and other basic animal reactions, it is almost always unsuccessful.

INTELLIGENCE
One of the least well understood terms in psychology: psychologists have not even arrived at a precise definition. Intelligence itself actually concerns those functions of the brain which have to do with the intellect—judgment, thinking and, to some extent, creativity. In common use the word has shifted its meaning slightly, and when we say that someone is intelligent we tend to mean that they are particularly well endowed with these intellectual qualities. The current view in psychology, however, is that intelligence refers to a creature's power to meet novel situations in a flexible way and make quick, sensible responses to changes in the environment. From this definition, it is obvious that all human beings are intelligent to some degree, and for that matter so are the majority of animals. If it seems surprising that animals can be considered intelligent, then this is probably because the concept of intelligence has been confused with conscious thinking and self-awareness. These qualities, when coupled with the use of language as an aid to thinking, are probably unique to man, but they represent only one aspect of intelligence as such.

INTELLIGENCE QUOTIENT (IQ)
A measure of relative intelligence which is obtained by taking the so-called mental age of a child or adult, dividing it by the chronological age and then multiplying the result by 100. Mental age is determined by a series of tests designed to bring out mental flexibility and versatility. The average IQ is 100 or, to be more correct, in the range between 90 and 110, where by far the greatest proportion of the population score. It needs to be stressed that IQ tests are not concerned with establishing how much a person knows (the number of facts he has in his head) but how good his brain is at coping with information and novel situations.

INTELLIGENCE TEST
Any one of a large number of formal tests which attempt to establish the mental age of an individual.

INTENTION
A desire to achieve a particular goal.

INTENTIONAL FORGETTING
Deliberate loss of memory, supposed by psychoanalysts to be caused by a wish to repress some unpleasant incident.

INTERBRAIN
An important part of the brain which also has the scientific name of *diencephalon*. It consists of the *thalamus* and the *hypothalamus*.

INTERCOURSE
The exchange of information or interaction between people or groups of people. In the case of sexual intercourse it refers to *coitus*, or the act of mating.

INTERECEPTOR
One of the internal senses which give information to the brain about the automatic movements of the organs.

INTERFERENCE
In psychology, the factors which intervene to prevent learning from taking place or memory from becoming established.

INTERMISSION
The state of relief or calm which sometimes occurs during mental disturbance, particularly in the so-called cyclic illnesses such as manic-depressive psychosis.

INTERNAL ENVIRONMENT
All the ongoing processes that take place inside the body—stomach movements, hormonal changes, and so on—which have a significant effect on human behavior, in the same way that forces in the external environment do.

INTERNAL INHIBITION
A concept developed by the Russian physiologist Pavlov in an attempt to explain why a conditioned or learned response gradually dwindles away if it is not continually reinforced or rewarded.

INTERNALIZATION
A psychoanalytic concept which states that as a child's personality develops it incorporates or "builds in" to itself the different kinds of attitudes and moral values it finds in other people. The superego, which Freud believed was one of the three main components of personality, is almost entirely developed as the result of the internalization of parental attitudes and serves as a kind of "conscience" which holds the rest of the personality in check.

Smouldering embers

If old flames cause flare-ups at bedtime, forget the past and love life now.

Making love brings a couple into an emotional closeness that excludes everything else. Physiology takes over and the lovers are aware only of their own reactions and their mutual passion. Yet at this most private moment some couples must cope with a "ghost in the mattress," a worm in the bud that can eat the heart out of a relationship. Even as they lie in each other's arms they embrace a third party, the memory of a previous love.

Only those couples who found each other—and recognized their mutual attraction—before they experienced love with another person escape the confusion of past with present. Of those who have loved before, some find they have learned from the encounter in ways that benefit the present; others hardly notice that there is a problem to be faced in what is, after all, a fairly common experience. But some find the specter of the past haunts their present involvement in ways that can only be harmful.

Saddest is the man or woman who preserves a memory of a previous love—perhaps a first love—that can never be matched. The reason might be death, leaving a widow or widower to lament an apparently irreplaceable emotional link, or just the previous lover announcing, "That's that," and walking out or seeking a divorce, creating a void. In this emptiness, a person can fantasize the perfect love—the dead or absent lover becomes the epitome of everything that can be right in a person, the relationship takes on a rosy hue that no real-life involvement could duplicate.

Only the Happy Memories

Selecting the high spots from a long-term affair and remembering just the first thrill of love, happy moment after happy moment, long sessions of love-making and the bliss of being certain of another's affection can obliterate the quarrels, suspicions and clumsy love-making that mar even the best of relationships. When the widow, widower or jilted lover finds someone else to share life with, the new partner may find that the standards set are unreachably high.

At first respect for the previous love may seem entirely natural. A man courting a widow does not expect that she will instantly forget her first marriage; equally, a woman aware of the intensity of her potential partner's earlier commitment will make allowances for it. But no one can continue making allowances when every action is dwarfed by the memory of a paragon. Gradually, a wedge is driven into the relationship as one partner insists on looking for disappointments after the "wonders" of the earlier partnership and the other partner comes to accept that there is no way to banish this vision of a time when skies were always blue and lovers always loving.

Shadow of Superman

"Vanessa's a wonderful woman but I'm at the end of my rope," explained George. "I never met her first husband Andrew. He died in a car crash shortly before I came to town. Sometimes I wish I had known him, a fine man by all accounts. When I first started to go out with Vanessa I was proud that she thought I could take his place—and friends they'd shared together welcomed me and gave me a great deal of encouragement.

"We talked about marriage very seriously before we finally went ahead—Vanessa made it clear that her feeling for me was not as deep as it had been for Andrew, and part of the reason for marriage was so that her four boys would have a father. I went into it with my eyes open, but I can't say I like the way it's turned out.

"Curiously the boys and I get on well, no problems there. It's Vanessa—she dwells on what happened in the past. If we go to the theater, during the intermission she'll just mention that Andrew taught her to love Shakespeare; on vacation she'll talk about how good a swimmer he was. And although she's never compared me with him in bed, she's made it fairly clear that she's happy to pleasure me but doesn't really expect to reach any ecstatic heights herself.

"I've insisted we talk to a marriage counselor—Vanessa and I could be very happy together, but I can't compete with an imaginary superman. One psychiatrist friend of mine came up with the convoluted explanation that subconsciously she believes if she truly loves a man he will die, so she hangs on to her love for Andrew rather than transfer it to me. That way, so he says, she's protecting me. Well, I just wish she'd let me take the risk rather than make me go through this half-and-half marriage."

Less far-reaching in effect but also worrying to a person involved in a second relationship are the memories that can be triggered off by activities shared with the new partner. Visiting a particular place or watching the partner doing something reminiscent of the first relationship; or noticing that an habitual sequence of love-making leads to different responses; or specifically avoiding comparisons between this and the first relationship: if the memories that come flooding in are tinged with regrets, they can affect the spontaneity and enjoyment of the present relationship.

And even when the person concerned accepts that the first relationship was unsatisfactory and realizes that buried within these memories are the indications that the end was coming, there may be a nagging feeling that a little more effort applied at the right moment could have extended and strengthened the connection. An insecure and immature person may import problems wholesale into the new relationship by harping on what happened in the past. Whether this takes the form of continually analyzing what went wrong or of extolling the wonders of previous partners in the hope that some of the gloss will rub off, the effects will not be helpful.

Continual Comparison

If the earlier relationship had enough significance to be mentioned at all, the new partner is tempted to seek comparisons. "Are we alike?" "Did you do this before?" "Am I as good?" These are questions that can apply to almost any activity from earning a living to carrying out household tasks to making love. When carried to extremes, and particularly over the matter of sex, continually demanding comparisons is a guaranteed way of tearing the guts out of the new relationship. Love-making must come to a virtual halt when, every time one or other makes a sexual move, there is the implied query "Did you do this with your previous partner?" And

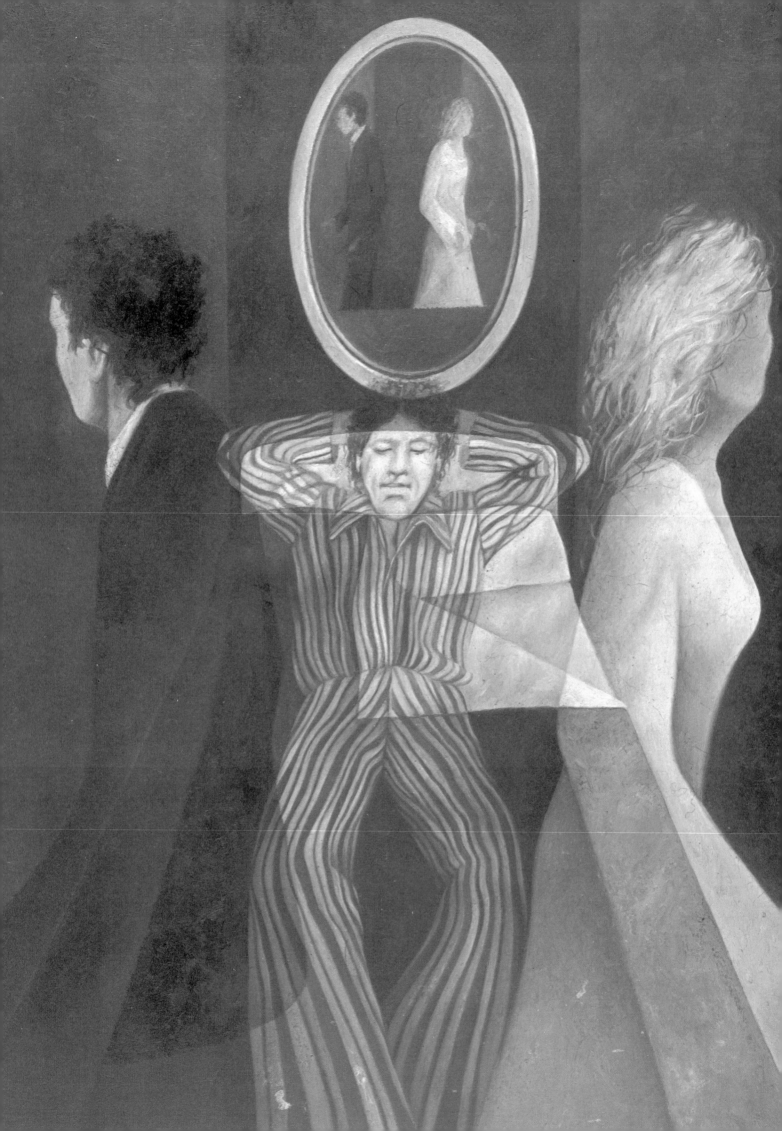

when a simple question such as "Do you enjoy this?" or "Would you like to try making love in this position?" suggests an urge to compete with a sexual specter, there can be no reassurance in lying in each other's arms, only a reminder of potential discord.

Habits acquired during an earlier relationship can certainly make difficulties for the new partner. Where lovers are splitting apart or husband and wife are heading for divorce, they can compensate for the failings they see in each other with sarcasm, bossiness or a tendency to leave all decisions to the other. If the break-up is prolonged, these bad habits can become ingrained and continue into the new relationship. The person is trapped by patterns of behavior that have no place in a successful relationship and the new partner must bear the burden until, together, they learn to substitute more pleasurable ways of dealing with each other.

Still Around

Friends can be another source of worry. Their feelings for the former partner can affect the welcome they give to a new one, making him feel guilty for breaking up the earlier relationship, even when it had fallen apart through its own flaws, and subjecting him to insensitive conversations about events in which the previous partner played a leading role. Relatives may be even worse as they may feel an urge to moralize and direct the developing relationship, where friends will accept and try to understand. Parents who believe their son or daughter has made a serious mistake in leaving one partner for another can exert a baneful influence on the new relationship.

Contacts with the ex-partner are probably the most difficult problem of all for the new partner, and this may be part of the reason why widowed people tend to be better able to establish a second relationship than the divorced. Except in special circumstances, a previous partner is likely to still be part of the same social scene, and if children and mutual property are involved regular meetings may be necessary.

Overreacting against the former partner may be the immediate temptation. Complaining if she is so much as present at a social gathering or pointedly ignoring her should there be a chance meeting in the street can cause a rift between the present lovers. When there has to be contact—whether just social or to make financial or other arrangements—there is

no point in trying to ignore the fact that there was once a bond. So long as the present involvement is soundly based, these encounters will be easy to manage on a fairly impersonal basis; if later all the people concerned become friends that is a bonus.

If the former lovers insist on intimate discussions during these meetings, going over past failures and successes and indulging in titillating sexuality, then the triangular situation produces tensions that do not vanish just because the new partner attempts to prevent these meetings. Lying beside a ghost in the mattress is one thing—wrestling with flesh and blood that has never effectively been banished from the bed is another.

Attempts to displace all reminders of the past also lead into a potential minefield of farce and failure. Redecorating the bedroom is fine—a sympathetic lover will almost certainly understand the desire to stamp a new personality on this room where the couple are most intimate—but to go through a house or apartment throwing out everything that shows the touch of someone else is impossible. Ripping photographs apart to destroy images of the threatening ex or forcing the partner to part with every gift invests the departed lover with a power he probably never had.

The problems pile up, however, when a couple, as well as confronting their own mixed reactions, have to deal with the behavior of an intrusive ex-partner. Recognizing and accepting that a relationship has ended is far more difficult than becoming engulfed in the excitement of a new involvement. An ex-partner who feels abandoned may just assume that the new relationship is a phase and that ultimately the lover will return. Late-night phone calls when loneliness strikes may meet a sympathetic response that confirms the illusion—and means the ex-partner makes more frequent phone calls, sends invitations to meet, and makes every effort to start up the previous relationship.

Arid Interchange

Ultimately the new couple have to cope with an ex-partner so convinced that the present relationship will not last that he or she takes up an apparently sophisticated attitude, starts talking openly about the partner's "fling" and adopts a patronizing air towards the new "young thing" which may include invitations to meet to discuss the well-being of the person at the apex of the triangle.

"Cheryl just would not see what had happened," said Harriet. "Isaac left her, that was the truth of it. He didn't leave her for me—I did already know him but we weren't yet lovers—he went because their relationship had turned into an arid interchange that sapped his psychic energies. Cheryl had become so emotionally dependent on him, so leechlike, that she could hardly make a telephone call unless he dialed it for her. The court recognized what was happening when they gave Isaac custody of the children—it's not that common for the children to go to the father.

Tender Spot

"Isaac feels sorry for her. He agreed to give her more alimony than she really needs and he helped to find her an apartment. But it's a very impersonal sympathy—I'm not worried that he has any regrets about leaving her or anything like that. What I can't take is the personal side. Isaac's at work all day, but Cheryl won't contact him there—even over the telephone, talking to the receptionist and his secretary before she gets through is more than she can take.

"So she phones me instead—I'm at home with the children all day as she well knows. There's always some question about the boys—would they like chocolate milkshakes next time they go to see her is typical—but then she's away into her own problems and what is Isaac going to do about them. The first couple of times I tried to help—I know myself how good Isaac is at sorting out difficulties—but then it began to grate. I've never met the woman, for example; I've got no wish to get mixed up in her life, and Isaac has already shown he wants out. Once or twice I've almost been rude to her—even though I know Isaac feels we ought to try to be sympathetic but now I just switch the telephone off around the times she's most likely to call. Isaac and I have our own life to make."

This cloying inability to come to terms with reality hampers the development of the new relationship; but malicious interference by a jealous ex-lover rips it apart. Jealousy and possessiveness can be the last emotions left when a relationship dies, and the previous close involvement provides exactly the awareness to slide a knife into a tender spot. Graham Greene, in a short story called "Mortmain," describes how Josephine kills stone-dead her ex-lover's marriage—by piling apparent kindness upon apparent kindness. The realization that Josephine still stalks

Ulrick Ross

through every aspect of his new relationship leaves Philip unable to sustain his carefree enjoyment of love-making with Julia.

The same combination of jealousy and possessiveness links the adolescent who moons around at a party and burst into red-faced tears every time the new couple enter the room with the matron who slides razor-sharp half-truths about her replacement into conversations over morning coffee. When this fever reaches its worst the couple may have to reckon with physical assault, poison-pen letters or even abusive telephone calls. In a very few cases official action may be necessary, but often, by carefully avoiding provocation and refusing to become involved in the ex-lover's "game," the couple themselves can defuse the situation.

On the positive side, a second relationship can have a lot going for it—properly tamed, the ghost in the mattress becomes a friendly spirit smoothing away the bumps and lumps in everyday matters. Ruthless honesty is the first step. The person who has been through a previous relationship—whether it ended through death, divorce, or just parting—must analyze

its strengths and weaknesses. Self-knowledge, which leads to the recognition that faults are never all on one side, provides the kind of guidance that helps avoid repeating previous mistakes. By being honest in this way a person can come to terms with the loss of confidence and the feelings of sexual and social inadequacy that can follow a breakup.

Only Second-Best

Honesty, too, helps a person in being necessarily ruthless with a previous lover. Commitment now is to the new relationship and can be made without antagonizing the previous partner. But where previous entanglements threaten the present involvement they must be dealt with firmly. This means no autopsies, no get-togethers to rehash the past, no intimacies—just a calm social contact when it is essential to meet.

For the new partner, too, honesty is the best policy. There is no point in dodging the fear of being second best. Talking together—and believing what the other says—is the quickest way of building the mutual trust that prevents any previous relationship from holding the present one to

Old love letters are all very well as long as happy memories do not sour the ones you're making now.

ransom. When the two partners are sure of each other's love and can discuss worries about this loving being as yet incomplete, they can look back on previous involvements with detached sympathy, seeing them as a potential source of guidance.

Next to talking about their problems the couple's task is to keep reminding each other that their difficulties are not because it is a second-time-around relationship. Blaming the one thing that seems to mark them out from other couples can be all too easy when adversity threatens. But all marriages, all serious relationships, go through difficult periods, and a couple may delude themselves if they deny the mundane causes of dissatisfaction. Their relationship may be more complex than a first romance just because more mutual friends, commitments, possessions—and even children—are likely to be involved, but although this may complicate problems it is hardly a reason for giving up in despair. Sorting out the complexities can itself be rewarding.

Improve your memory

Do you wish you had a better memory? Each year, thousands of copies of memory-training manuals are read, but they are not all based on sound psychological sense. More than fifty years of research has taught us a great deal about memory, yet some misunderstandings remain.

Memory is not a Muscle

If you practiced memorizing telephone numbers for ten minutes each day, you would almost certainly improve your capacity for memorizing telephone numbers. But you would be no better at remembering faces or names or dental appointments. The idea that one kind of learning improves another is called "transfer of training"; it works best when the two tasks are highly similar. The more different they are, the less likely is transfer to occur. Remembering is not just one kind of activity. If you wish to remember more effectively, you must first figure out what kind of material, and what kind of memory, is most useful to you. Exercises to improve memory are useless if they are not related to the remembering that gives you trouble.

Why We Forget

Freud's view that we forget what we do not want to remember sometimes holds true. Unpleasant tasks, difficult social occasions, letters, paying bills — if this is your remembering problem, the ability to memorize will not help you at all. You have to arrange for some signals of the task to jolt you into action. Do not rely on getting someone else to remind you; that merely shifts the burden of responsibility, and there is no guarantee that your deputy will remember, either.

When the task crosses your mind (usually at a time when you cannot do anything about it), write a large note to yourself and pin it up in a prominent place. Lipstick on the bathroom mirror works quite well for some people, or a big sheet of paper on the face of the clock. There is nothing necessarily wrong with your memory — it is your motivation that is lacking.

Remembering addresses, names, and birthdays boils down to the problem of paying attention. You may think you have no sense of direction because you cannot remember how to get back to a place you've visited once, but you were probably not concentrating when you first made the journey. Next time, notice the name of each street; tell yourself at each turn which direction you are going in. That alone may improve your memory, because more is being stored. When you meet people, repeat their names and look at them closely at the same time. If you do not hear the name, ask them to repeat it for you. What does not penetrate has no chance of being remembered.

More complex information is forgotten because it may have been imperfectly learned, or because it has not been in regular use. Information in the long-term memory becomes less detailed in time, leaving general outline and the odd detail.

Kinds of Memory

Most of us store information both verbally and visually, but some people have a marked preference for one or the other. If you can remember places and faces but not names, you are probably a good visualizer. Use this ability to help you remember what you need. Try to "photograph" a picture of the written name beside the image of the person, or attach a visual image to the words you want: a man named Stone could be represented by an image of a boulder. Translate ideas into the sort of code you remember best — if you are a verbalizer, put them into words; if you are a visualizer, fit them to an image.

Organizing Information

Test your ability on these three memory exercises. The first is a short prose selection, the second is a list of words, and the third is a group of nonsense syllables. Study each section for one minute and try to *remember it word for word*, then cover the page. Wait five minutes, and write down what you remember on a separate sheet.

1. Your brain stores information in "chunks"; any chunk can have several pieces of information — the more familiar or meaningful the material, the larger the "chunks" can be. When you learn something new, you take it in in small, separate bits, and much can be lost if you have no overall structure to relate them to. As you master the material, remember that one bit brings all the others in its train.

2.	location	journalist
	signal	window
	hammock	clergyman
	garden	geometry
	emphasis	intention
3.	ZEF	WOF
	PYV	RIT
	LUJ	DEP
	GOC	BAZ

Attacking the Task

1. You probably did not remember every letter of this rather difficult 70-word piece of prose, though you could reproduce the sense of the piece as a whole. The more sense anything makes to you, the more accurate your memory of it will be.
2. Did you make connections between these ten unconnected words. If you remembered hammock, you probably remembered garden by an association of ideas, too. Maybe you connected journalist and clergyman, as both being professions. The visualizer can "photograph" the words without making connections between them. Compare your accuracy with the first section. You may have managed to retain more of that piece than of the ten words.
3. These eight nonsense syllables have no meaningful structure in themselves. Most people would remember them less well than the first sections.

Learning a Part or the Whole

If you want to learn a poem or a part in a play, is it better to learn it a line at a time or to attempt the whole thing at once? Obviously, for a lengthy piece, it is not possible to learn it all at one go. But you will find it helpful to look over the whole thing to get some idea of its structure before you get down to the details.

Alternate practice and rest periods. The best thing you can do after learning something you want to remember is to go to sleep! But rehearsal of new information is essential for good remembering. If you do not practice what you learn, recall can be difficult. You will probably be able to recognize the items if you meet them again, but retrieving them from your memory store is a more complex process.

There is a tendency for memory to become less efficient with age. Partly, the longer you live the more you have to remember and the more different memories interfere with one another. It is likely, except where the brain tissue is damaged by accident or disease, that we do have very complete records stored in our skulls. Getting them out depends on brain efficiency, on motivation, and on the ways in which we connect knowledge. When you are searching for a piece of information, try to get to it through as many pathways as you can.

If practice, organization, and association do not work for you, then you will have to be honest and ask yourself just what you are gaining from being forgetful!

Lifting depression

We all have a favorite way of curing "down" feelings—a drink, a movie, a snack, calling up a cheerful friend. But what if it doesn't work? What if the low spirits persist? You could be suffering from clinical depression, an illness that seems to be growing more and more common.

No one is quite sure why this should be; it could be that we are living in depressing times, or that doctors are more enlightened and now make diagnoses of depression where they would once have prescribed a tonic, or that people are more willing to present their symptoms to physicians. If you have been lucky enough to escape depression, it is difficult to understand what it feels like. But you almost certainly know people less fortunate, and they will undoubtedly tell you that it is misery.

Symptoms of Depression

Clinical depression differs from ordinary low spirits in intensity and duration. Mood can vary from persistent unhappiness to blackest despair. Meanwhile, the sufferer's mental functioning is unimpaired, though he may be unable to concentrate and feel very fatigued. Well-meaning friends often suggest that he cheer up and pull himself together—cruel advice, because that is just what he cannot do. Counting your blessings is no good: the depressed person knows that he has a lot to be thankful for, that there are others much worse off, and that knowledge makes no

Marshall Cavendish

difference at all to the way he feels—except to make him even more guilty about feeling awful with no just cause.

Together with the mood of despair, eating and sleeping patterns are often disturbed. The sufferer may lose his appetite or eat compulsively; he may wake early every morning and lie awake in the bleak hours, or sleep far too much. The two sets of symptoms can even alternate in the same person; a common pattern is for the person to gain a lot of weight through overeating and oversleeping, then suddenly to lose it in a period of agitation.

One thing we know about depression is that, with or without treatment, it does get better in time. The trouble is that, for any one individual, it is impossible to predict how long the acute phase of the illness will last; it could be as short as three weeks, or it could go on for very much longer. The right treatment is likely to shorten the course of the depression and help to prevent its recurrence.

What is the Right Treatment?
Different schools of thought in psychiatric medicine argue for different kinds of treatment. At one extreme, an entirely physical treatment could be prescribed: ECT (shock treatment) or drugs, which often have dramatic effects. It is possible that some forms of depression are physiological in origin, and they would consequently respond well to drugs.

At the other extreme, you may find that entirely psychological treatment, like analysis or psychotherapy, is helpful. Where depression is of psychological origin, therapy is probably the best treatment, but the use of antidepressant drugs can relieve the worst of the symptoms—feelings of anguish or constant crying—enabling the sufferer to cope with the basic, underlying causes.

If you think you may be depressed, lose no time in consulting your doctor. A large range of antidepressant drugs is now available, and one of them could help you more than you would have thought possible.

Self-help in Depression
The first and in some ways the most difficult step is to recognize that you are, in fact, depressed. Intelligent, sensitive and conscientious people are often vulnerable to this disorder, and they find it hard to see that their feelings are not realistic. They believe that they are not worthwhile people, that the world really is as black as it looks, and consequently that there is no point in seeking help.

If you know someone like this, try to persuade him to ask for help. You may encounter problems, as the depressed person is usually afraid of wasting his physician's time and is convinced that he deserves to feel low. Once he decides to ask for help, he often feels much better. But if immediate help is not available, the depression creeps back.

Structuring Time
In severe depression, nothing in life seems worth doing. Even performing the most ordinary tasks, like getting up in the morning and getting dressed, takes great effort. Time seems endless, especially if insomnia accompanies the depression. Effective as the new antidepressant drugs are, they have one drawback: they do not start to work right away but take up to ten days for noticeable results. Meanwhile, you have to try to act as if your life mattered.

No one who has not experienced it can appreciate what it means to have no sense of purpose. But keep in mind that your sense of direction, your energy and your enjoyment of life *will come back.* Typically, the bad feelings slack off for a short time, and you may wake up feeling unaccountably better; then they return, and your short period of recovery seems like an illusion. But the good feelings do return. Gradually, the periods of depression grow shorter and less frequent, until they disappear or hit you only occasionally.

Looking for Causes
Psychiatrists used to distinguish between two kinds of depression—reactive depression, supposed to have its origins in an event, like a bereavement or loss of some kind; and endogenous depression, supposed to be constitutional. Now it is generally recognized that the picture is not so simple. So-called "endogenous" depression often has a precipitating cause, the "reactive" kind of depression it brings about becoming a chemical "habit"; for once having reacted with depression, a person may go on being depressed.

Very often, depression has its origins in childhood. Early feelings of unworthiness and the inability to match up to unrealistically high standards may cause depressive breakdowns in adult life. But the depressed person feels that his depression comes from nowhere, and may be blind to these causes.

Women frequently suffer from depression in the few days before menstruation. A wise husband usually knows what it is all about, but the woman herself may deny it! Psychological causes act similarly, and specialist help may be needed to uncover the links.

Mourning and Melancholia
Freud pointed out the parallels between depression and grief. Mourning, at death or any loss, is a natural reaction, but if the grief goes beyond a reasonable period of time, it becomes pathological. What is really being mourned? Is there a more subtle sense of loss at the bottom of the depression? Facing up to loss in a direct way can arrest depression and enable the affected person to take constructive steps.

Anger and Depression
Contemporary psychiatrists like Anthony Storr see depression as anger turned inwards. For some reason, the person cannot express direct anger, so he becomes angry with himself, even to the point of self-destruction. Turning the anger outwards again relieves the depression, and when a depressed person starts to get angry, this is usually taken as a sign of improvement. Who is he angry with? Again, this is a question that may be more quickly answered with professional help.

What To Do Until the Psychiatrist Comes
Searching deep-rooted causes of depression may take some time. Waiting is almost impossible for someone in an acute state of melancholy. If you are prone to depression, you learn to live with it, protecting yourself from all possible hazards. Once you have experienced it, you know what to expect and what measures bring some relief. But the first time around, it can be much more difficult.

First, you should tackle any physical symptoms. If you are exhausted, get some sedation, but not in quantities that would tempt you to take an overdose. If you cannot eat, try to get a whipped egg with glucose inside you. Plan your time; enlist the help of your friends. Recent medical research indicates that violent physical exercise helps lift stubborn depression. Forget your pride—ask for whatever help you can get. Even if it seems pointless now, *hold on.* The time will come when the depression seems like a bad dream. It can be a source of growth; you can come out the other side knowing yourself better and living more fully than ever before.

Could you be a psychologist?

In one sense, everyone is a psychologist. We are all interested in ourselves and others; we look for explanations of our actions and feelings and build up through experience our own theories to help us predict reactions and make sense of the past.

Is this your idea of what psychology is about? Many a student eager to discover more about the mind has been disappointed by courses of study in psychology. Interest in human behavior, in what makes people tick, is the first requirement, but other qualities are necessary too.

How Aware Are You?

Your responses to this questionnaire will tell you if you have what it takes to unravel the mystery of the mind.

Observation

For each statement, indicate whether it is true or untrue for you.

1. I often find that I notice things that others do not see.
2. I get impatient with detailed work.
3. I enjoy watching people when I travel or sit in a restaurant.
4. My head is so full of my own thoughts that I often pay no attention to my surroundings.
5. I am easily bored.
6. I enjoy doing accurate and detailed work.
7. I find it hard to sit still and watch even a good TV program.
8. I am often surprised by things which catch my attention.
9. I can rarely remember what people wear or the color of their eyes.
10. When something puzzles me, I find it hard to give up until I find a satisfactory answer.

Objectivity

Indicate which statements are true or untrue for you.

1. Once I make up my mind about something, I rarely change it.
2. I often lose my temper in arguments over ideas.
3. Before making decisions, I like to get as much information about different possibilities as I can.
4. I find it stimulating to hear views that are different from my own.
5. I have strong feelings which tend to influence my judgments of political and other situations.
6. I find that I do not always side with my friends when I do not agree with their actions.
7. I always try to be fair in summing up both sides of a question.
8. I would rather trust my own opinion than a factual survey.
9. When people try to convince me with facts, I find that I get more obstinate.
10. I believe that we should try to reason things out as far as we can.

Research Aptitude

1. How would you go about testing the truth of the statement "Gentlemen prefer blondes"?

Psychologist Roger Sperry delves into the workings of the mind.

Philip Daly

Rate Your Responses

Observation

Statements 1, 3, 6, 8, and 10. If you said these were true, you show the capacity for observation and curiosity which is essential for the good psychologist. Statements 6 and 10 indicate that you can follow up what interests you. All psychology is rooted in observation, but the observations have to be carried out with patience and must have relevance to particular questions; accuracy is vital. The whole process of scientific enquiry demands that the observations of one worker or team should be able to be repeated by others; and with a subject matter as vast as human (and animal) behavior, it is specially important to know whether the same things will happen again in the same conditions, or whether one set of results was a fluke. If you said these statements were untrue, you do not seem to be very observant at the moment. This could be partly corrected by training, but if your curiosity is also low, psychology is unlikely to be your vocation.

Statements 2, 4, 5, 7 and 9. If you checked 2 and 7 as true, you could be the sort of person who prefers ideas to action. Ideas are important in psychology, but testing them out can involve a good deal of painstaking work, forcing you to look outwards rather than inwards. If you checked 5, 7, and 9 as true, you could have a restless temperament, unsuited to the rigors of experimental work. There are some fine psychologists who have restless minds, spurting forth novel ideas which other people go on to develop. But you have to be pretty well-established to get research assistants to do the drudgery for you! You would probably do better in a more practical job.

If you checked these statements as untrue, you have patience and are probably observant. If you also agreed with 1, 3, 6, 8, and 10, or most of them, you rate highly on observation.

Give yourself +1 for every True in 1, 3, 6, 8, and 10; and for every Untrue in 2, 4, 5, 7, and 9.

Give yourself −1 for every Untrue in 1, 3, 6, 8, and 10; and for every True in 2, 4, 5, 7, and 9.

+5 to +10—high rating in observation and curiosity
−1 to +4—medium rating
−10 to −2—low rating

Objectivity

Statements 3, 4, 6, 7, and 10. If you said these were true for you, you attempt to be objective. We cannot be entirely objective, even with the help of well-planned experiments. Human beings perceive selectively; we see what we expect to see, and we may not all interpret the same information in the same way. But you seem to be flexible in your thinking and willing to be convinced by reason. You may well have strong feelings, but you try not to let them cloud your judgment. The ideal psychologist shares your lack of prejudice. The main difference between the layman's search for explanations for human behavior and strict psychological enquiry is in the rigor of the tests used to check theories or notions.

If you said these statements were untrue, perhaps your feelings are so strong that you are impatient with objectivity. You could be interested in psychology, but you would probably resent the procedures.

Statements 1, 2, 5, 8, and 9. If you checked these as true, you are a person of strongly-held views. That is an excellent qualification for a job like journalism, perhaps, or politics. But not for psychology.

If you checked these statements as untrue, you may sometimes wish that your opinions were not so fluid, but if you also agreed with 3, 4, 6, 7, and 10, you would find that an asset as a psychologist.

Give yourself 1 for every True score from 3, 4, 6, 7, and 10; and for every Untrue score from 1, 2, 5, 8, and 9.

Give yourself −1 for every True score from 1, 2, 5, 8, and 9; and for every Untrue score from 3, 4, 6, 7, and 10.

+5 to +10—high objectivity rating
+1 to +4—medium objectivity rating
−10 to −2—low objectivity rating

Research Aptitude

1. Do gentlemen prefer blondes?
Check the general plan that fits your approach.
a. Ask yourself (if you are a man) or ask a man you know (if you are a woman).
b. Check with several men that you know.
c. Ask a large group of men.
d. Set up a choice situation and record the results.

Score −2 for a.; −1 for b.; +1 for c.; +2 for d. Add +1 for every additional point you included from the following techniques:

e. The sample of "gentlemen" should be representative and not biased by such variables as age, education or occupation.
f. What are blondes being preferred to? You should compare not only with brunettes, but with other shades.
g. Did you check that it was blonde hair that was the criterion? All the girls should have been equally attractive in other respects.
h. Does the preference operate in all situations? You should specify several contexts, like taking a girl out, watching a girl in a show, getting married. If you thought of other relevant points, add 1 for each.

2. Score 2 for a.; 1 for b.; 0 for c.
3. Score 1 for each of the following questions:
a. What psychologists?
b. When was the study carried out?
c. Where was the study carried out?
d. How many children?
e. How were they selected?
f. What did they mean by "brighter"?
g. How did they define "healthier"?
h. How significant were the results?
i. Is there any other evidence in this field?
j. Is there any suggestion that being bright makes you healthy, or the other way around?
4. If you said Yes, give yourself −1.
5. Score +2 for a.; +1 for b.; −1 for c.

12 to 22—high research rating
5 to 11—medium research rating
−3 to +4—low research rating

---

2. Do you find yourself asking questions about why people do the things they do?
a. often
b. sometimes
c. rarely
3. "Psychologists prove that bright children are healthier." What questions would you like to ask when you read this statement?
4. Are you afraid of graphs and statistical tables?
5. Would you rate yourself in your work as
a. well-organized and methodical?
b. fairly well-organized and methodical?
c. low on organization and method?

Choose Your Field

If you scored medium or high ratings in any combination on the three sections, you could probably pursue successfully the study of psychology. But psychologists work in many different kinds of areas. You could choose from educational, clinical, industrial and academic work; and within these fields, you would probably have a speciality. Your own interest and previous experience is the best guide in making this choice.

Can you concentrate?

Are you amazed at how much you can do on those days when you find concentration easy? Have you ever wished it could always be like that? Unless you are very lucky your concentration will fluctuate, but by understanding more of how it works, you will be able to minimize bad days and get the best out of good ones.

Concentration depends on factors within and without the person. Some are beyond voluntary control; others can be harnessed to your interests.

Body over Mind

Some physical conditions make concentration almost impossible. If you are in a state of physical need—hungry or tired or even longing to go to the bathroom—your attention will be focused on satisfying the need before you can turn your energy to anything else. Drive states heighten your powers of concentration on those things which are relevant to the pressing need; but they lower the power to respond to other signals. Sometimes you have to get something done, though you are in a state of fatigue; but if you keep on driving yourself when your body needs rest, you become increasingly inefficient. Having a nap or going to bed then getting up early, far from wasting time, will help you to work more productively.

Your basic temperament affects your ability to concentrate. The introvert is in general able to concentrate for longer periods before reaching his level of inefficiency. The extrovert needs more rest pauses.

Very often, it is psychological factors which help or hinder our attention to the task at hand. Even a restless extrovert will spend long periods working at something which interests him, or which is important to him. It need not be the extreme case that Samuel Johnson spoke of—that nothing concentrates the mind so well as the knowledge that you will be hanged in the morning!

Motivation aids concentration. If you are motivated, there is no problem. It is when motivation is low that you feel like doing anything except what you know you should. The trick here is to engender some self-motivation, like giving youself a reward at the end of the task.

Outside Conditions

Concentration depends on the ability to exclude signals irrelevant to what you want to do. Even a peaceful environment may create distractions. Uncomfortable—or overly comfortable—conditions will interfere. Some people like to work in silence, others prefer some background noise, like a radio. Irregular noise is more distracting than an even level which you can learn to ignore, so the continuous flow of a radio broadcast could be tolerated, where intermittent conversation could not. If you find it hard to concentrate generally, it is worth taking time to arrange your room to make it as peaceful as possible. Cheap soundproofing, quiet colors, and not too many distracting objects all help.

Rate Your Concentration

To select the techniques that could improve your concentration, check out on the questionnaire just how much help you need.

1. Do you find that when you are reading, you have read the same page twice without taking anything in?
a. often
b. sometimes, if tired or bored
c. practically never

2. When you have a difficult job to do, do you start on it immediately?
a. hardly ever.
b. more than half the time
c. yes

3. If you encounter a problem in something you are doing, do you
a. give up?
b. stick at it for a while, but give up for the time being if it does not work?
c. keep going until you have solved it?

4. When you try to concentrate on one thing, do thoughts about other things come rushing in?
a. often
b. occasionally
c. practically never

5. Do you find it difficult to listen closely to other people?
a. often
b. only if tired or preoccupied
c. not often

6. Do you find that you make silly mistakes in adding up figures?
a. often
b. rarely
c. never

7. Do you daydream when you ought to be working?
a. often
b. sometimes
c. practically never

8. Do you spend more time worrying about what you should be doing than in actually getting on with your commitments?
a. often
b. sometimes
c. very rarely

How Do You Rate?

Mainly as—you find great difficulty in concentrating. Perhaps you have a grasshopper kind of mind that cannot rest for long on any one thing. If you manage to do what you should in short bursts of concentrated activity, this does not matter too much. But if you cannot settle down or become restless before you have accomplished much, you need to examine the reasons for your lack of concentration. Could it be anxiety? There may be unacknowledged worries in your life which you will need to sort out before you can expect improvement. Maybe you are being blocked (possibly by yourself) from doing what you really want. Trying too hard can also make you anxious to the point of interfering with ongoing behavior.

Mainly bs—your concentration is about average. Like most people, you find difficulty when you are unmotivated or if you are in a state of physical need. When you need to concentrate and find it hard, it would be helpful to have good work habits to fall back on. Getting down to work in the same place at the same time eases the process. Minimizing distraction helps, too. To stir up flagging motivation, give yourself frequent reinforcements: if you have six letters to write, promise yourself a break of ten minutes after the first one.

Making your own deadlines can spur you on. Instead of groaning at the size of the task, get down to it for 30 minutes or an hour. See how much you can get done in that time. Combine the deadline with a reinforcement: after an hour of work, give yourself 30 minutes of reading or watching TV or listening to music—you will come back to work refreshed. Nothing concentrates the mind like having to tell someone else about what you learn: enlist the help of someone who will lend an ear. If that is not possible, imagine that you will have to teach whatever you have been concentrating on to a class. This works best when you want to concentrate on learning something; more routine jobs are better tackled by the reinforcement method.

Mainly cs—lack of concentration is not your problem. But bear in mind that your efficiency decreases after an optimal amount of time at a task. You could do even better if you stopped when you got tired. You could sometimes be a little obsessional about sticking to a job until it is finished. A short break could help you to work faster in the long run.